# Contested Landscape

# Contested Landscape

## The Politics of Wilderness in Utah and the West

Edited by

### Doug Goodman

and

### Daniel McCool

The University of Utah Press
Salt Lake City

LIBRARY OF CONGRESS CATALOGING-IN-PUBLICATION DATA

Contested landscape : the politics of wilderness in Utah and the West
  / edited by Doug Goodman and Daniel McCool.
     p.    cm.
   Includes bibliographical references.
   ISBN 0-87480-604-6 (alk. paper)
    1. Wilderness areas—Political aspects—West (U.S.) 2. Wilderness
areas—Political aspects—Utah. 3. Wilderness areas—Government
policy—United States.   I. Goodman, Doug, 1963–    . II. McCool,
Daniel, 1950–    .
QH76.5.W34C65    1999
333.78'2'0978—dc21                             99-27465

To our parents:

Without them, this book
would not have been possible.

# Contents

*ABBREVIATIONS*

| | |
|---|---|
| ACEC | Area of Critical Environmental Concern |
| ADC | Animal Damage Control |
| APHIS | Animal and Plant Health Inspection Service |
| ARPA | Archaeological Resources Protection Act |
| AUM | Animal Unit Months |
| BLM | Bureau of Land Management |
| DEIS | Draft Environmental Impact Statement |
| EIS | Environmental Impact Statement |
| ESA | Endangered Species Act |
| FEIS | Final Environmental Impact Statement |
| FLPMA | Federal Land Policy and Management Act |
| IBLA | Interior Board of Land Appeals |
| IMP | Interim Management Policy |
| ISA | Instant Study Areas |
| NEPA | National Environmental Policy Act |
| NFMA | National Forest Management Act |
| NHPA | National Historic Preservation Act |
| NPCA | National Parks and Conservation Association |
| NPS | National Park Service |
| NWPS | National Wilderness Preservation System |
| OAD | Organic Act Directives |
| ORV | Off-road Vehicle |
| RARE | Roadless Area Review and Evaluation |
| RMP | Resource Management Plan |
| SE | Situation Evaluation |
| SITLA | School and Institutional Trust Lands Administration |
| SSA | Site Specific Analysis |
| SUWA | Southern Utah Wilderness Alliance |
| SWA | Secret Wilderness Areas (facetious) |
| SWC | State Wilderness Committee |
| UGS | Utah Geological Survey |
| UPLMUC | Utah Public Lands Multiple Use Coalition |
| USDI | United States Department of the Interior |
| USFS | United States Forest Service |
| USFWS | United States Fish and Wildlife Service |

| | |
|---|---|
| UWA | Utah Wilderness Association |
| UWC | Utah Wilderness Coalition |
| VER | Valid Existing Rights |
| WARS | Wilderness Attribute Rating System |
| WIH | Wilderness Inventory Handbook |
| WMC | Wilderness Management Commission (proposed) |
| WMP | Wilderness Management Plan |
| WSA | Wilderness Study Areas |

# Preface

In a recent conversation I had with a group of Austrian students visiting the University of Utah, one of them explained that many Europeans have a stereotypical image of American culture. "The stereotype is that America really has no culture of its own. Everything is so new and big, and so much seems artificial."

Another student added to the image. "When we think of Americans we picture people living in wide-open spaces, people with lots of open land around them."

A third Austrian also perceived America in terms of space. "The American West: I picture never-ending horizons, and roads leading straight into eternity."

I questioned their assumption that America did not have a unique culture. "Do you think all that undeveloped land affects culture? Could it be that a distinctively American culture has resulted from our relationship with the wide-open landscape?"

The Austrians, who came to America to dispel stereotypes rather than perpetuate them, were quite willing to consider this. They began to think about the essential elements of American culture.

"Our image of America always centers around cowboys, buffalo, huge national parks, and Indians riding across the plains," one student explained.

"Lots of space, with very few people living there. All of Austria would fit into a corner of Utah," another student added.

"Monument Valley—that's America," said another.

After some discussion it became quite clear that America does indeed have a unique and distinctive culture, one derived from our relationship with the land. From the beginning of European settlement on this continent, the single most important element was the nature of the land: wild, spacious, and dramatically varied. As we changed the land, it changed us, and the change forged an entirely unique culture.

In the early years of American settlement, the wildness of the land presented a dramatic challenge, a test that left an everlasting imprint on those who endured it. One of the best examples is the hole-in-the-rock trail chiseled out by the early settlers in southeastern Utah. It stands today as a singular example of tenacity, hard work, and the optimistic belief that a better life lay beyond the next ridge.

Today the challenges are different. We now must search for a way to preserve that cultural heritage as well as the land that shaped it. This debate has many facets, but perhaps none stir such passion as the conflict over wilderness. Some people of the rural West want to continue the lifestyle that has contributed so much to the American image, while others want to protect the remnants of the wild land that is so important to us as a people. Note that both sides want to *preserve* something distinctly American. This point was made quite clear recently when I attended a public speaker's forum on wilderness. I happened to sit between a passionate wilderness advocate and a long-time resident of Emery County—home to the San Rafael Swell. After the program, the man from Emery County, visibly upset, began talking to me.

"We don't want this wilderness designation. We just want to keep things the way they are. These people are going to ruin what we have," he explained.

The wilderness advocate listened, then replied, talking to me rather than to the man from Emery County. "We just want to protect the land. We don't want more mines and roads and developments to scar this beautiful land."

In other words, both of these individuals wanted to stop *change*. This is of course the one option that is not available. We can manage change, but we cannot stop the clock. This is especially true for the American West, with its booming population and dramatically changing economy. It is a region of the country that has a label for its recent metamorphosis: the New West.

The politics of wilderness in Utah and the West is in some ways a microcosm of all American politics: the interest groups, the dramatic claims, the media circus, the inflamed passions of the moment. But in other ways it is unique. The debate has continued virtually without reprieve for over twenty years. It involves local, state, tribal, and national politics. And it generates a level of interest and devotion that is unusual in a nation where political apathy seems to be a way of life. In a recent meeting with the authors of this book, Congressman James Hansen explained this quite succinctly: "I sit on the Defense Committee where we allocate tens of billions of dollars in public funds, and I seldom get a phone call from a constituent. But raise an issue over a few acres of wilderness and we get all kinds of calls."

Indeed, there is no shortage of passion and conviction on this issue. Unfortunately the heated debate has generated considerable misinformation, outrageous claims, and fundamental misunderstanding. What is clearly missing is a relatively objective discussion of the issue. A compilation of facts and an explanation of the relevant laws, policies, court cases, and political activity are needed if the wilderness debate is ever going to move toward resolution. That is the goal of this book.

*Contested Landscape* grew out of a class titled "The Politics of Wilderness in Utah and the West," taught in the winter and spring of 1997. This political science course was open to all majors and both graduate students and undergraduates. The first day of class I explained that every student would be expected to author or co-author a book chapter based on original research. I thought such a daunting challenge would scare off many students, but it did not; the class consisted of people with both a commitment to this critically important issue and a willingness to embark upon the difficult but rewarding task of writing a book about it. The students came from a variety of backgrounds and perspectives. Some of them were dedicated wilderness lovers; others grew up on the ranches and farms of rural Utah; and two students described themselves as "wheelers" (i.e., four-wheel-drive enthusiasts). In addition, some students signed up for the course simply to learn more about the issue and have an opportunity to write about it. In all, it was an eclectic group of people who reflected many different perspectives on wilderness.

The range of perspectives on wilderness is, of course, quite dramatic. The syllabus for the course began with two quotations:

"I have become tired of standing by and watching self-ordained 'eco-nuts' call for 5.7 million acres of wilderness." (Letter to the Editor, *San Juan Record*, April 30, 1996, from Ronald Thompson, District Manager, Washington County Water Conservancy District)

"The idea of Wilderness needs no defense, only more defenders." (Edward Abbey, from the Masthead of the *Wilderness Warrior* newsletter)

For this book we were not sure what to call the two sides in the issue. Simply calling them "pro" and "con" belies the range of opinions, and it also labels one side with a negative. Also, most "anti-wilderness" people are not opposed to all wilderness; the disagreement is over the extent of wilderness, not the existence of the policy. As a group we decided to standardize the labels to be used in the book. Thus, one side is called pro-wilderness, or some derivation of that, and the other side is referred to as multiple-use advocates.[1]

To effectively capture the range of opinion for the class, I used two strategies: guest speakers, and a field trip to southern Utah. The guest speakers included the following:[2]

Lawson LeGate, of the Sierra Club

Ken Rait, former Issues Director of the Southern Utah Wilderness Alliance

Ted Stewart, Executive Director of the Utah Division of Natural Resources

Mark Walsh, of the Utah Association of Counties

Margaret Kelsey, Wilderness Coordinator for the Bureau of Land Management

Utah Congressman James Hansen, Chair of the Public Lands Subcommittee

Jim Catlin, of the Wild Lands Project

Brad Barber, of the Governor's Office of Planning and Budget

Dick Carter, former director of the Utah Wilderness Association

Sheldon Kinsel, representing the Utah Farm Bureau

Glenn Eurick, of the Barrick Gold Corporation

Jeff Grathwohl, Director, University of Utah Press

Terry Tempest Williams, prominent author and wilderness activist

These guest speakers proved to be an invaluable source of information, perspective, and ideas, and we owe a great debt of gratitude to them.

The second strategy involved a field trip to San Juan County, Utah. Wilderness is an esthetic issue, and the best way to judge it is to see it. It is also an economic and lifestyle issue for rural people; they are the best spokespersons for their perspective. We traveled to Blanding, Utah, where we met with Janet Ross, a former wilderness inventory specialist for the Bureau of Land Management (BLM). Janet offered the revealing insights of an agency insider. We were then joined by Ken Sleight, owner of Pack Creek Ranch and long-time advocate of wilderness. Ken took us to Cedar Mesa and spoke eloquently of his vision for preserving the wild lands. We then met with Scott Edwards, BLM ranger at the Kane Gulch Ranger Station. He explained what it was like to manage hundreds of thousands of acres of federal land with only four rangers, in the face of dramatically increasing visitation.

From Kane Gulch we traveled to the La Sal Mountain Bed and Breakfast, owned by Hardy and Sunny Redd. Hardy took us on a tour of his grazing allotments. Then, after a sumptuous dinner, we met with a group of local citizens who came to the Redd home to share their perspectives on wilderness with us. It was an instructive, sociable experience. The exchange was friendly yet substantive. I got the sense that it was the first time many of the wilderness proponents and opponents in the room had ever met face to face; we all turned out to be human after all. In one particularly humorous exchange, Matt Adolphson, long-time SUWA activist, exchanged views on county roads with San Juan County Commissioner Ty Lewis.

"If you see me lying down in front of a bulldozer, don't run over me," Matt pleaded with mock seriousness.

"Oh, we won't hurt you," Ty replied. "We'll just rope you to the back of the dozer and keep going."

The room exploded in laughter.

Our frank discussion that night revealed an important element in the wilderness debate: both sides have vilified their opponents, but when we meet each other in person, we find many things in common. Indeed, it is a love of the land that binds us all together. Whether you want to live there, work there, or play there, the public lands of southern Utah provide the common source of our hopes and our vision for the future.

This book is an effort to move the debate beyond the present stalemate. There are many facets to that debate; although we cover many of them, we cannot include all of them. The book is divided into four topical sections. The first section, "A Foundation of Facts," contains essential background information about wilderness policy; one cannot understand the debate in Utah without first reading about wilderness policy in general. Chapter 1, "The Evolution of the Wilderness Concept," by Christopher Wehrli and Robin Clegg, explores the history of federal wilderness policy. Chapter 2, "The U.S. Constitution and Wilderness Designation," by Tina L. Compton, Kirsten Jansen, and Jerold N. Willmore, describes the constitutional framework for federal public lands. And chapter 3, "Weighted in the Balance: The Bureau of Land Management Wilderness Inventory," by Sara McCormick and Brent Osiek, explains the complex administrative process that the Bureau of Land Management has developed.

Section II, "The Wilderness of Politics," includes chapters that describe the raw politics of wilderness designation. Chapter 4, "Drawing Lines in the Desert Sand: The Politics of Public-Interest Groups," by Andrew Fitzgerald and Deborah Schwabach, explores the political strategies developed by the interest groups on both sides of the issue. Chapter 5, "Don't Cry Out Acreage Figures in a Crowded Theater," by Lucas Smart and Amber Ayers, describes how public-opinion polls have played a role in the wilderness debate. And chapter 6, "Babel in the Wilderness: The Rhetoric of Sufficiency/Release and Excepted Activities," by Meredith McKell Graff, concerns the conflict over specific types of language used in wilderness legislation.

Section III, "Competition for Resources," is the longest section of the book because there are so many resource conflicts on public lands. In a sense, the length of this section is a measure of how much is at stake in the wilderness battle. Chapter 7, "A Legacy of Conflict: Mining and Wilderness," by Joshua Footer and J. T. VonLunen, demonstrates how wilderness designation will affect mining in Utah. Chapter 8, "State Trust Lands: A Problem in Wilderness Designation," by Cyrus McKell and David Harward, discusses the conflict between wilderness values and the need to generate funds from state school trust lands. Chapter 9, "Beef and Backpackers: Grazing in Wilderness," by Christopher Krueger, Christian Senf, and Janelle Eurick, explains the relationship between wilderness designation and ranching. Chapter 10, "Divided Highway: The Politics of the Roadless Debate," by Christa Powell and Buck Swaney, describes the important conflict between county roads and wilderness. Chapter 11, "Pottery and Pithouses: Archaeological Resources in Wilderness," by R. Kelly Beck, covers an important but sometimes overlooked resource on public lands. The final chapter in this section, chapter 12, "The Cost of Solitude," by Chris Perri, provides an overview of the various economic studies regarding wilderness and other uses of public lands.

The final section of the book, "Lessons from the Past, Proposals for the Future," contains two chapters. Chapter 13, "The Year of Utah Wilderness: Lessons from 1984," by Richard Warnick, describes the successful passage of a Utah wilderness bill in 1984. The final chapter, "The Community Context Approach," by Doug Goodman and me, offers a proposal that will hopefully expand our view of what should be considered in any wilderness bill.

Writing this book was a challenging project, and we received a great deal of assistance from a wide variety of sources. It is essential to attempt to thank all the individuals who have helped us in this project, but that is a difficult endeavor; many, many people have aided our research efforts. Clearly, we need to thank all of our guest speakers and those who met with us on the field trip. We also owe a debt of gratitude to the University of Utah Teaching Committee, which financed part of our field trip. In addition, the Political Science Department, especially Professor Don Hanson, former chair of the department, and Susan Olson, current departmental chair, gave me the opportunity to offer this unusual class; they were supportive and encouraging even though this course was far from the typical teaching endeavor. We also thank Dean Donna Gelfand and Associate Dean Steve Reynolds of the College of Social and Behavioral Science for their assistance.

Paul Mogrin of the Marriott Library demonstrated how to utilize the library's many sources, including how to access the four thousand or so recent newspaper articles that have been written about Utah wilderness. We also extend our gratitude to Krista Rodin, formerly of the University's Division of Continuing Education, who arranged to have the field trip videotaped for use in future environmental policy classes. Doug and I owe a special debt to two of our own, Rich Warnick and Debbie Schwabach, who read the manuscript in its entirety and provided insightful feedback. And all of us gratefully acknowledge Jeff Grathwohl, the director of the University of Utah Press; thanks, Jeff, for having faith in us.

Finally I would like to personally thank my co-author and co-editor, Doug Goodman. His insights and hard work made an enormous contribution to this book; he did more than his fair share.

And speaking on behalf of all the authors of the book, we must thank all the people of Utah and the nation who have contributed so much to the wilderness debate. Some people decry the amount of time and energy that has been expended on this issue, but in a very real sense it is a perfect example of how an open, democratic process works; it is often unruly, inefficient, and turbulent, but we must all remember to be thankful for the right to be so contentious.

—Daniel McCool

## ℭ  NOTES TO PREFACE

1. Wilderness proponents might object to this labeling; they argue that wilderness *is* a form of multiple use. These uses are delineated in chapter 12.

2. I invited the National Federal Land Conference to speak to the class, but they declined. That group was established by rancher Wayne Hage to fight federal control of public lands.

# A Foundation of Facts

There is a certain irony in the debate over wilderness. The whole concept of wilderness is meant to preserve something that is remote and relatively untouched by the human hand. Wilderness is chiefly characterized by the absence of human activity. Yet it has become the subject of intense human activity and the center of a political storm where legions of activists, bureaucrats, and politicians utilize the latest in political strategy, electronic communication, and up-to-date analysis. There are hundreds of books and articles, thousands of newspaper articles, and ten thousand websites on the Internet that relate to wilderness. These "remote" lands are often on the front page of America's major newspapers, and a surprising number of Americans hold a strong opinion on the subject. The debate has involved America's top leaders for two decades. There is certainly nothing remote about the *politics* of wilderness.

We are deluged with political information regarding wilderness, most of it representing the viewpoints of the antagonists. For all this hoopla, there is precious little understanding of the basic facts underlying the politics of wilderness. There is a set of laws, policies, and regulations that form the historical, legal, and administrative context for the wilderness controversy. Unfortunately, this basic framework of facts is nearly impossible to discern among the polemics and diatribes that have characterized this debate for so long.

The chapters in this section are an attempt to establish this basic foundation of facts. Chapter 1, by Christopher Wehrli and Robin Clegg, explains the origins of the wilderness concept and the legislative history of the 1964 Wilderness Act. This chapter provides an understanding of how political pressures and trade-offs affected the final bill; it is a complex and fascinating legislative legacy.

The second chapter, by Tina Compton, Kirsten Jansen, and Jerold Willmore, explains how the Constitution provides a legal framework for the politics of federal lands. The Constitution is, of course, the supreme law of the land; all public lands legislation must comply with its precepts. This chapter lays the foundation for all subsequent discussion of law and policy regarding wilderness on federal lands.

Chapter 3, by Sara McCormick and Brent Osiek, explores the complicated world of BLM management and regulation. There is considerable detail in this chapter, but the astute observer will soon realize that seemingly trivial changes in bureaucratic procedures can have a profound impact on the outcome of the debate. To a great extent, bureaucratic discretion and the exercise of delegated authority have been at the center of the wilderness conflict for two decades; the BLM acts, and the rest of the world responds. McCormick and Osiek wade through the complex maze of regulations and procedures and demonstrate how they have affected the wilderness debate.

—The Editors

CHAPTER 1

# The Evolution
# of the Wilderness Concept

Christopher Wehrli

Robin Clegg

## WHAT IS WILDERNESS?

Wilderness, as defined in the Random House College Dictionary, is "1. a wild uncultivated, uninhabited region, as of a forest or desert; 2. a part of a garden set apart for plants to grow unchecked and; 3. a bewildering mass or collection." Dr. Greg Thayn, one of the Wilderness Coordinators for the Bureau of Land Management (BLM) in Utah during the wilderness review process, offered a different perspective: "Wilderness is whatever Congress says it is" (Thayn 1997). The Bible mentions several instances of people "wandering in the wilderness" for different spiritual reasons. Also, when one hears the term "frontier," the challenges associated with American expansion into the wilderness come to mind—an idea that has been romanticized since the Mayflower arrived. Although the idea of wilderness has been around since the beginning of history, the definition and modern-day concepts of wilderness have evolved into one of the most debated environmental issues of today.

The two men most associated with the development of the modern wilderness idea in terms of a type of land management are Aldo Leopold and Robert "Bob" Marshall. Leopold saw wilderness as "a continuous stretch of country preserved in its natural state, open to lawful hunting and fishing, devoid of roads, artificial trails, cottages, or other works of man" (Leopold 1921, 719). Marshall also wrote of his ideas of wilderness in forestry journals and other publications, and both fought most of their professional lives to bring about the preservation of wilderness lands.

## Congressional Wilderness

When the Wilderness Act of 1964 (Public Law 88-577) was passed, it defined what wilderness is, or should be, in the land management policies of the U.S. Forest Service (USFS), the National Park Service (NPS), and the U.S. Fish and Wildlife Service (USFWS). Under the guidelines and definitions of the Wilderness Act, the National Wilderness Preservation System (NWPS) mandated the USFS to study its previously set-aside "Primitive" or "Wilderness" areas for inclusion in a NWPS. As far as the definition of wilderness was concerned, the act also included the following guidelines:

> . . . an area where the earth and its community of life are untrammeled by man, where man himself is a visitor who does not remain . . . an area of undeveloped Federal land retaining its primeval character and influence, without permanent improvements or human habitation, which is protected and managed so as to preserve its natural conditions and which (1) generally appears to have been affected primarily by the forces of nature, with the imprint of man's work substantially unnoticeable; (2) has outstanding opportunities for solitude or a primitive and unconfined type of recreation; (3) has at least five thousand (5,000) acres of land or is of sufficient size as to make practicable its preservation and use in an unimpaired condition; and (4) may also contain ecological, geological, or other features of scientific, educational, scenic, or historical value. (78 Stat. 891)

With the passage of this act America had a legal basis for the preservation of lands, primarily within the national forests.

## The American Concept

The abstract definition of wilderness is stated clearly in the Wilderness Act, yet the actual identification of wilderness is largely subjective and often the point of much dissension. One idea of wilderness is a romantic vision of living off the land and removing one's self from the daily routine of modern conveniences. American culture has nurtured the idea of frontier and wilderness as a great asset throughout history. The tourist population throughout the world is aware of the vast expanses of undeveloped land within the United States.

The concept of setting aside lands for the public enjoyment started in 1864 when the federal government granted Yosemite Valley to the state of California, "to hold inalienable for all time" (Hendee, Stankey, and Lucas 1990, 7). In the designation of the first national park in 1872, the Yellowstone National Park Establishment Act clearly identifies the intent of Congress to create a ". . . public park or pleasuring ground for the benefit and enjoyment of the people" (1872). This social aspect of wilderness is unique to Americans and more specifically to those in the West (Hendee, Stankey, and Lucas 1990, 31).

## Spiritual Wilderness

Another concept of wilderness is not only as a physical place, but as a spiritual place where one can retreat to cleanse the soul. This idea has been around since biblical times, yet it is not necessarily a Christian idea. The Old Testament tells the story of Moses and the children of Israel, "wandering in the wilderness" for forty years as a form of spiritual cleansing and a preparatory stage before entering the "promised land." Other writings of the biblical wilderness suggest three general themes: first, as a sanctuary from sin and persecution; second, as a place to draw close to God; and, finally, as a testing ground to prepare spiritually for some specific "reward" (Nash 1982, 16).

In modern times this idea has become more and more popular. It focuses on the ability to master one's self and live apart from society and the technological world that surrounds us. Experiencing wilderness for some might be a spiritual rejuvenation of sorts, but it is not necessarily associated with religion. To go deeper into the spiritual aspects of wilderness uncovers the relationship of the individual to his environment. Native Americans have always considered themselves a small part of a greater whole, the Earth Mother. That is to say, every living thing, including the earth itself, is interconnected and related in some way to every other entity. Wilderness is, in the purest spiritual sense, getting as close to the center of spirituality as one might, while remaining mortal.

## A Personal Relationship

The personal views and definitions of wilderness number as many as there are people. Every person who cares enough about the issue will have an opinion. That opinion will tend to follow a particular side of a debate, yet very few people, if any, will have the same personal definition or place the same value on wilderness. The personal definition is by far the broadest definition. All of the previously mentioned types of wilderness are included in the personal definitions of wilderness. It would be nearly impossible to define one's own idea or concept of wilderness without including some legal, cultural, and spiritual characteristics. The personal definition also contains ideas that are specific to the individual, such as demographic factors. As an example, an individual who lives in a rural community might see wilderness entirely differently than someone who lives in the urban areas of Chicago or Boston.

*The Forgotten Lands*

The BLM's nearly 500 million acres were not addressed by the Wilderness Act. These were the lands left over after the federal program designed to transfer public lands to private ownership had been discontinued. Also, the 500 million acres do not include the withdrawn federal lands designated as national parks and monuments, military bases, wildlife refuges, or national forests. In 1970, it was estimated that BLM lands that could qualify as wilderness ranged from fifty million to ninety million acres in the lower forty-eight states (Hendee, Stankey, and Lucas 1990, 147). In 1976, with the passage of BLM's organic act, the Federal Lands Policy and Management Act (FLPMA) (P.L. 94-237), all of the lands under federal jurisdiction, specifically those lands managed by the BLM, were subject to an inventory and a land-use plan. FLPMA also required that within fifteen years a recommendation be made to Congress for all lands that fit the criteria for wilderness as defined in the Wilderness Act. With the passage of FLPMA and the Wilderness Act's criteria for designation of wilderness, the BLM had the monumental task of inventorying its lands for potential wilderness characteristics (the inventory itself is discussed in more detail in chapter 3).

## THE EVOLUTION BEGINS

An understanding of the various concepts of wilderness is essential to understanding the issues that created and perpetuate the Utah wilderness debate. It is important to remember that, although the Wilderness Act and FLPMA established a legal basis for the preservation of wilderness, the economic, cultural, and political issues surrounding Utah wilderness have changed almost daily. These perpetual issues are still evolving, and will, in the future, remain as points of contention regardless of any congressional act designating BLM wilderness in the state of Utah. The current wilderness debate may be understood more clearly through the historical background of wilderness in the United States and the West.

*The Birth of a Concept*

Since the early 1800s the protection of nature has been a subject of interest and conflict. Early efforts to protect nature can be traced to George Catlin, a lawyer and painter of Native Americans, who traveled extensively to remote regions and painted nature's beauty. In seeing the disappearance of wild areas and the general lack of regard for the land, Catlin foresaw the need to protect natural areas and gave birth to the idea of having "a nation's park . . . containing man and bear, in all the wild and freshness of nature's beauty" (Nash 1982, 101). Catlin's concept of long-term protection for the land fell by the wayside, virtually unnoticed, until Henry Thoreau, whose beliefs paralleled Catlin's, wrote of his experiences and relationships with the land. His books drew national attention to reckless behavior regarding the land and its resources. Through the influence of Catlin, Thoreau, and others, the world's first example of wilderness preservation for public interest on a grand scale occurred in 1872, when Congress created Yellowstone National Park. Although Yellowstone was not specifically created to preserve wilderness, it became an important precedent for natural preservation (Hendee 1990, 100).

*Primitive Areas*
The federal government's early preservation initiatives began with the Forest Service. Arthur Carhart, a landscape architect in Colorado, began thinking about wilderness preservation when the Forest Service hired him in March of 1919 as the first full-time, permanent, recreational engineer to landscape new roads (Nash 1982, 185). One of his first duties was to survey the Trappers Lake area in the White River National Forest of Colorado for summer home sites and to plan a road around the lake. A 1915 law allowed for long-term leases and construction of summer home sites in the national forests. While Carhart was laying survey lines around the lake, he met William McFadden and Paul J. Rainey, who, after some discussion, persuaded Carhart that the Forest Service should keep Trappers Lake undeveloped and roadless.

When Carhart presented the surveys to his supervisor, Carl J. Stahl, he planted the idea that further "improvements" would damage the natural landscape surrounding the lake. Stahl eventually agreed that the area should remain roadless and the many permit applications for home sites should be denied. This was a first in Forest Service history. Others in the Forest Service became interested and wanted more information about this nature-conserving concept. Aldo Leopold, Assistant Forester in Albuquerque, New Mexico, was one such man. In December of 1919, Carhart and Leopold met in the Denver District office, and as a result of that meeting Carhart put into writing a program for the preservation of nature in the Forest Service. Trappers Lake set a precedent in applying the wilderness concept. In 1921, Superior National Forest in Minnesota became the next example, due to Carhart's perseverance. Gila National Forest in New Mexico became the third example, through Leopold's influence.

## A "PRIMITIVE" MANAGEMENT POLICY

Aldo Leopold began working hard to influence surveys of roadless areas in other national forests. His efforts eventually led to the Forest Service L-20 Regulation in 1929. The L-20 Regulation allowed the Forest Service to establish a primitive area and mandated that it remain "primitive." By 1939, seventy-three primitive areas within the national forests had been established. Because timber cutting was still allowed, L-20 was viewed as not very protective, nor was it strictly enforced. Some writers have suggested that the L-20 regulation was used by the USFS to keep scenic lands in their jurisdiction that would otherwise have been transferred to the National Park Service (Hendee, Stankey, and Lucas 1990, 100).

Bob Marshall, a forester in Wyoming, recognized the inadequacy of the L-20 regulation (Zaslowsky and Watkins 1994, 202). In 1939, as chief of the Division of Recreation and Lands in the USFS, Marshall devised the U-Regulations. The U-Regulations expanded the purpose of wilderness, defined wild areas, and established roadless areas. The U-Regulations provided much more protection for wilderness areas. Intended to be permanent, they prohibited timber cutting and permits for home sites, and barred access by mechanical means, with a few exceptions. Neither the L-20 Regulation nor the U-Regulations were mandated by law; rather, they were administrative decisions that could be implemented at the discretion of the Forest Service. Wilderness proponents were concerned that some areas would not receive adequate protection under this administrative approach, which left prescribed wilderness values to the discretion of the agency's administrators.

In October of 1934, Bob Marshall met with Bernard Frank, Benton Mackaye, and his friend, Harvey Broome, at a forestry convention in Knoxville, Tennessee. This meeting soon evolved into a spirited discussion of how to save the vanishing wild lands in the country. As a result of this conversation the Wilderness Society was founded in January of 1935. Along with the four men from the Knoxville convention, Aldo Leopold became a co-founder. The stated objective of the Wilderness Society was "holding wild areas soundproof as well as sight proof from our increasingly mechanized life" (Nash 1982, 207). The co-founders were very selective about who could become a member. They wanted members who would remain committed to the cause. Mackaye told Marshall, "We want those who already think as we do, not those who have to be shown" (Zaslowsky and Watkins 1994, 205). Because of the selective style of the Wilderness Society, membership grew slowly at first but today has reached nearly 200,000. The creation of the Wilderness Society sparked what became the wilderness preservation movement.

*A Political Concept of Wilderness*
In 1956 the proposed damming of the Green River in Dinosaur National Monument prompted Howard Zahniser, executive secretary of the Wilderness Society at the time, to draft a bill to protect wilderness. Zahniser's love of "wild lands" came from his long association with the Adirondack Mountains. A journalist by trade, he worked his way up in the Wilderness Society, eventually becoming its executive director. Zahniser believed that all the lands would eventually be put to some developmental use. He stated, "If any of it is to be preserved in its natural condition it must be as the result of a deliberate setting aside of it for human use in a natural condition" (Zaslowsky and Watkins 1994, 207). Zahniser is the person who drafted the first version of the Wilderness Act and the majority of the sixty-six revised versions that followed.

*An Act of Congress*
The wilderness bill drafted by Zahniser allowed protection for a small percentage of federal lands that met the approved wilderness criteria. The various land managing agencies, the USFS, NPS, and USFWS, fell under this legislation. Each agency would be responsible and accountable for the management of wilderness land under its jurisdiction, and thus a new administrating agency would not be needed. Zahniser presented Senator Hubert Humphrey (D-Minnesota) with a copy of the proposed legislation.

In 1957 Senator Humphrey formally introduced the wilderness bill. Opposition to the bill was fierce. Senator Arthur Watkins of Utah was one of the bill's most outspoken opponents. Senator Watkins stated at a hearing in July of 1958, "Out our way millions of acres are already adequately preserved and reserved in the wilderness state, probably always will be because nature made it that way" (Zaslowsky and Watkins 1994, 209). The lines were drawn regionally, with the West generally against land management in any degree and opposed to the bill, and the South and Northeast for it. The U.S. Forest Service and the National Park Service also disliked it because they felt their agencies were already adequately protecting wilderness (Zaslowsky and Watkins 1994, 209).

The wilderness bill changed substantially during the eight years it was being considered in Congress. There were eighteen separate public hearings and thousands of pages of testimony before a final act emerged in 1964 (McCloskey 1966, 298). When the necessary votes were achieved for the passage of the Wilderness Act, Zahniser wrote: "We are establishing for the first time in the history of the earth a program, a national policy, whereby areas of wilderness can be preserved. That will not be the end of our efforts. That is just the beginning" (Zahniser 1964, 41). Now Congress could act independently to designate new wilderness areas for the National Wilderness Preservation System.

At its signing by President Lyndon Johnson, on September 3, 1964, the Wilderness Act immediately designated 9.1 million acres of national park, national forest, and wildlife refuge lands as wilderness. Each new wilderness area would be managed by the agency having jurisdiction over that area before its designation. The Forest Service prepared wilderness regulations and a management plan following the guidelines laid out by the act. Studies and recommendations of potential additions to the system were also under their jurisdiction, but none were made between 1964 and 1973. The agency's interpretation of the act followed strict standards that eliminated most areas that had been disturbed by man. The Forest Service gave the opinion that hardly any areas in the East were pristine or "untrammeled" enough to be classified as wilderness. But under pressure from preservationists, Congress passed the Eastern Wilderness Act in 1973 (P.L. 93-622). The 1973 act made it clear that if an area had recovered, or was in the process of recovering, from past use, it could be included in the National Wilderness Preservation System.

Similar pressure encouraged the Forest Service to take the initiative and survey its "de facto" wilderness and/or roadless areas for possible inclusion in the National Wilderness Preservation System. In 1972, the USFS initiated the process known as the Roadless Area Review and Evaluation (RARE). Two years later the final RARE report recommended 12.3 million acres for wilderness protection. Preservation groups were disappointed with the amount recommended and called for a second review. The Forest Service agreed and formulated a second review, called RARE II, which was much more comprehensive and established greater reliability and validity in the inventory process. Public comment was incorporated and more than fifty thousand people responded with suggested additions and deletions for the RARE II study. In response, the Forest Service identified a total of 65.7 million roadless acres. However, preservationists protested RARE II because only fifteen million acres of national forests were recommended as wilderness. There was a RARE III, but it had little support and was absorbed into the management process provided by the National Forest Management Act of 1976 (P.L. 94-588; Hendee, Stankey, and Lucas 1990, 134).

*Wilderness Designation in Utah*

Wilderness designation of Forest Service lands in Utah has been a slow process. Utah's first designation of wilderness in 1979 set aside the thirty-thousand-acre Lone Peak Wilderness near Salt Lake City. For sixteen years it was the only wilderness area in Utah. In 1982, Senator Jake Garn, who had promised conservationists a Forest Service wilderness bill, began the process of qualifying additional wilderness on Forest Service lands. Representative Jim Hansen played an active role in the negotiating process by bringing the opposing sides together to "hash out" their differences and find common ground resulting in a compromise acceptable to both sides. Governor Scott Matheson joined the Utah congressional delegation in support of the bill, thus creating a strong, united, political front that enabled the heart of the bill to remain intact throughout the negotiating process (Poulson 1984). President Reagan signed the bill September 28, 1984, setting aside 750,000 acres as Utah wilderness. The Utah Wilderness Act of 1984 (P.L. 98-428) proved politically that wilderness legislation can be passed through hard work and compromise (Bauman 1984). The politics surrounding the passage of this act are fully explored in chapter 13.

A month prior to the enactment of the Utah Wilderness Act of 1984, the Arizona Wilderness Act of 1984 (P.L. 98-406) was signed into law. The Arizona Wilderness Act encompassed some of Utah's BLM lands on the Utah/Arizona Strip into Paria Canyon–Vermilion Cliff and Beaver Dam Mountains Wilderness areas. This was the first time that BLM lands in Utah were considered for wilderness designation.

## FEDERAL LAND POLICY AND MANAGEMENT ACT OF 1976

Originally the Wilderness Act did not apply to the public domain lands managed by the BLM. This changed with the passage of the Federal Land Policy and Management Act of 1976 (FLPMA). The act is divided into seven titles and sixty sections, all of which regulate the management of all BLM lands from that time forward. Title I consists of the declaration of policy and the definitions of the act. The second title contains the regulations that cover planning, acquisition, and disposition of lands. Title III explains the administrative requirements of the act. Range management and rights-of-way are the next two titles, respectively, followed by Title VI, which is of great importance to the wilderness debate. The final Title (VII), covers existing rights and the repeal of existing laws.

Section 102(a)1 states that the public lands are to remain in federal ownership unless specific criteria of disposition are met for exchange or sale. Until FLPMA was passed, the policy was to allow the sale or acquisition of the lands by private citizens through such means as the Homestead Act. Section 102(a)2 requires that the "public lands and their resources be periodically and systematically inventoried and their present and future use projected through a land use planning process coordinated with other Federal and State planning efforts." Congress maintained its authority to "withdraw or otherwise designate or dedicate Federal lands for specific purposes." The executive is granted authority to do the same without legislative action. Other requirements of Section 102 include a requirement that the Secretary of the U.S. Department of the Interior (USDI) establish comprehensive rules and regulations with involvement by the public, and that goals and objectives of management be established on the basis of *multiple use and sustained yield*, two points of debate in the wilderness issue. An important subsection of Section 102 requires that the

> . . . public lands be managed in a manner that will protect the quality of scientific, scenic, historical, ecological, environmental, air and atmospheric, water resource, and archaeological values; that, where appropriate, will preserve and protect certain public lands in their natural condition; that will provide food and habitat for fish and wildlife and domestic animals; and that will provide for outdoor recreation and human occupancy and use. (Subsection [a]8)

The remainder of Section 102 discusses areas of critical environmental concern, disposal and exchanges of lands, the recognition of the nation's need for domestic sources of minerals, food, timber, and fiber from public lands, and the recognition of the Mining and Minerals Act of 1970. The final aspect of Section 102 concerns economics: the "Federal Government should, on a basis equitable to both the Federal and local taxpayer, provide for payments to compensate States and local governments for burdens created as a result of the immunity of Federal lands from State and local taxation." The importance of this section of FLPMA is addressed in chapter 14 of this volume.

The definitions in Section 103 are also important in the wilderness issues. As stated previously, the *personal* definition of wilderness is completely subjective and consists of spiritual, cultural, and experiential ideas. The BLM is required by law to set personal ideas aside and follow the *objective* definitions contained in FLPMA. Whether that is possible or not is debatable; however, the act establishes the definitions. Areas of critical environmental concern, or "ACECs," are defined as "areas within the public lands where special management attention is required to protect and prevent irreparable damage to important historical, cultural, or scenic values, fish and wildlife resources or other natural systems or processes, or to protect life and safety from natural hazards" (FLPMA P.L. 94-579). The definition of the term "multiple use" used in Section 103(c) is quite lengthy but bears quoting. Multiple use means

> . . . the management of public lands and their various resource values so they are utilized in the combination that will best meet the present and future needs of the American people; making the most judicious use of the land for some or all of these resources or related services over areas large enough to provide sufficient latitude for periodic adjustments in use to conform to changing needs and conditions; the use of some land for less than all of the resources; a combination of balanced and diverse resource uses that takes into account the long term needs of future generations for renewable and nonrenewable resources, including, but not limited to, recreation, range, timber, minerals, watershed, wildlife and fish, and natural scenic, scientific and historical values; and harmonious and coordinated management of various resources without permanent impairment of the productivity of the land and the quality of the environment with consideration being given to the relative values of the resource and not necessarily to the combination of uses that will give the greatest economic return or the greatest unit output. (Sec. 103[c])

Lastly, the remaining term to be defined is "Wilderness." According to FLPMA, wilderness as used in Section 603 shall have the same meaning as it does in Section 2(c) of the Wilderness Act of 1964. As stated earlier, the Wilderness Act defines wilderness in the broadest sense of the word and leaves many aspects open to interpretation.

Title II, which contains the land use planning and the acquisition and disposition of lands, has become a highly debated part of FLPMA. Section 201(a) requires the Secretary of the Interior to prepare and maintain an inventory of all public lands and their resource and other values. This inventory is also to be kept current and identify "new and emerging resources and other values." The final part of Section 201(a) is a stipulation that the identification and inventory "shall not, of itself, change or prevent change of the management or use of public lands."

Section 202 requires the Secretary to develop and maintain a land use plan for all the public lands, regardless of lands previously set aside or designated for a specific purpose. That is to say, even public lands that are part of a military withdrawal need to have a land use plan established and maintained. Section 202(c)1–9 sets out what is required in a land use plan. Section 202(c) states that in the development and revision of the land use plans, the Secretary shall:

> (1) use and observe the principles of multiple use and sustained yield . . .;

(2) use a systematic interdisciplinary approach to achieve integrated consideration of physical, biological, economic, and other sciences;

(3) give priority to the designation and protection of areas of environmental concern;

(4) rely, to the extent it is available, on the inventory of the public lands, their resources, and other values;

(5) consider present and potential uses of the public lands;

(6) consider the relative scarcity of the values involved and the availability of alternative means (including recycling) and sites for realization of those values;

(7) weigh long-term benefits to the public against short-term benefits.

Section 202(c)8 requires compliance with applicable pollution control laws. And the final part, Section 202(c)9, requires consistency with other government agencies, including state, local, and other federal agencies, and consistency with laws governing the administration of public lands.

Section 603 defines what is required of the BLM in regard to wilderness designation. There are some references to the 1964 Wilderness Act, which was discussed previously. Section 603 is such a significant part of FLPMA as it relates to wilderness that we are quoting it in its entirety:

> Within fifteen years after the date of approval of this Act, the Secretary shall review those roadless areas of five thousand acres or more and roadless islands of the public lands, identified during the inventory required by section 201(a) of this Act having wilderness characteristics described in the Wilderness Act of September 3, 1964 (78 Stat. 890; 16 U.S.C. 1131 et seq.) and shall from time to time report to the President his recommendation as to the suitability or nonsuitability of each such area or island for preservation as wilderness: *Provided,* That prior to any recommendations for the designation of an area as wilderness the Secretary shall cause mineral surveys to be conducted by the Geological Survey and the Bureau of Mines to determine the mineral values, if any, that may be present in such areas: *Provided further,* That the Secretary shall report to the President by July 1, 1980, his recommendations on those areas which the Secretary has prior to November 1, 1975, formally identified as natural or primitive areas. The review required by this subsection shall be conducted in accordance with the procedure specified in section 3(d) of the Wilderness Act.
>
> (b) The President shall advise the president of the Senate and the Speaker of the House of Representatives of his recommendations with respect to designation as wilderness of each such area, together with a map thereof and a definition of its boundaries. Such advice by the President shall be given within two years of the receipt of each report from the Secretary. A recommendation of

the President for designation as wilderness shall become effective only if so provided by an Act of Congress.

(c) During the period of review of such areas and until Congress has determined otherwise, the Secretary shall continue to manage such lands according to his authority under this Act and other applicable law in a manner so as not to impair the suitability of such areas for preservation as wilderness, subject, however, to the continuation of existing mining and grazing uses and mineral leasing in the manner and degree in which the same was being conducted on the date of approval of this Act: *Provided,* That, in managing the public lands the Secretary shall by regulation or otherwise take any action required to prevent unnecessary or undue degradation of the lands and their resources or to afford environmental protection. Unless previously withdrawn from appropriation under the mining laws, such lands shall continue to be subject to such appropriation during the period of review unless withdrawn by the Secretary under the procedures of section 204 of this Act for reasons other than preservation of their wilderness character. Once an area has been designated for preservation as wilderness, the provisions of the Wilderness Act which apply to national forest wilderness areas shall apply with respect to the administration and use of such designated area, including mineral development, access, exchange of lands, and ingress and egress for mining claimants and occupants. (Sec. 603[a])

*THE DEBATE*

The Federal Land Policy and Management Act of 1976 and the Wilderness Act of 1964 set forth the requirements of wilderness designation. They do not, however, require interest groups, states, or counties to follow their guidelines when recommending areas to be designated as wilderness. There are sections, phrases, and wording within the acts that are unclear, thus opening the doors of personal interpretation. Wilderness proponents and opponents alike have exploited and interpreted the wording of the law in the ongoing wilderness debate. This is illustrated in subsequent chapters.

This debate is especially contentious in Utah. The original intent of those who developed and brought forth the concept of wilderness preservation was *not* to designate all of the lands that meet the Wilderness Act's criteria. Rather, the emphasis was on preservation of selected lands. But the politics of wilderness has evolved into a debate over protection and political control of all wilderness lands. There are many people involved in the debate who would like to solve the wilderness issue with a determinative proposal. There are also those who do not want to give in to a compromise regardless of the end result. In other words, this debate has been driven by politics and emotion and not by rational, responsible discussion between the stakeholders. At the core of the debate is the issue of control versus protection. This will be brought out more substantively in the following chapters.

Issues such as grazing, mining, and other human uses of the land are at the heart of the wilderness preservation debate. With few exceptions no one wants to see all of the lands developed, yet when listening to the debate the environmentalists claim the multiple-use supporters want to strip mine, log, and develop all remaining untouched lands. On the other side, the multiple-use supporters claim that environmentalists want to go so far as to kill off humans for the betterment of the environment. We hope that this book will educate and inform as to the facts and relevant issues driving the wilderness debate in the West and specifically in Utah. This chapter described the history of wilderness policy in order to provide a historical foundation of facts. Hopefully that foundation will enhance the search for possible mitigation, compromises, and solutions. Subsequent chapters will shed further light on the Utah wilderness struggle.

## ℚ REFERENCES TO CHAPTER 1

Baldwin, D. N. 1972. *The Quiet Revolution: Grass Roots of Today's Wilderness Preservation Movement.* Boulder, CO: Pruett.

Bauman, J. 1984. "President Signs Utah Wilds Bill," *Deseret News,* September 29, B1.

*Federal Land Policy and Management Act.* 1976. Act of October 21, 1976. P.L. 94-579.90 Stat. 2743.

Hendee, J. C., G. H. Stankey, and R. C. Lucas. 1990. *Wilderness Management.* Golden, CO: North American Press.

Leopold, A. 1921. The wilderness and its place in forest recreation policy. *Journal of Forestry* 19 (7): 717–21.

McCloskey, M. 1966. The Wilderness Act of 1964: its background and meaning. *The Oregon Law Review* 45 (4): 288–321.

Nash, R. 1982. *Wilderness and the American Mind.* 3d ed. New Haven, CT: Yale University Press.

Poulson, M. 1984. Utah politics spark the call of the wild. *Utah Nature* (September): 19–20.

Thayn, Dr. G. 1997. U.S. Department of the Interior, Bureau of Land Management. Personal interview by authors, February 8.

*Wilderness Act.* 1964. Act of September 3, 1964. P.L. 88-577.78 Stat. 890.

*Yellowstone National Park Establishment Act.* March 1, 1872, ch. 24, 17 Stat. 32 (codified at 16 U.S.C. secs. 21, 22).

Zahniser, H. C. 1964. The people and wilderness. *The Living Wilderness* (Spring/Summer): 41.

Zaslowsky, D., and T. H. Watkins. 1994. *These American Lands.* Washington, DC: Island Press.

# CHAPTER 2

# The U.S. Constitution and Wilderness Designation

Tina L. Compton

Kirsten Jansen

Jerold N. Willmore

## INTRODUCTION

The United States is the oldest constitutional democracy in the world. The foundation document—the basic social contract upon which this nation was founded—is our Constitution. In this society, law is rooted in the U.S. Constitution—either authorized by or allowed by that document. It is, therefore, from the Constitution that all law derives its authority and finds its legitimacy.

This chapter will examine the constitutional issues involved in setting aside federal public lands as "wilderness." Ideally, in a government of law, politics is the process through which the public interest is distilled into public policy. This chapter will discuss that process—insofar as the constitutional roots of wilderness designation are concerned—as determined by the Congress; administered by the Executive Branch; and as ultimately ratified, modified, or nullified by the Supreme Court.

It is the Constitution alone that is the entire source of the duties, powers, and constraints of each of those three branches as they respectively make, execute, and adjudicate our laws (Constitution, Articles I, II, and III). And it is the Constitution, alone and supreme (Constitution, Article VI, Clause 2), that federally elected and appointed officials are sworn to ". . . preserve, protect and defend . . ." (Constitution, Article II, Section l, Clause 8).

It is, therefore, not unexpected that it is upon the Constitution that both sides of the wilderness debate have often based their arguments. In any event, it is the Constitution—or, at least, the Supreme Court's interpretation of it—that ultimately decides the issue. For, as the late Justice Charles Evans Hughes once observed, "The Constitution is what the judges say it is."

## THE CONSTITUTIONAL CONTEXT OF THE WILDERNESS DEBATE: TWELVE CLAUSES

Each of the provisions of the Constitution that relates in any way to wilderness designation is briefly explained in this section. A more detailed treatment of the two most pertinent clauses ("Property" and "Takings") appears in the following section. Table 2.1 summarizes these constitutional provisions.

There are twelve provisions (listed below, in textual order) of the U.S. Constitution that bear, explicitly or implicitly, on the debate, the political action, and the litigation concerning wilderness designation. Only a few of these provisions are ever cited by the debaters, however, or cited by the courts as the constitutional principle(s) on which wilderness cases turn. These twelve provisions do, nonetheless, create a fabric—a sociopolitical context—within which the debate takes place. This context clearly expresses a value system that operates as a guide and a foundation for basic aspects of the American character.

Concerning wilderness designation, these twelve provisions shape our policy formulation and control its implementation. In the aggregate, they comprise a body of principles and procedures that help us define where we stand on what has become one of the predominant issues in this century and one that will undoubtedly carry over into the next. That issue is whether, how much, and when to designate federal public lands as wilderness in order to secure the permanent protections afforded by the Wilderness Act of 1964.

### General Welfare Clause
Preamble: *We the People of the United States, in Order to form a more perfect Union, establish Justice, insure domestic Tranquility, provide for the common defence, promote the general Welfare, and secure the Blessings of Liberty to ourselves and our Posterity, do ordain and establish this Constitution for the United States of America.*

The Preamble could be called the constitutional "mission statement" for all who count themselves in the body politic referred to as "We the People of the United States. . . ." The Preamble plainly states the generic purposes for which the Constitution was established. As such, every part of the Constitution is interpreted in the context of the Preamble's language.

TABLE 2.1—Provisions in the Constitution that Create a Context for the Wilderness Debate

| Clause | | Section |
|---|---|---|
| General Welfare Clause | | Preamble |
| Commerce Clause | | Article I, Section 8, Clause 3 |
| Cession Clause | | Article I, Section 8, Clause 17 |
| Necessary and Proper Clause | | Article I, Section 8, Clause 18 |
| Equal Footing Doctrine | | Article IV, Sections 1, 2, 3, and 4 |
| Privileges and Immunities Clauses | (Federal) | Article IV, Section 2, Clause 1 |
| | (States) | Amendment XIV, Section 1, Clause 2 |
| Property Clause | | Article IV, Section 3, Clause 2 |
| Supremacy Clause | | Article VI, Clause 2 |
| Takings Clauses | (Federal) | Amendment V, Clause 2 and 3 |
| | (States) | Amendment XIV, Section 1, Clause 3 |
| People's Rights Clause | | Amendment IX and X |
| States' Rights Clause | | Amendment X |
| Equal Protection Clause | | Amendment XIV, Section 1, Clause 4 |

The interpretations, however, are often controversial, depending on the previous agendas the conflicting parties bring to the debate. The General Welfare Clause, for instance, could be used as a justification for, among many other things, conserving some natural habitat through wilderness designation. Conversely, the forest products industry could say that the General Welfare Clause should be interpreted to protect jobs in preference to spotted owls. In either case, wilderness designation has never been challenged on the ground that it violates the "General Welfare Clause."

## Commerce Clause
Article I, Section 8, Clause 3: *[The Congress shall have Power] . . . To regulate Commerce with foreign nations, and among the several States, and with the Indian Tribes.*

This clause has not been used as a justification of wilderness designation. It has been used—unsuccessfully—as a basis for attacking federal regulation related to wilderness areas (see *Kleppe v. New Mexico* [1976] discussion under Property Clause Overview, below).

## Cession (Enclave) Clause
Article I, Section 8, Clause 17: *[The Congress shall have Power] . . . To exercise exclusive Legislation in all Cases whatsoever, over such District (not exceeding ten Miles square) as may, by Cession of particular States, and the*

*Acceptance of Congress, become the Seat of the Government of the United States, and to exercise like Authority over all Places purchased by the Consent of the Legislature of the State in which the Same shall be, for the Erection of Forts, Magazines, Arsenals, dock-Yards, and other needful Buildings.*

Wherever such state-owned enclaves have been ceded to the federal government by a state or states it has been through negotiation and not through a "taking." The Takings Clause (below) applies only to private property taken for public use, and is, therefore, not involved here.

### Necessary and Proper Clause

Article I, Section, 8, Clause 18: *[The Congress shall have Power] . . . To make all Laws which shall be necessary and proper for carrying into Execution the foregoing Powers, and all other Powers vested by this Constitution in the Government of the United States, or in any Department or Officer thereof.*

This clause is an additional delegation of authority so fundamental and explicit that, while it is implicit in every congressional action, it has never been a basis for overturning federal wilderness regulations.

### Equal Footing Doctrine

Article IV, Section 1, Clause 1: *Full Faith and Credit shall be given in each State to the public Acts, Records, and judicial Proceedings of every other state.*

Article IV, Section 2, Clause 1: *The Citizens of each State shall be entitled to all Privileges and Immunities of Citizens in the several States.*

Article IV, Section 3, Clause 1: *New States may be admitted by the Congress into this Union. . . .*

Article IV, Section 4, Clause 1: *The United States shall guarantee to every State in this Union a Republican Form of Government. . . .*

The "Equal Footing Doctrine" is drawn from the aggregate of sections 1, 2, 3, and 4 of Article IV of the Constitution (above). The courts have interpreted them as a context to create a time-honored doctrine that all new states added to the original Union (of thirteen states) shall be admitted as equals, that is, on "equal footing" with every other state. In other words, there is no first-class versus second- or third-class statehood no matter the state's size, date of entry, population, wealth, and so on. This argument was invoked as a cause of action in a recent "county supremacy" case (*United States v. Nye County,* 1996), which is discussed in the Property Clause Case Law section, below.

### Privileges and Immunities Clauses

Article IV, Section 2, Clause 1: *The citizens of each State shall be entitled to all Privileges and Immunities of Citizens in the several states.*

Amendment XIV, Section 1, Clause 2: *No State shall make or enforce any law which shall abridge the privileges or immunities of citizens of the United States.*

These two clauses appear to bar any attempt by a state or county to deny or otherwise regulate citizen access to federal public lands, including wilderness, that citizens are otherwise entitled to enter. The philosophy inherent in these two clauses can even be construed to underwrite the modern public policy of requiring the construction or provision of amenities to facilitate the use of all public property, including wilderness, by physically challenged citizens.

### Property Clause

Article IV, Section 3, Clause 2: *The Congress shall have Power to dispose of and make all needful Rules and regulations respecting the Territory or other Property belonging to the United States.*

This clause—more than any other in the Constitution—is central to the discussion about, and the litigation over, the federal public lands in general, and those designated as wilderness in particular. An analysis of the clause's impact and its interpretation by the courts is illustrated in the Property Clause Case Law section, below.

### Supremacy Clause

Article VI, Clause 2: *This Constitution, and the Laws of the United States which shall be made in Pursuance thereof; and all Treaties made, or which shall be made, under the Authority of the United States, shall be the supreme Law of the Land; and the Judges in every State shall be bound thereby, any Thing in the Constitution or Laws of any State to the Contrary notwithstanding.*

This clause, more than most, leaves little room for interpretaion. It literally speaks for itself. Concerning control of the federal public lands, this clause is second in importance only to the Property Clause, which it reinforces (discussed more completely in the Property Clause Case Law section, below).

### Takings Clauses

Amendment V, Clauses 2 and 3: *Nor shall any person be . . . deprived of life, liberty, or property, without due process of law; nor shall private property be taken for public use, without just compensation.*

Amendment XIV, Section 1, Clause 3: *. . . Nor shall any State deprive any person of life, liberty, or property, without due process of law;*

These two clauses function as an impenetrable legal barrier protecting individuals from government tyranny—federal, state, or local. They are relied upon frequently by both government and private interests in disputes involving "private property . . . for public use . . ."; but only rarely, if ever, are these clauses operative on wilderness questions. They are, nevertheless, invoked by all sides on the wilderness issue, as discussed in the Takings Clause Overview, below.

### People's Rights Clause

Amendment IX: *The enumeration in the Constitution, of certain rights, shall not be construed to deny or disparage others retained by the people.*

This clause, although seldom if ever cited on wilderness issues, nevertheless serves as unspoken contextual reinforcement of two basic constitutional principles: (a) limited government; and (b) sovereignty retained by and residing with the people, who are the ultimate, sole source of all the powers delegated to the government. Wilderness designation, like all congressional action, must comply with those two realities.

### States' Rights Clause

Amendment X: *The powers not delegated to the United States by the Constitution, nor prohibited by it to the States, are reserved to the States respectively, or to the people.*

It is this clause, primarily, that gives substance to the idea of "dual sovereignty"—or sovereignty split between the federal government and state governments. A more complete discussion is offered in the Property Clause Case Law section, below.

### Equal Protection Clause

Amendment XIV, Section 1, Clause 4: . . . *[nor shall any state]. . . deny to any person within its jurisdiction the equal protection of the laws.*

This clause provides a clear mandate to the states to eliminate and avoid any personal discrimination in their law making or law enforcement. It was written for the specific protection of non-whites (see discussion in Takings Clause Case Law section, below), but could be construed to apply to physically challenged persons—including equal access to wilderness areas.

## THE CONSTITUTION AND WILDERNESS CASE LAW

### Introduction

Of all the twelve constitutional provisions discussed above that touch on wilderness designation, there are just two on which the majority of the cases turn. They are the Property Clause, primarily, and the Takings

Clause, secondarily. Most other constitutional provisions relevant to wilderness designation are treated by the courts as either contextual, tangential, or subordinate to those two clauses. The following analysis will illustrate.

*The Property Clause Case Law*
The Constitution's framers had vivid and sometimes bitter personal experience dealing with the unchecked, tyrannical power of a despotic government—the British Crown. Many of the framers were also well versed in both the modern and classical political history of European governments. They knew too well the pain, unfairness, and capricious domination that those monarchies had visited upon their subjects. And they knew, as well, of the endless bloody conflicts and intrigue those monarchies inflicted on each other. In light of that knowledge, the framers were determined to create a new American government with limited power and decentralized authority. Thus, the Constitution granted some powers to the federal government but denied others. Moreover, the federal government's authority to act was divided into the three separate, equal branches, each to act as a check and balance on the others.

If a delegation of federal power was neither expressed nor implied in the Constitution, then it was reserved, by default, ". . . to the states, respectively, or to the people." As a result, both the concept and the reality of "dual sovereignty" took root. For instance, the "police power" (the authority to act in all matters of health, safety, morals, and welfare) was reserved to the states—and, where they should so delegate—to their respective counties and cities. This idea of "dual sovereignty" structured into the Constitution has, no doubt, acted as a safeguard against some potential abuses of central power by the federal government. This concept also provided the central government with the power to function in the national interest where power fragmented among state or local governments would be at best inadequate and counterproductive. However—together with most Americans' traditional distrust of authority, generally—the idea of "dual sovereignty" has also been the source of endless confusion and conflict right up to the present day.

The Civil War was fought, at least in large part, to determine whether the "states" were sovereign and independent political entities—or whether they were, within the Constitution, subject to the supremacy of federal writ. In other words, the war was a contest between the "states' rightists" in the South and the "federalists" in the North to determine whether or not the term "United States" was singular or plural. History, of course, records that the North won, unconditionally. Given that all politics, ultimately, grows out of the barrel of a gun, one might think that would have settled the issue—that the "United States" is singular and sovereign—at least in areas where federal supremacy is clearly delineated in the Constitution, as it is in the Property Clause.

However, it has not settled the issue. Ever since the Civil War, for example, there have been both physical and legal challenges made to the federal government's authority, right, and power to regulate and control the federal public lands. In the last two decades alone, the "County Sovereignty," "Sagebrush Rebellion," and "Wise Use" movements have mounted direct challenges to federal authority over federal lands—sometimes physically, in the field; often rhetorically, in the news media; and occasionally with lawsuits, in the state and federal courts. In all cases, the issue has been decided in favor of federal supremacy. The primary operative authority is the Property Clause (below), especially when read in the context of the Supremacy Clause (Article VI, Clause 2):

> The Congress shall have Power to dispose of and make all needful Rules and Regulations respecting the Territory or other Property belonging to the United States; and nothing in this Constitution shall be so construed as to Prejudice any Claims of the United States, or of any particular State. (Article IV, Section 3, Clause 2)

This clause, on its face, appears to be simple, direct, and unequivocal. How, then, do the opponents of federal control of public lands justify a legal attack on that stewardship? They do it by reading the Property Clause in a "strict constructionist," restrictive way. However, an unbroken string of Supreme Court cases has interpreted it in a broad, unrestrictive way—a way that supports unlimited discretion in Congress to deal with federal property as it sees fit. But the opponents interpret the phrase "the Congress shall have Power to dispose of . . ." as a duty or an obligation for the federal government "to get rid of"—to completely divest itself of—most, if not all, territories acquired from other nations (Patterson 1949, 47–48; Brodie 1981, 721–22).

Another interpretation holds that the "power to dispose" or "divest," by definition, necessarily includes the "power to not dispose," to "not divest." The Supreme Court has consistently held that the clause does not mandate a "duty." It delegates a "Power." And delegated power, by definition, involves choice, which connotes latitude to be exercised at the discretion of the entity holding the power: Congress (Brodie 1981, 721–22).

The "sagebrush rebels" of the late 1970s and early 1980s (*Nevada ex rel. Nevada State Board of Agriculture v. United States* 1981; Gaetke 1985), as well as the "county supremacy" and "wise use" movements of the 1990s, filed suits based on the restrictive interpretation, coupled with an unprecedented interpretation of the "equal footing" doctrine, and proceeded to seek privatization of federal public lands (Hanna 1951; Erm 1994; Reed 1994). The rebels have interpreted the "equal footing" doctrine to mean that, since the original thirteen states (and most eastern states) were admitted to the Union with little or no federal public lands within their borders, then all other states should have little or no federal public lands within their borders. The rebels proposed to either privatize the federal public lands or turn them over to the states (Hanna 1951; Erm 1994; Reed 1994).

There were two insurmountable barriers to the success of the rebels' goals of either privatization or divestiture. The first barrier was the existence of "split estates"; and the second was the Constitution itself.

The insoluble problem posed by split estates was unforeseen by the rebels. The split estates idea had long been a rallying cry for the opponents of federal ownership of public lands. The term "split estates" embodies the concept that ownership is not a singular, simple, or seamless thing. In this view, generally recognized in the law, ownership of a single entity likens it to a bundle of sticks, where there can be different claimants on different sticks within the bundle. Applied to the federal public lands there are a variety of private claimants, not only to resources within those lands—resources with real, commensurable economic value—but sometimes even to privately owned, fee simple land enclaves within the federal land (Hage 1994).

Wayne Hage (1994) relates some examples of the resources privately claimed within federal public lands:

(a) Water rights justified initially by western use customs and later by congressional authorization in 1866 (Hutchins 1971);
(b) Grazing rights (*Taylor Grazing Act* 1934);
(c) Subsurface mineral extraction rights (*Mining Act of 1872*);
(d) Timber harvesting contract rights (*National Forest Management Act* 1976);
(e) National park concessions (*National Park Concession Policy Act* 1965).

Beyond all this are the "improvements" supplied by the claimants, either on the public lands or on adjacent private land, to facilitate use of the public lands improvements, such as buildings, roads, fences, ditches, watering troughs, pipelines, and storage tanks, corrals, hotels, service stations, concession facilities, campgrounds, and rights-of-way.

The law recognizes "possessory interest" in these facilities for those who supplied them. Hage (1994) claims that acts of Congress have withdrawn from the public domain the rights-of-way to many of these facilities and recognized the physical facilities themselves as private property assets with real, commensurable economic value having full private-asset protections, rights, and obligations—including the right to sell, subject to the same conditions under which the asset was originally acquired—as well as being subject to taxation.

It is interesting, and a fundamental distinction worth noting, that those who oppose federal stewardship of the public lands invariably refer to the private use or exploitation of any of the above resources, i.e., water, grazing, mining, access, etc., as a "right," whereas proponents of federal stewardship of public lands view that use or exploitation as a "privilege," permitted by the federal government, with conditions of the permit that must be observed if the privilege is to be retained. This latter view has been consistently supported by the Supreme Court, as the case law presented below will show.

Whether seen as a private property "right" or a federally permitted "privilege," the sagebrush rebels' drive for privatization or state ownership of the federal public lands was stymied by the existence of the "split estate" under which they had laid claim to private ownership rights in public lands. What the rebels came to realize was that there was, in fact, no "practical way to transfer all the millions of split estate ownerships belonging to miners, grazers, loggers, cabin owners and all the rest into state ownership" (Hage 1994). Privatization seemed equally difficult, since many of the claims overlapped. Also, given the new emphasis on protection of the environment, natural resources, wildlife habitat, and wilderness recreation, the existence of split estates made privatization complex to the point of being nearly impossible. Accordingly, "the Sagebrush Rebellion failed because it had only an ideology and no real philosophy" (Hage 1994, 91).

The second insurmountable barrier to the sagebrush rebellion, county supremacy, and wise use movements was the Constitution itself. Among the many cases, five stand out. First, beginning in 1840, the Supreme Court held that congressional power over the public lands has no conditions or limitations (*United States v. Gratiot* 1840). Then, in 1897, the Court extended the power even to adjacent private lands when the owner's fences also enclosed public land, saying, "The general Government doubtless has a power over its own property analogous to the police power of the several States. . . . A different rule would place the public domain of the United States completely at the mercy of state legislation" (*Camfield v. United States* 1897).

In another case, handed down in 1911, the defendant, by grazing his cattle in a national forest, had flouted the Forest Service rules requiring a grazing permit. He claimed that the United States had no power to create a national forest on federal public land without consent from the state within which the forest was located. The Supreme Court unanimously rejected his views, saying, "The United States can prohibit absolutely or fix the terms on which its property may be used. As it can withhold or reserve the land it can do so indefinitely. . . . 'All the public lands of the nation are held in trust for the people of the whole country.'. . . And it is not for the courts to say how that trust shall be administered. That is for Congress to determine" (*Light v. United States* 1911).

In 1928 the Court denied Arizona's claim that the federal government's wildlife managers had to obtain state licenses to kill deer to thin out starving deer populations on a federal reservation (*Hunt v. United States* 1928).

Finally, in *Kleppe v. New Mexico* (1976), a unanimous Court, speaking through Justice Thurgood Marshall, ruled against "dual sovereignty" concerning federal public lands. The Justices unequivocally reinforced the Court's earlier decisions resolving the issue of absolute congressional authority and federal supremacy in the control of federal public lands. The case arose when New Mexico, having captured and sold several wild horses that had strayed off federal land, claimed that it was unconstitutionally outside the Property Clause for the Congress to legislate to protect wild animals (*Wild Free-Roaming Horses and Burros Act of 1971*) on a federal reservation. However, the Court held that the act was well within Congress's Property Clause power, and that "the power over the public lands thus entrusted to Congress is without limitations" (*Kleppe v. New Mexico* 1976, 539). That power, ruled the Court, extends not just to the public lands, but to the wildlife that lives on them. "The foremost question used to be the extent of congressional power over the public lands; it was settled with apparent finality by the *Kleppe* court in 1976" (Coggins and Glicksman 1995, 3–2).

In the same case, the Court held that states may enforce their laws on federal lands, but only until contrary congressional action. Then, "where those state laws conflict with . . . legislation passed pursuant to the Property Clause, the law is clear: the state laws must recede" (*Kleppe v. New Mexico* 1976, 540). Thus, for over 150 years, the United States Supreme Court has consistently said that, concerning the Property Clause, the Congress has a free hand to do, or not do, whatever it chooses; its actions supersede all conflicting state law (Supremacy Clause); and any state claims to the contrary are, as the Ninth Circuit said, "legally frivolous" (*Ventura County v. Gulf Oil Corp.* 1979, 1080 and 1083).

Notwithstanding that unbroken string of Supreme Court decisions supporting Congress's Property Clause supremacy under the Constitution, "the Wise Use, property rights, and county movements have picked up the disputes over federal lands where the most recent sagebrush rebels have left off" (Davis 1997, 25). Of the scores of state laws and county ordinances that have been enacted since 1990 to either diminish federal control over public lands or transfer that control to the states or counties, three are illustrative: Catron County, New Mexico; Nye County, Nevada; and Boundary County, Idaho.

The Catron County Ordinance of 1991 required that "all federal and state agencies shall comply with the Catron County Land Use Policy Plan . . . within . . . Catron County, New Mexico." After more seasoned reflection, it was repealed by Catron County nearly eighteen months later (Catron County 1992). Nonetheless, the Catron County Interim Land Use Policy Plan was published and sold, for $250 each, by the National Federal Lands Conference, a wise use organization in Bountiful, Utah. It has been purchased and discussed or enacted by "about 75 counties in the western states" (Meske 1995).

Starting in 1993, Nye County's ordinance has sought to overturn federal authority over federal lands within the county by, among other things, attempting to reopen the Jefferson Canyon road through the Toiyabe National Forest in defiance of the United States Forest Service. The county ordinance relied on the Equal Footing Doctrine as a basis for gaining county control of the federal public lands, stating that "Nye County in cooperation with the State of Nevada, is the public land management authority within the borders of Nye County on all public lands" (Nye County, Nev., Board of Commissioners 1993).

Nye County, in line with Nevada statute (Nevada Revised Statute Annotated 1994, 596–99), asserted that federal jurisdiction over public lands did not go beyond what was specified under Article I, Section 8, Clause 17 of the Constitution. The county's ordinance expressed the position that ". . . title to the public lands passed to the State of Nevada under the equal footing doctrine upon Nevada's admission to the Union in 1864." The federal government filed suit against the county (later amended to join Nevada as a co-defendant) challenging the constitutionality of the Nye County Ordinance (and, later, the Nevada statute), seeking a declaratory judgment to negate the ordinance and the Nevada statute as unconstitutional. The federal complaint asserts that the Equal Footing Doctrine neither promises nor requires equality of land ownership among the states—only that the states be equal with each other politically within the Constitution (*United States v. Nye County* 1996b, 1117). Judgment was for the plaintiff, the federal government (*United States v. Nye County* 1996a). The court found that "the entire weight of the Supreme Court's decisions requires a finding that title to the federal public lands within Nye County did not pass to the State of Nevada upon its admission pursuant to the equal footing doctrine" (*United States v. Nye County* 1996b, 1117).

In a third "county supremacy" case, Boundary County, Idaho, passed an ordinance much like Catron County's in its intent, which was to make it illegal for federal action to reduce the value of private property. Citizens and environmental groups filed suit on the ground that the ordinance contradicted the Supremacy and Property Clauses of the Constitution. The Idaho Supreme Court agreed and struck it down. Relying on the long-established doctrine of federal preemption, the court declared that "portions of the ordinance are preempted by federal law and are therefore unconstitutional," and invalidated the entire ordinance (*Boundary Backpackers v. Boundary County* 1996).

The court found that many parts of the Boundary County Ordinance directly conflicted with federal public land use laws, specifically the Wild and Scenic River Act of 1994, which authorized "the Secretary of the Interior and Secretary of Agriculture to acquire land within the boundaries of any component of the wild and scenic rivers system" (*Boundary Backpackers v. Boundary County* 1996); the Federal Land Policy Management Act, ". . . authorizing the Secretary of the Interior to acquire . . . by purchase, exchange, donation or eminent domain, lands or interests therein" (43 U.S.C. Art. 1715[a] [1994]); and the National Forest Management Act, which authorizes the "Department of Agriculture to acquire land, or interest therein, by purchase, exchange or otherwise, as may be necessary to carry out its authorized work" (7 U.S.C. Art. 428a). The court also found that subordinating federal agencies to county authority violated portions of the Endangered Species Act and the Wilderness Act (*Boundary Backpackers v. Boundary County* 1996, 1147–48). The net effect of these findings is to once again reinforce a century and a half of consistent court rulings supporting federal authority under the Property and Supremacy Clauses of the Constitution.

*The Takings Clause Case Law: Overview*

In all sovereign societies the government has an inherent power of "eminent domain," that is, the right to appropriate private property for public use. In the United States, governments at all levels—federal, state, and local—are restricted by the Constitution in their exercise of that power. Eminent domain cannot be invoked in an arbitrary, capricious, or unfair manner. The standard that government must meet in taking private property is explicitly set out in the Constitution, as interpreted by "takings" case law that has developed over time.

The "Takings Clauses" themselves are found in two different locations in the Constitution. The first location is in the Fifth Amendment of the Constitution, part of which states: ". . . nor shall private property be taken for public use without just compensation." The second location is in the Fourteenth Amendment, which states: "No state may deprive any person of life, liberty, or property without due process of law; nor deny to any person within its jurisdiction the equal protection of the laws."

These two amendments, at first glance, appear to be redundant. However, the Fifth Amendment was ratified on December 15, 1791, as part of a package of the first ten amendments called the "Bill of Rights." It was necessary because the public distrusted centralized governmental power and was reluctant, therefore, to support ratification of the new Constitution. To allay those fears, the Constitution's supporters promised that they would, as the first order of business after ratification, add the Bill of Rights to the new Constitution as a condition of ratification. The purpose was to place, in that document, these codified restrictions on the new federal government—as well as to place codified guarantees of rights, protections, and powers to the citizenry and their local government(s).

The Fourteenth Amendment had a different purpose in that it is one of the three "reconstruction amendments," namely, the Thirteenth, Fourteenth, and Fifteenth Amendments. They were ratified in 1865, 1868, and 1870, respectively—all within five years of the end of the Civil War.

The reconstruction amendments represented the Congress's (the North's) commitment to make sure that all constitutional guarantees, safeguards, prohibitions, and requirements applied equally to all citizens—regardless of ethnicity—and to the states wherein they resided. These reconstruction amendments reflected the North's determination to end the South's arguments asserting "states' rights" as a barrier to Congress's enforcement of the Constitution's provisions on the states. That is why the Fourteenth Amendment's Section One uses very explicit language to say "No State shall . . . abridge . . .; nor shall any state deprive . . .; nor deny. . . ." The initial, overriding purpose was to provide all Americans with full and equal citizenship of the United States—with all its federally guaranteed rights and privileges.

However, a constitutional protection that was written for one primary purpose eventually can serve another. In this instance, the Fifth and Fourteenth Amendments' prohibitions against the government's—federal, state, or local—taking of private property for public use "without due process" and "without just compensation" is a powerful safeguard, for multiple users and conservationists alike. The Constitution provides a mechanism to help ensure that any conflicts over "takings" can be resolved on common ground and within the "rules."

### Classification of Takings

All takings cases fall into one of two classifications: "1) Regulatory taking, where government action restricts the use of property; and 2) Physical taking, which involves entry onto the property" (Patton-Hulce 1995, 292). Physical taking may also involve seizure, condemnation, or fee simple transfer from private to public ownership.

The Constitution's Takings Clauses apply only to ". . . private property taken for public use. . . ." Since virtually all land designated as wilderness (under the Wilderness Act) was already public land before its wilderness designation, the case law for "physical takings" does not apply other than to private inholdings. Therefore, "physical takings" is outside the scope of this chapter, which deals only with wilderness issues.

On the other hand, the question of whether or not there have been or are "regulatory takings" of private property for public use in wilderness areas is, as yet, not definitively ruled on by the courts. In the past, the court cases alleging regulatory takings based on federal modification or elimination of grazing permits, timber allotments, water rights, rights-of-way, and the like have almost exclusively dealt with non-wilderness federal lands.

However, there is a wilderness-related case filed with the United States Court of Federal Appeal that is not yet resolved (*Hage v. United States* 1996). The plaintiffs, E. Wayne and Jean N. Hage, ranchers in Nye County, Nevada, claim, first, that the federal government took compensable private property from them in the form of grazing permits, water rights, ditch rights-of-way, rangeland forage, cattle, and their ranch. Second, the plaintiffs also contend that the grazing permit is a contract, breached by the U.S. government, entitling them to damages. Third, the plaintiffs want compensation for improvements they claim to have made to the public rangeland. The government asked for a summary judgment on each of the three claims.

Courts render summary judgment only on the application of the law, not the facts, and then only in cases where there are no factual issues in dispute. Accordingly, the court granted summary judgment in favor of the government on the grazing rights issue, holding that the grazing permit was a mere license, the cancellation of which does not create damages and is, therefore, not compensable. The court denied summary judgment on the other two claims, finding that questions of fact were at issue, and ruled that limited evidentiary hearings and a trial should proceed to resolve the issues still outstanding (*Hage v. United States* 1996). A government request to dismiss was denied, and a trial date is set for April, 1999 (*Hage v. United States* 1998).

In an earlier case, the Supreme Court said that grazing permits are only licenses—use privileges—and that when a base ranch was condemned upon which grazing rights were dependent, the owner's loss of grazing privileges is not compensable (*United States v. Fuller* 1976). In that same case the Court said that "The provisions of the Taylor Grazing Act . . . make clear the congressional intent that no compensable property right be created in the permit lands themselves as a result of the issuance of the permit." Consistent with that ruling, a later opinion held that the government's condemnation of a site on which a hydroelectric plant was located did not entitle the condemnee to compensation beyond the term of the hydroelectric license because the interest generating the disputed value is owned by the condemning authority (*United States v. 42.13 Acres* 1996). The courts seem to be saying that the majority of free-access rights are also held not to be compensable property rights (*Wilderness Public Rights Fund v. Kleppe* 1980). The same is true of limited occupancy permits (*Paulina Lake Historic Cabin Owners Association v. United States Department of Agriculture* 1983) and hunting licenses (*Baldwin v. Montana Fish & Game Commission* 1978). Similarly, the courts have held that there were no compensable property rights in a coal prospecting permit as a prerequisite to the granting of a preference right lease (*Grueger v. Morton* 1976) and in the prospect of timber contracts in the future (*PVM Redwood Co. v. United States* 1982). In summary, the government can restrict, eclipse, or otherwise regulate these and similar interests without it being a compensable "regulatory taking" under the Fifth and Fourteenth Amendments of the Constitution (Nelson 1986). There must first be an existing private property right before it can be taken.

When analyzing whether or not there has been a proper "regulatory taking" under the Constitution's provisions, the following questions must be addressed: (1) Was there a private property right? (2) If so, was it either damaged or destroyed through government action? (3) Was the purpose of the taking for public, rather than private, use? (4) Was the property owner fairly compensated? (5) Did the government provide due process for the taking?

Analysis of whether or not a regulatory taking has occurred is a "work in progress." About the only aspect of it that has been definitively decided by the courts is that a permit or license is only a privilege that can be revoked or changed any time without compensation. The other issues having to do with physical improvements, structures, and the like are still being resolved.

## CONCLUSION

The courts have been unable to fix a "bright-line test" to determine when there has been a regulatory taking. In fact there is probably more frustration and controversy about it now than at any other time. That is, at least in part, because of the extraordinary variety of circumstances indigenous to the cases that come before the courts, particularly in the area of regulatory takings. However, the Constitution is a living document. Its interpreters, the courts, could be likened to a living Constitutional amendment system of sorts. As the public dialogue over wilderness issues evolves, history indicates that public policy—and the court's interpretation of it—will continue to evolve also. So, the Constitution serves both as a frame—to contain and preserve that which should remain constant; and a framework—to support the growing, adapting parts of our society that need to adjust.

## ℂ REFERENCES TO CHAPTER 2

*Baldwin v. Montana Fish & Game Commission*. 1978. 436 U.S. 371 (1978).

*Boundary Backpackers v. Boundary County*. 1996. 913 P.2d 1141, 1148 (Idaho 1996).

Brodie, Albert W. (1981). A question of enumerated powers: constitutional issues surrounding federal ownership of the public lands. *Pacific Law Journal* 12: 693, 721–22.

*Camfield v. United States*. 1897. 167 U.S. 518, 525–26 (1897).

Catron County, New Mexico. 1991. Ordinance 004-91, May 21.

———. 1992. Ordinance 003-92, Oct. 6.

Coggins, George Cameron, and Robert L. Glicksman. 1995. Federal Control (vol. 1 of *Public Natural Resources Law*, 10th ed.) New York: Clark Boardman Callahan.

Davis, Sandra K. 1997. The war over the West. In *Western Lands and Environmental Politics*, edited by Charles Davis. Boulder, CO: Westview Press.

*Endangered Species Act and the Wilderness Act*. 1973. 16 U.S.C., 1147–48.

Erm, Rene, III. 1994. The "Wise Use" movement, the constitutionality of local action on federal lands under the preemption doctrine. *Idaho Law Review* 30: 631.

*Federal Land Policy Management Act*. 1976. 43 U.S.C. Art. 1715.

Gaetke, Eugene. 1985. Refuting the "classic" property clause theory. *North Carolina Law Review* 63: 617.

*Grueger v. Morton*. 1976. 539 F.2d 235 (D.C. Cir. 1976).

Hage, Wayne. 1994. *Storm Over Rangelands: Private Rights In Federal Lands*. Bellevue, WA: Free Enterprise Press.

*Hage v. United States*. 1996. 35 Fed C1 147 (1996), no. 91–1470 L.

*Hage v. United States*. 1998. WL775484 (Fed. Cl.), November 5.

Hanna, John. 1951. Equal footing in the admission of states. *Baylor Law Review* 3: 519.

*Hunt v. United States*. 1928. 278 U.S. 96 (1928).

Hutchins, Wells A. 1971. *Water Rights Laws in the Nineteen Western States*, vol. 1, Department of Agriculture Miscellaneous Publication 1206. Washington, DC.

*Kleppe v. New Mexico.* 1976. 426 U.S. 529 (1976).

*Light v. United States.* 1911. 220 U.S. 523 (1911).

Meske, Michele. 1995. U.S. files suit to quash sagebrush rebellion II. *Environmental News Briefing* 3 (3): March 1995.

*Mining Act.* 1872. 30 U.S.C.A. SS 22–45 (1872).

*National Forest Management Act.* 1976. 16 U.S.C. (1976).

———. 1994. 7 U.S.C. Art. 428a (1994).

*National Park Concession Policy Act.* 1965. 16 U.S.C. SS 20 et seq. 462 (1965).

Nelson, Robert H. 1986. Private rights to government actions: how modern property rights evolve. *University of Illinois Law Review* 3, 361.

*Nevada ex rel. Nevada State Board of Agriculture v. United States.* 1981. 512 F. Supp. 166 (D. Nev. 1981).

Nevada Revised Statute Annotated. 1994. 9. Article 321.596 (Michie [1994]), 596–99.

Nye County, Nevada, Board of Commissioners. 1993. Resolution No. 93-48 (December 7, 1993).

*Omachaevarria v. Idaho.* 1918. 246 U.S. 343 (1918).

Patterson, C. Perry. 1949. The relation of the federal government to the territories and the states in landholding. *Texas Law Review* 28: 47–48.

Patton-Hulce, Vicki R. 1995. *Environment and the Law: a Dictionary.* Santa Barbara, CA: ABC-CLIO, Inc., 291.

*Paulina Lake Historic Cabin Owners Association v. United States Department of Agriculture. 1983. 577 F. Supp. 1188 (D. 1983).*

*PVM Redwood Co. v. United States.* 1982. 686 F.2d 1327 (9th Cir. 1982).

Reed, Scott W. 1994. The county supremacy movement: mendacious myth marketing. *Idaho Law Review* 30: 25.

*Taylor Grazing Act.* 1934. 43 U.S.C. (1934).

*United States v. 42.13 Acres.* 1996. 73 F.3d 953 (9th Cir. 1996).

*United States v. Fuller.* 1976. 409 U.S. 488 (1976).

*United States v. Gratiot.* 1840. 39 U.S. (14 Pet.) 526 (1840).

*United States v. Nye County.* 1996a. 920 F. Supp. 1108 (D. Nev. 1996).

———. 1996b. 920 F. Supp. 1108 (D. Nev. 1996) SS 1117

*Ventura County v. Gulf Oil Corp.* 1979. 601 F.2d 1080, 1083 (9th Cir. 1979).

*Wild and Scenic River Act.* 1968. U.S.C. Art. 1271–1287 (1968).

*Wilderness Act of 1964.* 1964. 15 U.S.C. 113 (1964).

*Wilderness Public Rights Fund v. Kleppe.* 1980. 446 U.S. 982 (1980).

*Wild Free-Roaming Horses and Burros Act.* 1971. 16 U.S.C. Sec. 1331–1340 (1971).

# CHAPTER 3

# Weighted in the Balance

*The Bureau of Land Management*
*Wilderness Inventory*

Sara McCormick

Brent Osiek


## INTRODUCTION

This chapter analyzes the wilderness review process for lands administered by the Bureau of Land Management (BLM). As the first chapter notes, the Wilderness Act of 1964 established the wilderness review process in other federal agencies such as the Forest Service and the National Park Service. The Federal Land Policy and Management Act of 1976 (FLPMA) made it applicable to the BLM. To set the stage for a discussion of wilderness and the BLM, several sections of FLPMA are reviewed, including sections covering the declaration of policy, land use planning, and the BLM wilderness study.

### WILDERNESS AND THE FEDERAL LAND POLICY AND
### MANAGEMENT ACT OF 1976

FLPMA is referred to as the organic act for the BLM because it established policy guidelines for the agency and provided the BLM with the authority to enact them. In Section 102 of FLPMA, Congress established the federal policy of retention of the public lands, required the BLM to create land-use plans, including the review of lands classified but not previously designated for specific uses, reiterated Congress's constitutional authority to withdraw public lands, and required the Secretary of the Interior (referred to hereafter as the Secretary) to establish rules and regulations to administer the public lands. FLPMA also requires that the BLM manage its lands "in a manner that will protect the quality of scientific, scenic, historical, ecological, environmental . . . values; [and] that where appropriate will preserve and protect certain public lands in their natural condition" (Sec. 102[8]). At the same time, the BLM must establish goals and objectives as guidelines for public land-use planning, and land management must be based on a multiple-use, sustained-yield philosophy unless otherwise specified by law (Sec. 102[7]).

The Secretary is instructed to "prepare and maintain" an inventory of all public lands and their resources and values with a priority on "areas of critical environmental concern" (Sec. 201[a]). The inventories should be kept current but should not necessarily change the management or the use of public lands. As appropriate, land-use plans, planning, and management should be coordinated with other federal departments and agencies such as the National Forest systems and Indian tribes as well as state and local governments (Sec. 202[b]).

Section 603 of FLPMA instructs the Secretary to review roadless areas of five thousand or more acres identified by the public lands inventory for the wilderness characteristics described in the Wilderness Act. Mineral surveys are to be conducted by the United States Geological Survey and the Bureau of Mines to determine the mineral value of materials present in the areas under review. Based on this review, the Secretary is to recommend to the President the suitability of an area for wilderness designation. Within two years of receiving the recommendation from the Secretary, the President is to advise the Senate and the House on recommendations for wilderness designation and provide any supporting documentation.

## COORDINATION BETWEEN THE STATE AND THE BLM

FLPMA requires the BLM to consult with local and state governments in developing land-use plans, so states have a voice in determining the outcome of the wilderness study and inventories. In September 1978 the Governor of Utah, Scott Matheson, and the BLM State Director signed a cooperative agreement. This agreement guaranteed that the state and the BLM would "identify, communicate, and coordinate actions of common concern" (Cooperative Agreement 1978, 1). Coordination of planning was an important part of this agreement because it provided for early notification of any proposed planning or policy formation. Also, the BLM agreed to "ensure optimal consistency with State and local plans and zoning," to the fullest extent possible under federal laws and regulations. Correspondingly, the state agreed to inform and involve the BLM in the development of land-use plans and other decisions concerning state lands.

The size of this extensive wilderness inventory and survey made communication between the state and the BLM vital. Local concerns could be heard more easily, advocated, and possibly placated by the governor's office, so the opinion and concern of the governor greatly interested the BLM. The governor was to be promptly notified of all actions inconsistent with his recommendations, and the BLM was to "consult frequently with the Governor on matters of mutual concern" (Cooperative Agreement 1978, 3). The level of consideration and deference given to the governor was so extensive that the state office agreed to involve the national BLM Director to resolve areas of disagreement (Cooperative Agreement 1978).

## THE BLM WILDERNESS PROCESS

The BLM divided the wilderness review into three phases in compliance with FLPMA: first, an inventory per section 201(a), followed by a study of the areas, and, finally, reporting to the President per section 603(a). The inventory phase was divided into two separate processes: the Initial and the Intensive Inventories.[1] Table 3.1 provides a time line of the process in Utah.

The Wilderness Inventory Handbook (BLM 1978), referred to as the WIH, provided the initial procedures for the inventory, which stated four objectives for the inventory process. The first was to identify lands that had wilderness characteristics as established in Section 603 of FLPMA.

TABLE 3.1—Time Line of Wilderness Process in Utah

| Date | BLM Wilderness Process Key Event |
| --- | --- |
| September 27, 1978 | Wilderness Inventory Handbook issued |
| December 1, 1978 | Initial inventory begins |
| March 1979 | Intensive inventory begins |
| April 4, 1979 | Initial Inventory Proposals published |
| June 28, 1979 | Clarification of Selected Initial Inventory Policies and Procedures issued (OAD 78-61 change 2) |
| July 2, 1979 | Public Comment Period on Initial Inventory ends |
| July 12, 1979 | Clarification and supplemental guidance for aspects of the Intensive Inventory issued (OAD 78-61 change 3) |
| August 8, 1979 | Final Initial Inventory completed |
| October 4, 1979 | Final Initial Inventory effective |
| April 2, 1980 | Proposed Intensive Inventory results announced |
| November 4, 1980 | Final Intensive Inventory completed |
| January 31, 1986 | Draft EIS issued |
| November 1990 | Final EIS issued |
| October 18, 1991 | Utah Statewide Wilderness Study Report |

The second was to determine lands that do not qualify for Wilderness Study Area (WSA) status and from which therefore the Section 603 restrictions on the management and use of lands could be removed. The third was to document in map and narrative form the inventory considerations. The final objective was to provide the public with an opportunity to be involved in the inventory process.

The draft procedures were published for public comment and the final document issued September 27, 1978. During the public review process of the WIH, the four issues of most significance were the definition of "roadless," adequate public involvement, environmental values including non-wilderness environmental values, and the impact on non-wilderness areas of the wilderness review (WIH). The BLM stated that the WIH was reviewed intensively by the public. This has been challenged on the basis that the Federal Register notices did not provide the substance of the proposed guidelines. In addition, the central issues raised during the public comment and the BLM's response were not published as is the usual process to comply with the Administrative Procedures Act (Torrey 1992).

The WIH guidelines were clarified and expanded upon through Organic Act Directives (OADs) and Instruction Memorandums that provide additional instructions and clarification of policy. As policy guidelines were revised, the state BLM offices were to comply with the new directives.

Prior to beginning the inventory process, each State Director determined whether to conduct a statewide review or whether to conduct the inventory on a smaller, regional basis. In Utah, the decision was reached to conduct a statewide review that encompassed over twenty-two million acres of BLM lands. The WIH also established a two-year deadline for identification of Wilderness Study Areas (WSAs), so the entire inventory process would be completed by September 30, 1980.

Section 603 of FLPMA also requires that lands previously identified as natural or primitive be declared as Instant Study Areas (ISAs). During the Initial Inventory, thirteen areas were declared ISAs by the BLM. These lands were studied prior to other units to determine their suitability for wilderness designation, with final recommendations to be sent to Congress by July 1, 1980. Of the thirteen ISAs in Utah, eight were recommended for designation as wilderness in the Final Environmental Impact Statement (FEIS) of 1990 (BLM Utah 1990).

*Initial Inventory*
The goal of the Initial Inventory was to determine which public lands clearly and obviously do not meet the criteria for WSA status. These lands could then be eliminated from further review and Section 603 restrictions

on use and management lifted. Conversely, if a unit did not clearly and obviously lack the criteria, an Intensive Inventory would be conducted on it. The Initial Inventory in Utah was started in December 1978, and the proposed Initial Inventory decision was issued April 4, 1979. The publication of the proposed decisions initiated a ninety-day comment period ending July 2, 1979. Following the incorporation of the public comment, the Final Initial Inventory Report was issued August 8, 1979, effective October 4, 1979 (BLM Utah 1980b).

The Initial Inventory guidelines provided in the WIH are brief. To conduct the Initial Inventory "existing or readily available information" on land status and roads were combined; "the resulting 'inventory units' will be roadless areas or islands, bounded by either a road, non-public lands; or water" (BLM 1978, 10). Once units were identified, using the knowledge of district personnel and existing materials, Situation Evaluations (SEs) were prepared to provide "a description of the general condition and present situation of a unit" (BLM 1978, 10). Only limited field work was to be completed. The District Manager used the SEs to formulate an initial recommendation on which lands should be intensively inventoried; these recommendations in both map and narrative form were forwarded to the State Director.

The State Director finalized the proposed Initial Inventory decisions and the draft proposals were made available for public review. During the public review, if valid questions were raised about whether an area should be part of the Intensive Inventory and the "State Director agrees, these areas [were to be] returned to the District Manager of the Intensive Inventory" (BLM 1978, 11).

FLPMA Section 202(f) requires an opportunity for public involvement including public hearings. Public involvement is defined in FLPMA as

> [an] opportunity for participation by affected citizens in rulemaking, decision making, and planning with respect to the public lands, including public meetings or hearings held at locations near the affected lands, or advisory mechanisms, or such other procedures as may be necessary to provide public comment in a particular instance. (43 USC 1702[d])

Using this legislative guidance, the BLM determined that to ensure a thorough public review, public meetings were to be held during evenings and weekends in the areas close to the units. In addition, news releases, mailings, and all other methods to involve the public were to be incorporated (BLM 1978). Some have argued that designing the public involvement process with hearings and public notices in the vicinity of the public lands benefits multiple-use proponents (Allin 1997).

In June 1979, after the release of the Initial Inventory results for public comment, a clarification of Initial Inventory policies and procedures was issued via OAD (Organic Act Directive) 78-61 change 2. The OAD restated the BLM's commitment to conducting the review in an open manner with "meaningful public involvement throughout the process" (BLM 1979a, 1). Second, it clarified language in the WIH by stating that if, during the Initial Inventory, any valid doubt existed as to whether a unit contained wilderness characteristics, the inventory unit should be analyzed in the Intensive Inventory. Further, "responsibility rests with the State Director to demonstrate that areas do indeed fit the standard of 'clearly and obviously' lacking characteristics" (BLM 1979a, 2). As a result, it is not the public's responsibility to prove that the characteristics are present but "to demonstrate that there is a reasonable question about the absence" (BLM 1979a, 2). Also, this OAD clarified that the inventory process was only to evaluate which lands possess wilderness characteristics and that "inventory decisions *do not* involve consideration of other factors such as competing resource values" (emphasis in original, BLM 1979a, 1). Changing the guideline from the State Director having to agree that the questions raised are valid according to the WIH, to the State Director having to demonstrate that an area clearly and obviously lacks the characteristics, put the State Director in a more defensive position. Also, the changing guidelines caused confusion for personnel.

The Initial Inventory in Utah has been criticized because it was completed so quickly—it covered over twenty-two million acres of Utah's public land in four months. Another criticism of the process relates to how boundaries were determined. The Utah BLM office finalized WSA boundaries during the Initial Inventory. In contrast, several other states did not determine the final boundaries until more explicit guidance regarding boundaries was issued via OAD 78-61 change 2 (Torrey 1992). The WIH instructions that guided the Utah BLM office's decisions on boundaries state that the inventory unit will be "bounded by either a road, non-public lands; or water, in islands or coastal situations" and that "inventory units may be divided or grouped . . . as long as all of the qualifying area is inventoried and the wilderness integrity is not compromised" (BLM 1978, 10). In contrast, OAD 78-61 change 2 instructed that "when a boundary adjustment is made due to imprints of man, the boundary should be relocated on the physical edge of the imprint of man" (BLM 1979a, 5). An analysis of the impact of this different approach to determining boundaries indicates that more acreage was excluded during Utah's Initial Inventory than was excluded in neighboring states (Torrey 1992).

Given the contentious history of the wilderness debate in Utah, it is interesting that BLM Director Arnold Petty noted in June 1979, "A thorough and professional inventory process should insure that there will be no valid basis for questioning the inventory results" (BLM 1979a, 1). Petty seemed to have a premonition of how the wilderness debate would evolve, or perhaps he just realized the difficulty of the task facing the BLM.

Over 6.3 million acres were proposed for the Intensive Inventory (see table 3.2 for summary). Based on comments from 1,600 people statewide, seven units were added, nineteen units were deleted, and boundary adjustments were made on thirty-seven units, resulting in 942,159 acres being deleted from the final recommendation (BLM Utah 1979b). Once the Final Initial Inventory was made effective, 14.6 million acres of public lands were released from wilderness consideration and restrictions on uses of the land were lifted.

*Intensive Inventory*

The purpose of the Intensive Inventory was not "to make judgments about whether the unit would be a good or outstanding addition to the National Wilderness Preservation System" nor its suitability for other resource uses; these issues were to be analyzed in the study phase (BLM 1979b). Instead, the Intensive Inventory was to focus on an evaluation of the wilderness characteristics of the units, because if a unit lacks the necessary wilderness characteristics it cannot be designated as wilderness. The characteristics to be assessed were size, naturalness, outstanding opportunity for solitude or a primitive and unconfined type of recreation, supplemental values, and the possibility of the unit returning to a natural condition. The characteristics as defined in the WIH are noted below; if a definition was notably modified after the WIH was issued, the change and source are noted.

*Size*—This was reviewed in the Initial Inventory but the on-site inventory of the unit was expected to reveal additional information that would reduce the size of the unit. Therefore, the size criterion had to be re-evaluated. Basically, the size criterion would be met if the unit was roadless and greater than five thousand acres or was a roadless island. A unit less than five thousand acres could also meet the size criterion if it was contiguous to lands that have wilderness values (or potential values) and (1) the unit was managed by another agency; (2) public support was strong for the unit and it was large enough to be managed as wilderness; or (3) the unit was contiguous with an area under five thousand acres that is administered by another federal agency that has the authority to study and preserve wilderness values. It was further clarified that private and state inholdings or lands owned by other federal agencies were not to be included in the acreage calculation (BLM 1979a). The OAD also states that it is not valid to drop an area solely on the basis of its size if it fits one of the three special categories noted above.

*Naturalness*—As noted in the Wilderness Act, the area must be primarily affected by the forces of nature and man's imprint must be substantially unnoticeable. If the impact is substantially noticeable, that portion of the unit could be excluded. Some specific impacts allowed in designated wilderness areas include, in part, trails, trail signs, bridges, fire towers, snow gauges, and pit toilets. The OAD also states that "an overly pure approach to assessing naturalness must be avoided" (BLM 1979a, 5). In addition, the apparent naturalness is the issue to be considered, not the natural integrity of the land (BLM 1979a).

*Outstanding opportunities for solitude or a primitive and unconfined type of recreation*—Although solitude and primitive and unconfined recreation might be expected to coexist, they often do not. Therefore, either factor may qualify an area for WSA designation. Primitive and unconfined recreation has been defined by the BLM as nonmotorized and nondeveloped recreation, including horseback riding, hiking, fishing, and sightseeing. The factors influencing solitude are size, natural screening, and a person's ability to find a secluded spot. These factors are to be considered only as they impact the ability to avoid sights, sounds, and evidence of other people. As a result, the impact will vary depending on size and shape of the unit.

OAD 78-61 change 3 restates that for an area to be excluded on the opportunities criterion, it must be documented that the area has neither outstanding opportunities for solitude nor a primitive and unconfined type of recreation. Also, areas are not to be compared and no type of rating system can be used.

In the introduction to the Final Decision on WSAs for the Intensive Inventory, Gary Wicks, the State Director for the BLM, clarified that a unit cannot have just "an opportunity"; it must be "an outstanding opportunity," and no objective standards had been established to guide this determination (BLM 1980a).

*Supplemental values*—These are not required for wilderness, but their presence is to be noted as well as the quantity and quality. These values include ecological, geological, or other features of scientific, educational, scenic, or historical value.

*Possibility of returning to a natural condition*—If a unit contains a substantially noticeable imprint of man, but it is reasonable to expect the imprint of man to return (or to be returned) to a substantially unnoticeable level through natural processes or hand labor, the unit may be considered further for designation. It was later clarified that the unit must qualify as it is; the rehabilitation potential should not be the basis for a wilderness recommendation except in rare and extreme cases (BLM 1979b).

In March 1979, prior to the Initial Inventory being completed, the Intensive Inventory was initiated. Over 5.4 million acres had to be studied intensively, so the Utah office hired temporary workers as Wilderness Specialists to assist permanent BLM personnel. Guidance was provided in the WIH and augmented by OADs and Instruction Memorandums. A permanent documentation file was to be created for each unit. The file was to include a map and narrative of the unit, a road inventory, a wilderness inventory, a plan for obtaining public input as well as all public input received on the unit, the preliminary and final recommendations, and the State Director's approval (BLM 1978). All field work for the Intensive Inventory was completed in the summer and fall of 1979. The districts completed the intensive inventory February 2, 1980, proposed Intensive Inventory results were issued April 2, 1980, and final decisions were issued the following November.

As noted above, boundaries were to be adjusted only to exclude major imprints of man. If the boundary was relocated it should be to the edge of the physical imprint of man, not to a more nebulous zone of influence of the imprint (BLM 1979a). Boundary adjustments were not to be made on the basis of outstanding opportunities for solitude and primitive and unconfined recreation, nor did outstanding opportunities have to exist in all areas of the unit (BLM 1979b). Exceptions to the adjustment criterion were to be approved by the BLM Director.

An adjustment exception was requested in March 1980. The Utah State Director, in a one-page memo to the Director of the BLM, requested boundary adjustments to nine areas because there was a "high degree of character change within the units" and he wanted to delete areas without outstanding opportunities (BLM Utah 1980a). The BLM Director approved the action on March 13, 1980, but the exceptions were appealed to the Interior Board of Land Appeals (IBLA)[2] by the Utah Wilderness Association (UWA). The IBLA ruled that a one-page document did not provide the BLM Director with adequate supporting materials for the Director to make an independent judgment. In addition, the IBLA ruled that the BLM did not fully document the rationale for deleting the lands as is required by BLM policy. The IBLA remanded the areas to the BLM for a reassessment (IBLA 1983).[3]

The criteria and standards used for the inventory changed throughout the process. The ongoing changes in definition caused problems for individuals conducting field work. Two wilderness specialists reported a lack of cohesiveness in the process. In addition, directions on how to conduct the inventory were received too late in the process (Cleave and Ross 1979). While the WIH was published for public review, the OADs and the Instruction Memorandums were not published and therefore were not open to public scrutiny. After numerous OADs and memos were issued, and nine months after the Intensive Inventory started in Utah, the BLM ultimately decided it was inappropriate to issue revised or additional guidelines during the Intensive Inventory (Gregg 1980).

The final intensive inventory found that almost 1.9 million acres of the over five million acres reviewed had the required wilderness characteristics. Including ISAs and previously identified WSAs brought the total acreage with wilderness characteristics to 2.46 million. Table 3.2 summarizes the acreage analyzed during each stage.

Scott Matheson was Governor of Utah during the Initial Inventory, Intensive Inventory, and Study Phase, and desired an early completion to the wilderness study process. He was unhappy with the process and commented that "both sides of the wilderness issue have been shortchanged by the lack of flexibility dictated by Congress and the Department of the

TABLE 3.2—Summary of Utah Wilderness Inventory Acreage

| Stage of Wilderness Inventory Process | Wilderness Review | ISAs and Contiguous Lands | Existing WSA Previously Identified | Total |
|---|---|---|---|---|
| Approximate acreage included in Initial Inventory | 22,000,000 | — | — | — |
| Proposed Initial Inventory acreage to be intensively inventoried | 6,359,669 | — | — | — |
| Final Initial Inventory acreage to be intensively inventoried | 5,427,621 | — | — | — |
| Proposed Intensive Inventory WSA recommendations | 1,751,951 | 248,630 | 427,503 | 2,428,084 |
| Approximage acreage designated as WSAs in response to appeals to IBLA | — | — | — | 600,000 |
| Final acreage of designated WSAs | — | — | — | 3,235,834 |

Interior" (Matheson 1980). The governor wanted an accelerated wilderness study process because he had serious concerns about the effect of the process on state lands and economic resources while under the wilderness review process, and he believed many of the units would eventually not be suitable for designation as wilderness due to resource conflicts and local concerns. Matheson even told the State Director he would ask the Utah congressional delegation to provide "accelerated funding" to the BLM to expedite the completion of the inventory (Matheson 1980). Although BLM would not consider the governor's desires and recommendations concerning resource values during the initial inventory (BLM Utah 1979c), then Under-Secretary of the Interior, Donald Hodel, agreed with the governor's desire for a statewide study approach, immediate release, and more flexibility given to state directors to accelerate wilderness inventories (Hodel 1981).

The environmental community was also not satisfied with the results of the inventory process. After going through the BLM protest process, a coalition of fourteen environmental organizations led by the UWA appealed the BLM's decision to the IBLA. The 1,400-page appeal was described by one attorney as "awesome and intimidating in scope" (*Deseret News* 1981). The appeal included 300 photographs and 120 affidavits and covered 925,000 acres in twenty-nine roadless areas (Utah Wilderness Coalition 1990). The IBLA reversed the BLM on two units that cover a little over 16,310 acres and remanded to the BLM for further review nineteen areas covering over 800,000 acres (IBLA 1985). Although ruling in the UWA's favor for the most part, the IBLA stressed that the appellant must raise substantial questions concerning the BLM's consideration of wilderness characteristics and show that the conclusions reached by the BLM are not supported by the unit's record (IBLA 1983). The IBLA also stated that if the BLM demonstrated firsthand knowledge of a unit and public comments have been considered, then "the BLM's subjective judgments of the unit's naturalness . . . are entitled to considerable deference" (IBLA 1982a; IBLA 1983).

The BLM conducted additional field work on the remanded areas and approximately 525,000 acres were given WSA status. The UWA appealed again, contending that approximately 248,000 acres remanded by the first appeal, but not designated as WSAs, should be reviewed again. After more work by the BLM, another 77,000 acres were designated as WSAs. The IBLA's language in the response to the second appeal by the UWA strongly reiterates the subjective nature of the decisions and that judgments could not be overcome by simply expressing disagreement with the BLM's decision (86 IBLA 91, 1985).

Remands typically resulted from the BLM not following established guidelines or not adequately documenting a decision. For example, in discussing Mancos Mesa, the IBLA notes that close inspection of the summary sheet for the unit reveals that an answer had been changed using "white-out" when OAD 78-61 change 2 clearly stated that the original documentation of unit decisions is not to be modified by erasures, or by other additions or deletions (72 IBLA 185, 1983). On the Newfoundland Mountains unit, the IBLA ruled that the appellants did establish an error in the BLM's assessment of recreation opportunities and that a different determination of opportunities might result from a reassessment (72 IBLA 137, 1983). In the Carcass Canyon Unit, the IBLA ruled that "a lack of outstanding screening" did not equate with a "lack of outstanding opportunity for solitude" and therefore a reassessment of the solitude criterion would have to be performed (72 IBLA 139-140, 1983). In an appeal of the elimination of Negro Bill Canyon unit from further study, the IBLA found that the BLM had failed to document internal disagreement over a unit; sections addressing opportunities for primitive and unconfined recreation had been deleted from the final inventory file, which is contrary to BLM guidelines (62 IBLA 263, 1982).

The quality of the inventories has also been questioned by some members of Congress. In 1983, after visiting Utah on a fact-finding mission, Congressman John Seiberling (D-Ohio), Chairman of the Subcommittee on Public Lands, concluded that areas had been left out of the process that should have been included (Utah Wilderness Coalition 1990). In addition, the Subcommittee on Public Lands and National Parks conducted oversight hearings on the BLM Wilderness Review Process in 1982, 1984, and 1985 and found that the substantial evidence presented suggested that a reconsideration of two million acres should occur (Udall et al. 1989). Based on Secretary of the Interior Donald Hodel's offer to review areas of concern, Representative Seiberling requested that eighteen specific units representative of the problems identified in the inventory process be reviewed (Seiberling 1985). The Interior Department replied that "the inventory in Utah was as accurate and consistent as possible" and the time for initiating an appeal had expired (Utah Wilderness Coalition 1990). Representative Seiberling is also noted as saying, "It's rather interesting that in many cases those areas which they dropped happened to coincide with things like tar sands, or coal fields" (Utah Wilderness Coalition 1990, 38). This allegation—of inappropriately excluding units during the inventory based on the mineral value of the land—has been made by several individuals within the wilderness debate, but evidence that this was intentional has not been identified.

Criticism of the inventory also came from other agencies. The EPA regional administrator ranked Utah's performance in the inventory to be the lowest of all the states (Torrey 1992).

Another contentious issue in the debate was the "Watt Drops." In 1983, the Secretary of the Department of the Interior, James Watt, determined that units under five thousand acres and split estate lands[4] would be dropped from wilderness designation, further wilderness review, or management under the Interim Management Plan, although the lands could be reviewed for other designation such as Areas of Critical Environmental Concern (BLM 1982). In Utah, fourteen units covering 25,187 acres were impacted by this decision. In 1985, the district court ruled that Secretary Watt's actions were illegal and all the units impacted by the drops should be returned to wilderness study status (*Sierra Club v. Watt* 1985). Ultimately thirteen of the Watt Drops in Utah were established as WSAs; one unit was excluded because changes to the boundary of the Forest Service Deseret Peak Wilderness Area resulted in the unit no longer being contiguous (BLM Utah 1990).

*Study Phase*

Following the intensive inventory, the wilderness study phase began. Two criteria were used to determine the extent of wilderness characteristics in each WSA. The first criterion involved an evaluation of wilderness values, including principal characteristics, special characteristics, multiple resource values, diversity in the NWPS, and identification of areas within a one-day drive of an urban center (BLM Utah 1990, I). Under this criterion, some of the WSAs, in whole or in part, did not meet the qualifications for wilderness designation. The BLM found 937,033 acres of WSA land without outstanding opportunities for solitude and 1,194,367 acres not possessing outstanding opportunities for primitive and unconfined recreation (BLM Utah 1990, I).

The second criterion was that of the manageability of a proposed wilderness unit. Some WSAs have characteristics that make it difficult for wilderness values to be maintained. Manageability problems may occur when a WSA has irregular boundaries that cannot be monitored, or when extensive private or state inholdings, pre-existing uses, and land withdrawals make wilderness characteristics hard to protect. Current manageability concerns include private inholdings in eight WSAs comprising 3,988 acres and special land withdrawals, such as power projects, public water reserves, and oil shale withdrawals, affecting 206,841 acres in 51 WSAs (BLM Utah 1990, I).

In addition to the two criteria, six quality standards were developed to ensure the gathering of consistent information from each WSA. Using these six standards, each WSA was studied to determine (1) energy and mineral resources; (2) impact of designation on other resources; (3) impact of non-designation on wilderness values; (4) public comment; (5) local social and economic effects; and (6) consistency with other wilderness studies (BLM Utah 1990, I).

The public participation requirement consisted of solicitation of public comments and numerous regional meetings. In July 1982, comments were requested from interested individuals and groups on the Site Specific Analyses (SSAs) prepared for each WSA. Also, public meetings were held in rural and urban areas to gather a broad spectrum of opinions. During the early part of 1984, the BLM held meetings in Vernal, Logan, Tooele, Price, Moab, Monticello, St. George, Kanab, Escalante, Loa, Delta, and Salt Lake. These meetings were to help the BLM determine the issues and concerns regarding the study process, opinions about the diversity of wilderness, and possible alternatives to be examined in the Draft EIS (BLM 1984).

In October 1991, the Utah Statewide Wilderness Study Report was issued. The report contains information about resource values, public input, manageability constraints, mineral surveys, and environmental consequences of designation for each WSA. The report was submitted to the Secretary, the President, and Congress and contained the BLM's official rationale for wilderness designation or nondesignation in each of the WSAs (BLM Utah 1991).

## THE ENVIRONMENTAL IMPACT STATEMENT

The BLM prepared an Environmental Impact Statement (EIS) in accordance with the National Environmental Policy Act (NEPA), which requires all federal agencies to use "a systematic, interdisciplinary approach . . . in decision making which may have an impact on man's environment" (Battle 1986, 116). The statewide EIS provided environmental analysis of wilderness designation, public information, and a summary of information for the Secretary and Congress to use in planning and determining wilderness suitability (BLM Utah 1990, I). Although the EIS provides objective analysis and information for the public, it is not a final decision document, nor does it resolve the conceptual issues of wilderness, such as purpose and amount of land appropriate for wilderness designation (BLM Utah 1990, I). The EIS evaluated eighty-three WSAs located in five regions of the state and identified major issues and impacts, including naturalness, solitude, unconfined recreation, water uses, mineral exploration, mineral leases, local economic conditions, local employment, local sales, and impacts to federal revenues

(BLM Utah 1990, I). From this evaluation the BLM's preferred action was developed. The preferred action included 1,975,219 acres in sixty-six WSAs. Additionally, eighteen alternatives were suggested and six were studied in detail. These six alternatives provided an overview of wilderness opportunities and analyzed various WSA combinations, ranging from a low of no acres, the No Action alternative, to the All Wilderness Alternative of 3,235,834 acres in eighty-three WSAs and thirteen ISAs (BLM Utah 1990, I).

Significant changes from the Draft to the Final EIS were an increase in acreage, redefinition of statewide alternatives, and revisions of maps. Changes in BLM's preferred alternative acreage resulted from changes in boundaries of partial alternatives and addition of private inholdings acquired by federal land exchanges (BLM Utah 1990, I). State land inholdings were also treated differently. At the time of the EIS process, the state reversed its opinion on inheld lands and refused to consider a single massive trade-out of inholdings. BLM then re-analyzed the effects of these inholdings on wilderness designation, assuming the state would need access to its lands. Recently the state and the federal government concluded a land-swap in the new National Monument that may provide a template for future trades (see chapter 8).

*Public Comments on the EIS*
Public awareness of the environmental impact of federal actions is required by the EIS process (Battle 1986). To achieve public participation, scoping of the opinions of various interested individuals and groups was done to guide development of the Draft EIS (BLM Utah 1990, I). Of the approximately 6,200 public comments on the Draft EIS, most centered on a few key issues: the need for wilderness, study and inventory procedures, road designations, interim management, buffer zones, inholdings, and the BLM's rationale for proposed actions (BLM Utah 1990, I). Sometimes public comment forced the BLM to use more realistic evaluation techniques. In the Draft EIS, the BLM used the anticipated surface disturbance to determine the future degradation effects of pre-existing mining claims, assuming all potentially economically valuable areas would be developed sometime in the future. However, public comment forced the BLM to change its analysis of surface disturbance in the Final EIS to "activities projected to be feasible within the foreseeable future" (BLM Utah 1990, I, 30–31). This reduced the estimated amount of future surface disturbance to approximately one-quarter of the previous estimate, 58,968 to 215,967 acres, respectively.

Many comments received on the EIS concerned perceptions that scoping was inadequate and ignored vital environmental issues. The BLM responded that its proposed alternative minimized conflicts and allowed beneficial use of wilderness and non-wilderness resources (BLM Utah 1990, VII-B Sec. 3). The BLM also responded that NEPA requires all significant impacts to the human environment to be included in the EIS, but other potential impacts need only to be assessed (BLM Utah 1990, VII-B Sec. 2).

Several groups contended the BLM misunderstood, or did not fully comprehend, the idea of wilderness, when it rejected designation of study areas in favor of other uses. Also, several groups commented on the inconsistencies in decisions between the five BLM districts. The BLM responded that wilderness policy requires consideration of diversity, manageability, and the balance between wilderness and other resource values when considering suitability recommendations; additionally, the assessment of wilderness reflects the individual judgment of various BLM personnel (BLM Utah 1990, VII-A Sec. 2). Many individuals wanted the entire wilderness process delayed while these issues were resolved, but the BLM again indicated that problems with wilderness designation or nondesignation resulted from the uncertainty of future resource demands and from individual subjectivity (BLM Utah 1990, VII-A Sec. 2). The BLM reiterated that WSAs are not automatically suitable for designation and that significant differences exist between suitability and desirability (BLM Utah 1990, VII-A Sec. 8).

Other individuals believed the BLM gave too much deference to local interests. Conversely, many local interests felt the BLM ignored city and county land-use planning. However, the BLM responded that wilderness values are to be balanced against other resource values and uses that would be forgone by wilderness designation (BLM Utah 1990, VII-B Sec. 2). The BLM "endeavors to make the land use plans for Federal lands consistent with . . . resource related plans of other federal agencies, state and local governments, and Indian tribes" (BLM Utah 1990, VII-B Sec. 2, 12).

A portion of the respondents questioned the BLM's boundary definitions. The BLM responded that it has no authority to study private or state lands for wilderness characteristics, and they contended that boundaries "were drawn to be inclusive of the required wilderness characteristics" (BLM Utah 1990, VII-B Sec. 3, 6). The BLM also reiterated its national policy of recommending only areas that could be managed as long-term wilderness. Many questioned the BLM's manageability concerns as a rationale for possible nondesignation; the BLM responded that effective management of certain areas would be administratively difficult and expensive because these areas would require extensive policing or fencing to prevent degradation of existing wilderness values (BLM Utah 1990, VII-B Sec. 3).

Another common response to the wilderness study was a perceived commodity bias in the BLM's preferred alternative. The BLM responded that the Wilderness Study Policy states, "Recommendations . . . will reflect a thorough consideration of any identified or potential energy and mineral resource value present in the area" (BLM Utah 1990, VII-B Sec. 3, 33) and, additionally, both the Wilderness Act and FLPMA required a review of mineral resources.

*INTERIM MANAGEMENT*

The BLM 's *Interim Management Policy and Guidelines for Lands Under Wilderness Review* (IMP) is the guideline for managing "lands under wilderness review until Congress either designates these lands as wilderness or releases them for other purposes" (BLM 1995, 1). The IMP is in effect when an area is declared a WSA. Thus, WSAs are treated as *de facto* wilderness. FLPMA is replete with public participation requirements, and management of WSAs is no exception. The IMP requires notification of all interested parties who have jurisdiction over WSA land, followed by a thirty-day public comment period, prior to making a final decision on any proposed action in a WSA (BLM 1995). IMP guidelines require the State Director to prevent unauthorized activities in WSAs and to notify the public if unauthorized disturbances occur (BLM 1995). The IMP also requires that adequate personnel be available to prevent degradation, but the BLM has been historically under-funded and adequate monitoring and surveillance are not always assured (Allin 1997).

Although the creation of buffer zones around wilderness is part of neither the Wilderness Act nor the FLPMA, BLM managers have been advised to evaluate the nature of any proposed action within half a mile of a WSA boundary. This action is a management tool that prevents unauthorized degradation of WSAs. However, there are no existing legal restrictions on these boundary lands (BLM Utah 1990, VII-B Sec. 7).

*Allowable Activities Under Interim Management*
"Management under the nonimpairment standard does not mean lands will be managed as though they had already been designated as wilderness . . . certain activities are allowed during the inventory and study phases if their impacts [can] be reclaimed by the time the Secretary forward[s] recommendations to the President" (BLM 1995, 5). Temporary uses that do not create ground disturbances or involve new construction in WSAs are also allowed, but these activities may be prohibited in designated wilderness (BLM 1995, 1). However, since the BLM has sent their

Utah wilderness recommendation to the Secretary, this rule no longer applies. In addition, grandfathered uses and Valid Existing Rights (VERs), such as oil drilling, mining, and grazing, that existed before FLPMA became law, are allowed.

In determining access to non-federal inholdings in WSAs, the BLM considers many variables. "The BLM has the discretion to evaluate . . . construction methods . . . reasonable alternatives (trails, alternate routes, including aerial access or the degree of development), and to establish such reasonable terms and conditions necessary to protect the public's interest" (BLM 1995, 30).

*Exceptions to the Interim Management Plan*
VERs in WSAs are protected by Section 701(h) of FLPMA and are subject only to the undue degradation provisions of FLPMA. However, these restrictions may not unreasonably interfere with the benefit of existing rights, which usually consist of pre-FLPMA grazing rights and developed mining claims. A special VER exception does exist. The Director of the BLM may suspend pre-FLPMA VERs in a WSA when the President is expected to recommend a special WSA for wilderness designation. Although Congress is expected to act quickly, the VERs could be suspended for a maximum of two years (BLM 1995).

Impairment exceptions besides VERs do exist. Search and rescue operations and emergency suppression of certain wildfires are allowed, as is reclamation of degradation caused by emergency actions, IMP violations, and pre-FLPMA impacts. Structures and other conveniences may be constructed in WSAs, but they should be "facilities that clearly protect or enhance the land's wilderness values or that are the minimum necessary for public health and safety" (BLM 1995, 9).

Special exceptions exist for wilderness declared under Section 202 of FLPMA. Section 202 lands are not required to have interim management protection and are not protected from degradation of wilderness values. However, the State Director may elect to keep Section 202 lands and adjacent areas under the IMP to allow land-use plans to remain consistent in a particular area. Stricter controls than the IMP can exist in areas that had special protection before the passage of FLPMA. For example, most Instant Study Areas (ISAs) are protected under stricter management guidelines, which augment the level of protection given to an area (BLM 1995).

When the restoration or improvement of a designated wilderness or WSA is required, the BLM uses the "minimum tool" method to reduce the amount of impact in these areas. The minimum-tool concept is a key component of wilderness management and "can be *useful as a guide* when applied to the interim management of the WSAs" (emphasis in original, BLM 1995, 18). For example, when the BLM plans to improve the quality of a wilderness experience by improving supplemental wilderness values, it reviews the activity plan for any other possible solution that may be less impacting to the primary wilderness characteristics (BLM 1995). This management philosophy implies that the simplest and least impacting tools or means to accomplish an action will be used when the BLM attempts to enhance wilderness characteristics.

*Development During Interim Management*
At the time the FEIS was written, there were eight developments proposed in WSAs. Construction of a reservoir by the Washington County Water Conservancy District in a WSA, and development of the Burr Trail adjacent to a WSA, were quite controversial.[5] Also, the pre-FLPMA right-of-way of I-70 is included in the Devils Canyon and Sids Mountain WSAs and future development of the interstate may alter the wilderness characteristics of these areas (BLM Utah 1990, I). The BLM must decide what values are important to citizens. As the Interim Management Plan states, "The BLM is responsible for the balanced management of the public lands and resources . . . that will best serve the needs of the American people" (BLM 1995, 95).

The BLM has accidentally, or through poor management, allowed at least fifty-seven IMP violations to occur in WSAs (Baker 1984). Some violations may be accidental because of boundary uncertainties or inaccurate maps, but other violations have occurred because of improper administrative procedures regarding mineral extraction and oil and gas leases. The BLM allowed certain WSAs to be developed improperly, failed to follow specific administrative procedures, relied upon administrative exclusions of areas, and failed to give adequate public notice of development occurring in WSAs. These IMP violations were usually associated with the extraction of minerals and hydrocarbon resources, including the Exxon well inside the Mount Ellen WSA and the multiple violations involving oil and gas leases that occurred in the Book Cliffs WSAs (Baker 1984).

## MANAGEMENT OF DESIGNATED WILDERNESS

Management plans are an important aspect of designated wilderness management and must be carefully designed to protect and preserve the special qualities of wilderness areas. The BLM attempts to achieve several wilderness management goals: preserving wilderness character; fostering a naturally functioning ecosystem by allowing fire, insects, and disease to act as a natural system; protecting natural conditions; limiting acceptable

change; and maintaining both special features and outstanding opportunities for solitude (BLM 1983). However, the BLM's primary objective is
to manage and protect wilderness for future use; and nonconforming uses
of wilderness, such as VERs, will be managed to prevent undue and
unnecessary degradation of wilderness areas (BLM 1983). History of use,
various environmental factors, and management considerations are also
evaluated in designing and implementing a management plan. In addition, the plans must be updated periodically and respond to changes in
wilderness use (BLM 1983).

The BLM generally uses management to preserve wilderness, not to
control people. However, the BLM does determine the use capacity of land
and can manage visitor use of areas to stop degradation of wilderness characteristics. To limit visitor impact, the BLM prefers indirect methods of
people management, like trail design modification and education. However,
party size, length of stay, and the number of parties may be limited as more
protective measures of wilderness are needed. The BLM also has various
other tools at its disposal to limit the impact on wilderness, such as removing existing improvements—for example, camp grounds—in wilderness
areas; improving access to and encouraging use of lightly used areas; minimizing promotion of wilderness areas; encouraging visitors to use nondesig-
nated areas; rerouting transportation corridors; and decreasing the quality
and design of access roads and parking lots. Stricter management may also
include permits, restriction of grazing, and regulation of pack stock.
Because preservation of wilderness values is paramount to the BLM's management philosophy, visitors may be entirely prohibited (BLM 1983).

*AREAS OF CRITICAL ENVIRONMENTAL CONCERN*

ACECs are "areas within the public lands where special management attention is required . . . to protect and prevent irreparable damage to important
historic, cultural, or scenic values, fish and wildlife, or to protect life and
safety" (BLM Utah 1990, I, 129). Because of these special characteristics,
ACECs are given priority in identification during the inventory by Section
201(a) and priority in designation and management in land use plans by
Section 202(c)(3) of FLPMA. This allows extended protection of these
"most environmentally important and fragile lands" (BLM 1980c, 2).
Currently, ACECs exist in eight WSAs (BLM Utah 1990, I). However, an
ACEC does not need to be located inside a WSA or Wilderness Area, nor
is designation of an ACEC the equivalent to wilderness designation.
Similar to WSA procedure, identification of an ACEC does not necessarily
mean designation will occur. The BLM must first consider the interest of

the public and potential resource uses before designation occurs, and must also consider the relevance of the site, importance of the special features, and the qualities that make the ACEC special (BLM 1980c). Management of ACECs is different from that of wilderness and can include many special requirements and stipulations to protect special values. For example, an ACEC may be withdrawn from appropriation under the Mining Law of 1872 and "limited development, when wisely planned and properly managed, can take place in these areas . . .," but it must be "consistent with protection of the ACEC" (BLM 1980c, 3).[6]

## MANAGEMENT OF H.R. 1500 LANDS

Congressional legislation such as H.R. 1500 has proposed additional wilderness areas outside of existing designated WSAs (to be referred to as the H.R. 1500 lands). Former Representative Wayne Owens (D-Utah) originally submitted H.R. 1500 in 1989, proposing that 5.7 million acres be designated as wilderness; this legislation has been reintroduced several times by Representative Maurice Hinchey (D-New York). This proposal is significantly larger than the 3.2 million acres currently established as WSAs. How the lands contained in this and other proposals are managed has been a contentious issue. Bruce Babbitt, Interior Secretary, instructed the BLM Director to ensure that any BLM management decisions "affecting potential wilderness on BLM lands in Utah, whether within formally designated WSAs or not, are given your careful attention" (Babbitt 1993). In a 1994 memo to Representative Jim Hansen (R-Utah), the USDI Assistant Secretary of Land and Minerals Management reiterated that "particular care" was being taken to review proposals that might impact Congress's ability to designate an area as wilderness, but that does not mean that they are being managed as WSAs (Armstrong 1994). Instead, H.R. 1500 lands are being managed under Section 302 of FLPMA, which requires the Secretary "to take appropriate action to prevent unnecessary or undue degradation of the values found on those lands, including wilderness values" (Armstrong 1994).

Mat Millenbach, BLM State Director, described the management process in more depth in a letter to Hansen (Millenbach 1995). When considering an action, possible alternative locations outside of H.R. 1500 lands are first considered. If an alternate location is not feasible, actions are allowed on H.R. 1500 lands. Some actions that have been allowed include issuance of a multi-year permit for the Jeep Safari, issuance of approximately twenty-five film permits, and development of a water pipeline and range improvements (Millenbach 1995). Not all BLM employees feel that the particular care given to H.R. 1500 lands is appropriate. In March 1994, a group of twenty-five BLM employees, mostly from the Cedar City district, wrote the State Director, James Parker, voicing their concerns regarding instructions they had received on the management of H.R. 1500 lands (Pack et al. 1994). Specifically, they stated that they had been verbally instructed to manage H.R. 1500 lands in a manner that was not in accordance with existing laws and court decisions. Instead, if there was opposition to a specific action, such as chaining, by a specific interest group, such as the Southern Utah Wilderness Alliance (SUWA), the action would not be approved. A written response to the employees' concern could not be located.

Responding to an inquiry from Booth Wallentine, Executive Vice President of the Utah Farm Bureau Federation, BLM Utah State Director William Lamb indicated that only four permittees had been requested to delay or had been denied a range improvement permit due to the location of the improvement being within a WSA or H.R. 1500 area (Lamb 1996c). Lamb also noted that no inquiries for range improvements had been made on lands being reinventoried as part of the wilderness review. Special attention is being given to the management of H.R. 1500 lands. Whether the care is excessive is a matter of opinion.

*THE WILDERNESS REVIEW*

In a congressional hearing on April 24, 1996, Secretary Babbitt and Representative Hansen discussed how much acreage should be designated as wilderness in Utah. During that discussion Hansen questioned Babbitt's statement that about five million acres were worthy of wilderness protection, and stated: "Rather than shouting at each other why don't we just come up with some work" to determine what the correct acreage should be (Babbitt 1996). Since "the original inventory of BLM Utah lands . . . has been enmeshed in controversy from the time it was completed," Babbitt decided to conduct a review (often referred to as a reinventory) of the BLM lands that are included in wilderness legislation H.R. 1500 or H.R. 1745 but are not designated as WSAs (Babbitt 1996).

Since the deadline established in Section 603 of FLPMA for review of the lands for their wilderness value had passed, Babbitt claimed authority to conduct the review under FLPMA Section 202 requirements for land-use planning and the mandate in Section 201 "to prepare and maintain on a continuing basis an inventory of all public lands and their resource and other values" (Babbitt 1996). A team of career BLM employees with extensive experience in BLM's wilderness program was assembled from Utah and other states (Lamb 1996a). The team did not have a particular acreage target but was supposed to perform a thorough review of the areas of concern.

The detailed memo Babbitt sent to Representative Hansen on July 24, 1996, provided guidance for conducting the review until the Utah Wilderness Review Procedures were issued in September 1996. The review was to use the same legal criteria that were used in the original wilderness inventory, and "to consider each unit on its merits solely to determine if it has wilderness characteristics" (Walker 1996). Field work began in September 1996, and the goal was to complete the review by December 1996 (Millenbach 1997). Review units were identified via aerial photos and existing maps. Any potential man-made impacts were noted and field work performed to verify observations and to collect additional data regarding the review units. Public input was not included in the review. Instead, Babbitt stated that once he had the findings, he would make them public and consult with Hansen and other interested parties as to the next step. The options noted by Babbitt included "going through the public process under FLPMA, including compliance with NEPA," or formulating via a NEPA legislative process new recommendations (Babbitt 1996).

Babbitt's letter received an immediate response from Representative Hansen and Senators Orrin Hatch and Robert Bennett of Utah (Hansen, Hatch, and Bennett 1996). Calling the review a "misguided and ill-conceived proposal," they contested the legality of the action under FLPMA and whether the strict definition of wilderness was being correctly applied. They also questioned whether Babbitt's comments, about five million acres possibly being an accurate amount of wilderness, had established a target. Finally, they stated the action being taken was going to further damage state and federal relations and could have a long-term negative impact on Forest Service and National Park System lands as well as BLM lands throughout the system (Hansen, Hatch, and Bennett 1996).

As the wilderness review progressed, acrimony increased. In mid-September 1996, thirteen county councils or commissions wrote letters to the BLM requesting to be involved in the review. The BLM responded that the team was "busy examining existing information" and public meetings or hearings would not be held during the review, although documents from previous public meetings would be consulted for relevant information (Lamb 1996a). Local newspaper headlines reflect the sentiment of some Utahns: "As Babbitt Backs Up, Utahns Say Back Off" (Woolf 1996); "Stoking Wilderness War" (*Salt Lake Tribune* 1996); and "Let's Put Wilderness Study on Endangered Species List" (*Deseret News* 1996).

Babbitt did not back down from his position. On October 14, 1996, the State of Utah, the Utah Association of Counties, and the State Office of Trust Lands Administration filed a lawsuit in the U.S. District Court against Secretary of the Interior Bruce Babbitt, the USDI, the Acting Director of the BLM, Michael P. Dombeck, and the BLM. The lawsuit sought to block the wilderness review for a variety of reasons, including the following: the wilderness review is based on different criteria than the original inventory; the public had not been given the opportunity to comment on the criteria; the process did not include public participation as required by Section 202 for planning activities; the legal time period for a wilderness review under FLPMA section 603 had expired on October 21, 1991; and the BLM was studying state lands that were not under their jurisdiction (U.S. District Court 1996a). The plaintiffs were also concerned the defendants would place under *de facto* wilderness management any lands identified as having wilderness characteristics. The BLM continued the wilderness review and on November 12, 1996, the plaintiffs filed for a temporary restraining order and preliminary injunction. Ruling that "the Plaintiffs are substantially likely to prevail on their legal claims," District Court Judge Dee Benson granted an injunction six days later against further work on the wilderness review (U.S. District Court 1996b).

One of the most significant differences between the original inventory and the wilderness review was the way state inholdings were handled. In the original inventory, the boundary lines were drawn to follow man-made imprints and to exclude state lands, resulting in very convoluted boundaries for some units. In the wilderness review, state inholdings were evaluated "to determine their affect, if any, to wilderness characteristics found on adjacent Federal lands" (Lamb 1996b). Justifying this approach, the Wilderness Review Procedures state that "the boundary of a review unit will not be altered to avoid state lands . . . and [the review] will document wilderness characteristics on both. Recent wilderness proposals by the Utah delegation have included state lands . . . and the Secretary of Interior has directed this review to consider the same lands" (BLM 1996, 1). In addition, the procedures cite as a justification the State of Utah's expressed desire to exchange lands within designated wilderness areas.

The goal was to complete the review by December 1996; the field reviews on the estimated 2.5 million acres were approximately 90–95 percent complete when the injunction stopped the review (Millenbach 1997). Claiming a deliberative process privilege, the BLM withheld from the appellants and the public many of the review documents. The rationale for this privilege is that it gives employees and management the ability to work to the best of their ability without opening their initial drafts to public scrutiny. Since the findings and opinions had not been reviewed by the whole team, including BLM management, they were subject to further review and modification (Millenbach 1997).

Fifteen months after the injunction, the U.S. Court of Appeals vacated the preliminary injunction and remanded the case with instructions to dismiss seven of the eight causes of action. The court held that the BLM was acting within the boundaries of Section 201 of FLPMA in conducting an inventory of public lands. If the BLM decided to use the data to engage in land-use planning, then they would be required to seek public participation as required by Section 202 of FLPMA. The one area in which the plaintiffs could still take legal action regarded the imposition of wilderness management standards on non-WSA acreage. The plaintiffs requested a rehearing of the appeal from the entire Court of Appeals, but this was rejected and the injunction has been lifted.

In February 1999, the BLM released the findings from this wilderness review. The BLM identified an additional 2.6 million acres possessing some type of wilderness characteristics, bringing the total amount of potential wilderness to 5.8 million acres. A series of public hearings will be held to determine if the new areas now under wilderness consideration should be subject to interim protection. Additionally, the new acreage will be subject to more comprehensive reviews in the near future to determine if WSA status is warranted (Davidson and Spangler 1999).

*CONCLUSION*

FLPMA requires that BLM lands be inventoried, areas that meet the wilderness criteria studied, and a presidential recommendation made to Congress of what lands should be designated as wilderness areas—all within fifteen years. Over twenty years later the debate over wilderness in Utah is as fierce as ever, and a compromise is not on the horizon. The factors that feed this ongoing controversy can be categorized into two groups: first, the larger political context of wilderness in the West, and, second, internal factors affecting the BLM's ability to function.

There are three facets of the larger political context that directly affect the BLM wilderness review process. First, the BLM is acting in a political fish bowl, with the players on both sides of the fence watching. Every time the BLM takes action someone is waiting to criticize and accuse it of favoring the other party. This criticism comes from within the agency as well as from external sources. This contentiousness prolongs the administrative process because, no matter what action is taken, someone objects.

Second, because the BLM wilderness review process has taken so many years, it has been significantly impacted by successive Congresses and presidential administrations with different perspectives on wilderness. Reagan's Secretary Watt tried to exclude acreage, while Clinton's Secretary Babbitt completed a "reinventory" of wilderness that potentially could expand WSAs. Both were challenged in court. Different members of Congress also influence the process over time. Representative Seiberling criticized the original inventory and conducted subcommittee oversight hearings on the public land management policy and the BLM wilderness program; Representative Wayne Owens, in conjunction with the Utah Wilderness Coalition, developed an alternative wilderness proposal. In contrast, the current Utah delegation has supported congressional legislation that would designate a smaller amount of wilderness than currently established WSAs.

A third factor in the political context is the political influence of the state legislature and local governments. In contrast with federal inconsistency, their position has been very consistent. The Utah Legislature has passed resolutions against both Forest Service and BLM wilderness. The BLM's statewide report says unequivocally that the policy of local governments is that Utah has "enough wilderness and other single use designation" (BLM 1991, 6). In addition, some state and local governments protested the reinventory and joined in the lawsuit that halted it.

In addition to these elements in the larger political context, there are factors within the BLM and its procedures that have affected the agency's ability to do its job. First, at least some of the conflict is a result of the way the inventories were conducted. The BLM acted quickly to exclude areas from the intensive inventory so they would not be subject to as many management restrictions. The BLM's haste may have been to protect the interests of its traditional land users. But the haste meant that the Initial and Intensive Inventories were unpalatable to some important parties. Because the foundation for making decisions on WSAs is not agreed upon, it hurts the overall process and creates ongoing conflict.

The wilderness review process was, at least in concept, designed to allow the BLM, as a multiple-use agency, to achieve a balanced approach to wilderness designation in relation to other multiple-use benefits of the land. Wilderness was a new resource the BLM had to consider, and the process emphasized the multiple-use aspects of wilderness and provided for a system of analyzing the value of wilderness designation. The wilderness review process—a set of rules, policies, and guidelines that over time were adjusted to meet practical realities—provided the framework for a significant shift in land management policy. Although the subjective nature of wilderness determination was always a factor, the guidelines and policies attempted to mitigate personal feelings and allow for professional and objective consideration of land proposed for wilderness.

In practice, however, the agency bumped up against internal conflicts and the larger political context described above. The BLM acted quickly in establishing areas to be intensively inventoried. During the initial inventory, all BLM lands were removed from development until the acreage to be intensively inventoried was determined. Since the concept of wilderness was new to the BLM, this may have created conflicts with previously established land use legislation and traditional land use. Because early statutes of the Grazing Service required personnel to have practical range experience, Grazing Service employees, some of whom would become BLM managers, were usually ranchers or ranchers' sons (Bradley and Ingram 1986). Although the BLM currently has a diverse staff with various specialties, one long-term employee noted that in the 1970s personnel came mostly from resource management schools (Thayne 1997).

The BLM also had to face political reality. Lengthy initial and intensive inventories would have withdrawn millions of acres of land for a politically unacceptable amount of time. The State of Utah requested the BLM to do a statewide inventory, although a regional approach to the inventory might have been logistically and politically easier in the long run.

The BLM's wilderness review process attempted to mitigate some of the contentious wilderness issues by seeking a reasonable balance between multiple-resource use and wilderness designation. However, the lawsuits and political maneuvering have made it very difficult to identify a "reasonable balance." Pro-wilderness groups and those groups favoring less wilderness have criticized the process at every step. Although neither group was pleased, the process was the BLM's attempt at finding the balance between use and preservation.

Utah's wilderness dilemma has become an example of what not to do. Senator Harry Reid (D-Nevada) says that he will not try to push a wilderness bill through Congress until the divergent parties reach a compromise first (*Great Basin News* 1996). This has yet to happen, at least in Utah. Instead, the BLM has become the referee in the fight between the polar interests of environmentalists and multiple-use groups.

## ℂ NOTES TO CHAPTER 3

1. For a more detailed description of the wilderness review process see K. Jack Haugard's *Wilderness Preservation: A Guide to Wilderness Selection on BLM Lands* (Stanford Environmental Law Society, 1985, Palo Alto, CA). Another detailed source: U.S.

Department of the Interior, Bureau of Land Management, Utah BLM Statewide Environmental Impact Statement issued November 1990.

2. The IBLA is the judicial branch of the U.S. Department of the Interior and rules on cases regarding land use decisions within that department.

3. In a remand, the IBLA finds that the BLM failed to follow its guidelines or there is doubt about the adequacy of the original assessment. As a result, the BLM must perform a reassessment. In a reversal, the appellant establishes that the BLM failed to follow its guidelines and that this failure resulted in the BLM reaching an incorrect conclusion. As a result, the IBLA reverses the agency's decision (IBLA 1983).

4. Split estate is defined in the *Utah BLM Statewide Wilderness Final Environmental Impact Statement* as "situation(s) where the subsurface mineral estate is owned or controlled by a party other than the owner of the surface of the same land area" (BLM Utah 1990, 395).

5. The reservoir proposal in Parunuweap Canyon WSA has been withdrawn as part of a land exchange program. The Burr Trail is adjacent to, but not inside, WSAs.

6. Wilderness areas are also withdrawn from appropriation under the mining law of December 31, 1983. Valid claims staked prior to the deadline can be retained and developed—for example, in the Mount Nebo Wilderness (see chapter 7).

## ₵ REFERENCES TO CHAPTER 3

Allin, Craig. 1997. Wilderness policy. In *Western Public Lands and Environmental Politics*, edited by Charles Davis. Boulder, CO: Westview Press.

Armstrong, Bob. 1994. Letter to Honorable James V. Hansen. April 22.

Babbitt, Bruce. 1993. Letter to Director of the BLM. Subject: Utah Wilderness. November 1.

———. 1996. Letter to Honorable James V. Hansen, Chairman, Subcommittee on National Parks, Forests and Public Lands. July 24.

Baker, James. 1984. "The BLM's Wilderness Policy Probed by a Skeptical Congressional Committee," *High Country News*, July 9, 10–12.

Battle, Jackson B. 1986. *Environmental Decisionmaking and NEPA*. Cincinnati, OH: Anderson Publishing Co.

Bauman, Joseph. 1986. "Rich in Scenery, Minerals and Controversy," *Deseret News*, May 6–7, A1.

BLM (Bureau of Land Management of the U.S. Department of the Interior). 1978. Wilderness Inventory Handbook. September 27.

———. 1979a. OAD 78–61 change 2. June 28.

———. 1979b. OAD 78–61 change 3. July 12.

———. 1980a. Instruction Memorandum No. 80-236. January 22.

———. 1980b. Intensive Wilderness Inventory Proposals. April 2.

———. 1980c. Areas of Critical Environmental Concern: Policy and Procedures Guidelines. June.

———. 1982. Instruction Memorandum No. 83-188. December 23.

———. 1983. Management of Designated Wilderness Areas. Document 8560, release 8-22.

———. 1984. Public Scoping Issues and Alternatives. July 20.

———. 1985. *Interim Management Policy and Guidelines for Lands Under Wilderness Review*. Document number H-8550-1. Release 8-36. July 5.

————. 1995. H-8550.1. *Interim Management Policy and Guidelines for Lands Under Wilderness Review*. Supersedes Handbook 8550.1. November 10, 1987.

————. 1996. Utah Wilderness Review Procedures. September 9.

BLM Utah. (Utah State Office, Bureau of Land Management of the U.S. Department of the Interior). 1979a. *BLM Utah Proposed Initial Wilderness Inventory*. April. Salt Lake City, UT.

————. 1979b. *BLM Utah Final Initial Wilderness Inventory*. August. Salt Lake City, UT.

————. 1979c. Letter from Associate State Director to Scott Matheson. August 13.

————. 1980a. Letter from the Utah State Director to the Director of the BLM. March 6, 1980.

————. 1980b. *BLM Intensive Wilderness Inventory Final Decision on Wilderness Study Areas*. Washington, DC.

————. 1990. *Utah BLM Statewide Wilderness Final Environmental Impact Statement, vol. I–VII*. Washington, DC.

————. 1991. *Utah Statewide Wilderness Study Report, vol. I–III*. Washington, DC.

Bradley, Dorotha M., and Helen M. Ingram. 1986. Science vs. the grass roots: representation in the Bureau of Land Management. *Natural Resources Journal* 26, no. 3 (Summer 1986): 494–518.

Cleave, Bobbie, and Janet Ross. 1979. "Summary Problems with Utah BLM Wilderness Process." Field Notes, September 19, 1979.

Cooperative Agreement. 1978. Agreement between the Governor of Utah and the State Director, Bureau of Land Management, U.S. Department of the Interior, September 1978.

Davidson, Lee, and Jerry Spangler. 1999 "Utah Environmentalist Cheer BLM—Babbit Releases New Wilds Inventory—5.8 Million Acres," *Deseret News*, February 5, [http://www.desnews.com/cgi-bin/libstory_state?dn99&9902101135].

*Deseret News*. 1981. "Group Files 1,400-page Wilds Appeal," August 24–25, 8D.

————. 1996. Editorial, "Let's Put Wilderness Study on Endangered Species List," August 7, A12.

*Great Basin News*. 1996. What can Nevada learn from Utah? *Great Basin News* 1, no. 1 (Winter).

Gregg, Frank. 1980. Memo to State Director. Instruction Memorandum No. 80-236. Subject: Final Guidance on Application of Wilderness Criteria During Intensive Inventory. January 22.

Hansen, James, Orrin G. Hatch, and Robert F. Bennett. 1996. Letter to Bruce Babbitt. August 1.

Hodel, Donald. 1981. Letter to Scott Matheson. June 16.

IBLA (Interior Board of Land Appeal of the U.S. Department of the Interior). 1982a. Sierra Club, Utah Chapter. 62 IBLA 263 (decided March 15, 1982).

————. 1982b. Don S. Orlando, et al., 64 IBLA 7 (decided May 4, 1982).

————. 1983. Utah Wilderness Association, et al. 72 IBLA 125 (decided April 18, 1983).

————. 1985. Utah Wilderness Association, et al., Clive Kincaid. 86 IBLA 89 (decided April 12, 1985).

Kelsey, Margaret. N.d. Summary of the wilderness inventory, study and report process.

Lamb, William G. 1996a. Letter to R. Lee Allen, Chairman of the Box Elder County Commission. September 18.

————. 1996b. Letter to Brad Barber, Deputy Director, Governor's Office of Planning and Budget. October 2.

————. 1996c. Letter to Booth Wallentine, Utah Farm Bureau Federation, November 12.

Matheson, Scott. 1980. Letter to Gary Wicks, BLM Utah State Director, June 30.

Millenbach, Matthew N. 1995. Letter to Honorable James V. Hansen. Response to a letter from Representative Hansen dated March 6, 1995. March 20.

————. 1997. Declaration No. 97-4015 in U.S. Court of Appeals for the 10th Circuit. *State of Utah, et al. v. Bruce Babbitt, et al.* March 20, 1997.

Pack, Gina, et al. 1994. Letter to James Parker dated March 2, 1994, and signed by twenty-five BLM employees.

*Salt Lake Tribune.* 1996. Editorial, "Stoking Wilderness War," August 4, AA-1

Seiberling, John F. 1985. Memo to Donald Paul Hodel, Secretary of the Interior. December 9.

*Sierra Club v. Watt.* 1985. 608 F. Supp 305 (E.D. Cal 1985).

Thayne, Greg. 1997. Bureau of Land Management. Personal interview by authors, April 10.

Torrey, Ricky Shepherd. 1992. The wilderness inventory of the public lands: purity, pressure and procedure. *Journal of Energy, Natural Resources and Environmental Law* 12: 453–520.

Udall, Morris K., Bruce F. Vento, George Miller, Peter H. Kostmayer, and Nick Joe Rahall, II. 1989. Letter to Honorable Manuel Lujan, Jr., Secretary of the Interior. April 18.

U.S. District Court, District of Utah. 1996a. *State of Utah, et al. v. Bruce Babbitt, et al.* Order, 2:96-CV-870B. Complaint for Declaratory and Mandatory Relief and a Preliminary and Permanent Injunction. Dated October 14, 1996.

————. 1996b. *State of Utah, et al. v. Bruce Babbitt, et al.* Order, 2:96-CV-870B. Temporary Restraining Order Granted October 18, 1996.

Utah Wilderness Coalition. 1990. *Wilderness at the Edge.* Layton, UT: Gibbs Smith.

Walker, Tom. 1996. Instruction Memorandum No. 96-176 to Utah State Director. Subject: Utah Wilderness Review Procedures—Interim Guidance. September 6, 1996.

Woolf, Jim. 1996. "As Babbitt Backs Up, Utahns Say Back Off," *Salt Lake Tribune*, August 2, 1996, A1.

Zumbo, Jim. 1981. Rebellion or ripoff. *American Forests* 87(3) March: 25.

# The Wilderness of Politics

Democracy is a sloppy process. The debate is often acrimonious, the competition among special interests intense, and the opportunities for political grandstanding endless. Toss in a large measure of hyperbole, photo-ops, and a public that makes endless demands on government—but does not want to pay for any of them—and you have American politics in a nutshell. It may seem odd that we should be so thankful for such a system of government. But in fact our government is more open, inclusive, and deliberative today than it ever has been. There was a time when the Senate was a rich man's club, the electoral college actually selected presidents, and only propertied white males had the right to vote.

The democratization of American politics is reflected in the federal government's changing policy on public lands. At one time huge swaths of public land were given to railroads; timber companies ravaged entire forests without regard to consequences; and enormous cattle ranches, many of them foreign-owned, dominated the range. The public lands were a vast source of wealth to be plundered by those who could force out the competition and buy enough politicians to make it all legal.

But gradually the age of the robber baron gave way to the age of the bureaucrat. The U.S. Forest Service was created in 1905, the National Park Service was authorized in 1916, and the U.S. Fish and Wildlife Service was formed out of existing agencies in 1940. The remaining public lands remained under the control of the General Land Office and the Grazing Service until those two agencies were merged in 1946 to create the Bureau of Land Management. These agencies developed close relations with their clientele—timber companies, concessionaires, anglers and hunters, and ranchers—and exercised virtually unlimited control of the public lands until the 1960s.

The open, participatory bureaucratic process we know today, with scoping sessions, public hearings, comment periods, and open meetings, is a relatively recent development. Even the language is new; when we spell-checked this manuscript, the spell-checker rejected the following words: scoping, nonimpairment, reinventory, biodiversity, redrock, backcountry, and recreationist (it suggested "receptionist"). And of course the spell-checker could not recognize any of the acronyms listed at the beginning of this book, even though some of them are practically household words for many Utahns. In short, the process by which we are trying to resolve the wilderness question is quite new, and much more open and democratic than in the past.

Before the advent of progressive legislation, federal land agencies and their clientele ruled the public lands as their own private domains. But beginning with the Administrative Procedures Act of 1946, a series of laws began to pry open the bureaucratic process and allow a variety of interests to play a role. The passage of the National Environmental Policy Act of 1969, the Forest and Rangeland Renewable Resources Planning Act of 1974, the 1976 National Forest Management Act, and the 1976 Federal Lands Policy Management Act forced these agencies to open their deliberations to the public. The result is a decision-making process that is considerably more democratic, but also much more vitriolic and conflictual. The age of the bureaucrat has been replaced, or at least altered, by the age of interest-group competition.

The highly politicized process of designating wilderness in Utah is the subject of this section of the book. Chapter 4, by Andrew Fitzgerald and Deborah Schwabach, explains the strategies used by the opposing interest groups. It is an object lesson in how to win—or at least keep from losing—in the potboiler of contemporary interest group politics. Chapter 5, by Luke Smart and Amber Ayers, focuses on another source of political power, the people. They describe how each side in the debate has attempted to exploit the numerous public opinion polls on wilderness. And the final chapter in this section, by Meredith McKell Graff, describes the heated political controversy over two issues: exceptions language and release language. It is a sure sign of prolonged political conflict when the debate generates its own special jargon, with terms such as "hard release" and "soft release."

When reading these chapters, it is important to remember that none of this would have occurred in an earlier period when robber barons and bureaucrats ruled the public lands. The competing interest groups, the public opinion polls, the prolonged debate over bill language—all of these are telling signs that the democratic process is alive and well.

—The Editors

# CHAPTER 4

# Drawing Lines in the Desert Sand
*The Politics of*
*Public Interest Groups*

Andrew Fitzgerald

Deborah Schwabach

*In your mind's eye hold the perfect complexion of the desert's face, the*
*smell of sagebrush and the silence. Then imagine all of it ravaged,*
*scarred by the sights and sounds of savagery of county bulldozers, dis-*
*qualifying it as wilderness.*
———Activity Flier, Utah Wilderness Coalition

*We believe that formal wilderness designation is essentially a selfish, sin-*
*gle-use, exclusionary concept that discriminates against the sportsman,*
*recreationists, the elderly, the handicapped, and the vast majority of*
*Americans who support responsible resource use and development to*
*grow the nation's economy.*
———Wilderness Position Paper,
Utah Public Lands Multiple Use Coalition

## INTRODUCTION: THE ROLE OF PUBLIC INTEREST GROUPS, GENERAL

By the nature of our governmental processes, interest groups play a role
in all public lands debates. The public-interest groups participating in
the Utah wilderness debate have divided into two opposing coalitions:
the Utah Wilderness Coalition (UWC), an alliance of environmental
organizations, and the Utah Public Lands Multiple Use Coalition
(UPLMUC), an alliance of land and resource user interests and local
government organizations. This chapter compares the ways in which
these two coalitions have evolved and exerted political influence through

three strategies: forming alliances, defining the issues, and delineating the scope of conflict.

*FORMING ALLIANCES*

Advocates on both sides of the Utah wilderness debate have found it advantageous to form coalitions to broaden and strengthen their influence. The UWC was organized to ally interest groups concerned with Utah wilderness under a united front with one goal. The UWC consists of 150 interest groups that support an initiative based on UWC's own inventory of BLM lands in Utah, which it refers to as the Citizens' Proposal (McCoy 1997).[1] Descriptions of key member groups in the Coalition are summarized in table 4.1.

Utah multiple-use advocates have also formed an alliance as an essential strategy in advancing their side of the Utah wilderness debate. These sixteen groups have joined under the banner of the UPLMUC, which represents a variety of business, industrial, agricultural, urban, and rural interests as summarized in table 4.2. The UPLMUC draws its leadership from chairman Booth Wallentine of the Utah Farm Bureau Federation and vice chairman Mark Walsh of the Utah Association of Counties.

The UWC promotes a united, no-compromise position based on the assumption that a united proposal is more effective than a variety of disparate proposals (McCoy 1997). This philosophy represents an important shift from the locally oriented, compromise-based political tactics used by the now-defunct Utah Wilderness Association in the 1980s. In 1984, certain Forest Service lands in Utah were designated wilderness (see chapter 13). The principal environmental group involved in negotiating that bill was the Utah Wilderness Association (UWA). The UWA worked within the Utah political atmosphere of the 1980s, which was generally hostile to wilderness designation, and required compromise from environmental advocates. The result was a 1984 wilderness bill that set aside approximately 800,000 acres of wilderness on Forest Service land.

The Sierra Club and other environmentalists outside of the UWA were reluctant to support the 1984 bill, feeling that the acreage was too small and that many acres qualifying for wilderness designation would now remain open to logging and mining. In the eyes of many wilderness advocates, UWA's willingness to compromise was unacceptable (Rait 1997). This view reflected a national trend recognizing that "there has been no reward, historically, for NGO [nongovernmental organization] leaders' public participation in any process leading to compromise" (Cutler 1995, 192).

TABLE 4.1—Utah Wilderness Coalition Key Members

*Sierra Club*—National and international broad-based organization advocating on clean air, clean water, toxic waste, and public lands issues

*The Wilderness Society*—National group formed to protect public lands through wilderness designation

*Wasatch Mountain Club*—Recreation oriented, Salt Lake City–based group with focus on local canyons

*Southern Utah Wilderness Alliance*—Pro-wilderness interest group with national membership and mission of preserving wildlands of Southern Utah

*Grand Canyon Trust*—National group dedicated to conservation of the natural and cultural resources of the Colorado Plateau

TABLE 4.2—Utah Public Lands Multiple-Use Coalition Membership

*Agriculture and Ranching*—Utah Cattlemen's Association, Utah Farm Bureau Federation, Utah Wool Growers Association, Utah-Idaho Farmers Union, Utah Forest Products Association

*Business and Industry*—Salt Lake Area Chamber of Commerce, Utah Taxpayers Association, Utah Manufacturers Association

*Mineral and Oil & Gas*—Utah Mining Association, Utah Petroleum Association, Coastal States Energy

*Off-Road Recreation*—Utah Snowmobile Association, Utah Trail Machine Association

*Water*—Utah Association of Conservation Districts, Utah Water Users Association

*County Government*—Southeastern Utah Association of Counties, Utah Association of Counties

Local observers attribute the rise of the Southern Utah Wilderness Alliance (SUWA) and the UWC to dissatisfaction among environmentalists over UWA's position of compromise on the 1984 Utah Wilderness Act. "The 1984 Forest Act prompted these interest groups to come about. We did not want to see BLM wilderness go the way of the Forest Service wilderness" (Rait 1997). Dick Carter, a leader of the former UWA, notes that, while his group sought a local resolution to wilderness issues, there was growing pressure from interest groups on both sides to seek resolution in Washington, D.C., where these groups have strong lobbies (Carter 1997).[2]

According to Carter, the 1984 experience led groups on both sides of the wilderness debate to seek new strategies and alliances. While environmental groups have joined ranks through the UWC, the extractive users in Utah have joined ranks not only with each other, but with state, local, and county governments as well through the UPLMUC. These groups have identified common concerns such as potential limitations on public land multiple use, reduction in state and local tax revenues stemming from those uses, and economic viability of rural communities. As author Charles Davis has observed:

> Not only are user groups demonstrating an ability to funnel PAC monies to like-minded legislators but they have finally overcome the tendency to operate independently on political issues such as hardrock mining or livestock grazing on public lands. Organizational leaders have recognized the importance of building coalitions that transcend specific issues and have created multi-issue umbrella groups. . . . (1997, 195)

Similarly, the member entities of the UPLMUC share a resistance to federal agency control. Mark Walsh of the Utah Association of Counties describes his group's mission: "The Association of Counties . . . was formed by county elected officials getting together and trying to influence public policy decisions that are made by levels of government that are above them. And that's everybody. That's the state, the feds, it's agencies . . . it's basically anybody that makes rules and regulations that affect county government" (1997). Like the Association of Counties, other members of the UPLMUC want to secure a voice for public land users in the Utah Wilderness debate.

Coalition building is important to multiple-use advocates because they share common interests, and also because the individual groups making up the coalition do not normally concentrate on wilderness issues and must devote their resources to other priorities. The Utah Farm Bureau Federation, for example, is part of a nationwide parent organization, the American Farm Bureau Federation. The American Farm Bureau advocates for agricultural interests on a variety of environmental and non-environmental regulatory issues such as wetlands, endangered species, agricultural commodities, tax incentives for ethanol production, farm subsidies, and worker's compensation insurance. Other UPLMUC members such as the Utah Petroleum Association, Utah Mining Association, and Utah Manufacturers Association are in a similar position. Wilderness issues are a small part of these groups' overall missions, and coalition formation has enabled these groups to share resources and develop a unified position representing sixteen member organizations.

With their constituencies and spokespersons well defined and organized, the UWC and UPLMUC wage their opposing campaigns for political influence on the Utah BLM wilderness battlefield. Extractive users and local government interests align in support of rural economic viability and freedom from federal control. Conservationists rally for the wilderness acreage identified in the new Citizens' Proposal.

## DEFINING THE ISSUES

In order to analyze how public-interest groups are influencing Utah wilderness policy, it is important to understand the different ways the two coalitions define the issues. The UPLMUC has defined the wilderness debate primarily in terms of rural resource and economic issues, while the UWC has defined the debate primarily in terms of how much acreage qualifies for wilderness designation. Not only do the two sides frame the wilderness issue differently, but each side tends to dismiss the other as arguing from a non-germane standpoint.

The UPLMUC has formulated unified positions on ten issues, which are listed in table 4.3. Their positions reflect the economic interests shared by extractive users, rural communities, and local governments. The UPLMUC proposes that any future congressional bill designating Utah wilderness should address the "substantive and procedural issues" reflected in their positions.

TABLE 4.3—UPLMUC Summarized Positions on Wilderness Issues

1. *Water Rights*—There must be no reserved water rights, stated or implied, in any future Utah wilderness act.

2. *School Trust Lands*—Trust sections captured within WSAs should be traded out, and the federal government should bear the administrative cost of the trades. Wilderness legislation should protect access to school trust lands.

3. *Grazing*—Utah wilderness legislation should guarantee and protect livestock grazing in wilderness areas and prohibit reductions in grazing as a result of wilderness designation.

4. *Oil, Gas, and Mineral Exploration and Extraction*—The future of energy and mineral production in Utah is dependent on access to public lands, which would be restricted by wilderness designation.

5. *Wildlife and Recreation*—access to lands for wildlife management, hunting, fishing, and recreational activities should be preserved.

6. *Timber*—Wilderness legislation should prohibit the management of adjacent land as a buffer zone and should permit timber harvest in adjacent lands.

7. *Tourism*—Wilderness designation seeks to restrict human access to and impacts on designated lands, thereby reducing activities including tourism.

8. *Watershed Management and Fire Control*—Wilderness legislation should either exclude watershed lands or be written to allow watershed management (including mechanized activities) and mechanized fire control.

9. *Tax Base and Private Property Rights*—Wilderness legislation should include consideration of tax revenue impacts on rural counties.

10. *Jobs*—Wilderness designation reduces job opportunities in rural areas.

Source: UPLMUC, 1997

Ken Rait (1997), former Issues Director for SUWA, dismisses these issues as irrelevant to the Utah wilderness debate. "What drives this issue is not germane to the issue. . . . A lot of people in San Juan County believe there is no grazing in wilderness. . . . To have a conversation in these (public) meetings is difficult because of myths. . . ." SUWA and the UWC define the issue in terms of the total number of acres of land that meet Wilderness Act and FLPMA criteria for wilderness designation.

As discussed in chapter 3, currently in the state of Utah there are 3.2 million acres of BLM lands in WSA status, protected and managed as wilderness until a congressional decision is made. In essence, Utah has 3.2 million acres of land that is for all intents and purposes protected wilderness, at least until Congress passes a Utah wilderness bill. The Utah delegation wilderness bill proposes nearly 2 million acres for designation. The UWC's position for several years was that there are 5.7 million acres of land that qualify as wilderness, an increase of 3.5 million acres over the delegation proposal. The most recent UWC inventory increased that claim to approximately 8.5 million acres (SUWA 1998, 11).

Mark Walsh of the Utah Association of Counties refutes the claim that acreage is the central issue in the debate, contending that this was not the original congressional intent of the Wilderness Act. According to Walsh,

> When the Wilderness Act was passed, in 1964 . . . there were very strong statements made that we're not going to designate *every* acre that qualifies, we're going to have a representative system here. What that meant was that, instead of designating for instance all of the Kaiparowits . . . as wilderness, we're going to designate a part of the Kaiparowits. And the wilderness founders intended that the parts that were designated were the parts that created the least amount of burden for anybody. (Walsh 1997)

The issues and positions articulated by the UPLMUC represent the interests of its member groups, but they also reflect a political strategy. The UPLMUC has managed to link the concerns of three subgroups: extractive users, who have an interest in maintaining access to mineral, grazing, timber, and water rights; local governments, who want to maintain their autonomy and tax revenues; and rural residents, who are concerned about job availability and economic prosperity (these issues are discussed further in chapters 12 and 14).

Defining wilderness issues in this manner has helped promote the influence of multiple-use advocates throughout the West:

> Associational leaders have also capitalized politically on some of the issues ignored by environmental leaders, such as the social costs of change accompanying resource-dependent communities as they make the transition to

recreation or amenity-based economies. Protecting jobs has become a useful wedge issue for industries seeking to abate or delay the implementation of resource management decisions. In other cases, political alliances are formed with local governmental officials who have become dependent upon the revenues generated by extractive land use activities such as energy royalties, grazing fees, or timber receipts. (Davis 1997, 195)

Similarly, the issues and positions articulated by the UWC reflect their political strategy. With 3.2 million acres of WSAs currently managed and protected as wilderness, the Wilderness Coalition has no incentive to negotiate its position. With this scenario in place, SUWA has drawn a line in the desert sand regarding any proposal less than the Citizens' Proposal as non-negotiable and undesirable. In their own words, "Do good, fight evil. And when you feel weary from the battle, lay your back down on the rock whose stunning beauty lays bare our very souls" (SUWA 1997, 16).

One way in which SUWA has communicated this good versus evil definition of Utah wilderness issues is in a full-color publication promoting its wilderness vision. The booklet contains spectacular color photographs of proposed wilderness lands contrasting visions of preservation versus destruction. A photograph of the Kaiparowits Plateau is captioned, ". . . a rich, living testament to our cultural and natural heritage . . ." and is compared on the next page to a black-and-white photograph of a miner standing on a coal heap, representing the future of the Kaiparowits if not protected as wilderness. The booklet goes on to state, ". . . what anti-wilderness zealots see when they look at the Kaiparowits is coal" (SUWA n.d.).

In this way the UWC attempts to define both the issue and the opposition interest group. The UPLMUC refutes this definition of their stance:

[We are] . . . not anti-wilderness. It's the pro-wilderness group in the political arena that tries to paint the other side as anti-wilderness and they define what anti-wilderness and pro-wilderness is. . . . It's sort of like the old notion, you're either with me or you're against me. If you don't support 5.7, then you're anti-wilderness. You can support a lesser amount but you're still anti-wilderness, and that's the way they try to make the public believe. (Walsh 1997)

The political argument over Utah wilderness has thus become characterized not by differing views on common issues but by polarized definitions of the issues themselves. Whereas "debate" refers to the discussion of opposing sides of a question, the two coalitions are not prepared to agree on a common question at this time.

## NATIONALIZING THE SCOPE OF CONFLICT

The Utah wilderness debate of the 1980s, which centered largely around Forest Service lands, was characterized by attempts to resolve issues locally. A Utah wilderness committee created by former Governor Scott Matheson in 1979 provided a forum for wilderness opponents and proponents to present their viewpoints and negotiate differences before congressional hearings in 1983. Dick Carter of the Utah Wilderness Association (UWA), a participant in these early efforts, observes that nationally oriented public interest groups on both sides of the debate would have preferred to "hammer out the bill in Washington D.C.," where they already had strong lobbies in place (Carter 1997).

In the intervening years, the Utah wilderness conflict has indeed become increasingly polarized and nationalized. Two competing versions of Utah BLM wilderness bills have been brought to Congress, each representing one of the polarized viewpoints described above. The public-interest groups have distanced themselves from local processes aimed at achieving common resolution, and they are instead lobbying for their individual positions on a national scale. As a consequence, each side has been successful in blocking the aims of the other, yet neither can break the resulting political stalemate.

A prime example of this strategy has been the campaign waged by the UWC to defeat the Utah delegation wilderness bill (H.R. 1745 and S. 884) from January 1995 to March 1996. According to Rait, UWC's lobbying efforts "utilized the Sierra Club's muscle and their political prowess within the beltway in Washington," as well as the Wilderness Society's lobby there (1997). Utah's Sierra Club representative, Lawson LeGate, says the UWC's tactic was to

> . . . approach members of Congress who we felt were persuadable, including some Republicans, and convince them that this was a bad idea, particularly moderate Republicans who can swing votes. They in turn communicated to [Utah Congressman] Hansen's office that they had serious misgivings about this legislation. It was enough that . . . Lee Davidson, Washington correspondent for the Deseret News, reported there was serious concern that Hansen's bill, if brought to the floor might actually be defeated. It was enough that it spooked Jim Hansen so that he never did bring that bill up. (LeGate 1997)

The UWC drew attention to the bill's hard release language, exemptions for dam building, recognition of R.S. 2477 rights,[3] and vehicle use within wilderness areas. According to LeGate, the hard release language was the "key concept [that] really made a difference" in persuading Congress to vote against the Utah delegation bill (LeGate 1997). According to Pam Eaton of the Wilderness Society, "our main role last Congress was to point out the national implications of H.R. 1745. The Utah delegation was challenging the very concept of wilderness" (Eaton 1997).

Similarly, the UPLMUC is clear in expressing its position on congressional bills. The UPLMUC argues that any wilderness designation of BLM lands by Congress is unnecessary and inappropriate. As an alternative, the UPLMUC endorses the designation of BLM lands as Areas of Critical Environmental Concern (ACECs), saying, "In those areas needing special protection of the resource, this prescription can be and is being used, while allowing some multiple uses" (UPLMUC 1997, 5). The UPLMUC contends that the existence of "scenic, pristine areas" in Utah constitutes evidence that non-wilderness public land management provides adequate protection, and argues that "it is a colossal misconception that only wilderness designation will protect our resources for future generations" (UPLMUC 1997, 5).

Further, the types of legislative provisions that made the delegation's bill unacceptable to environmental groups are the ones that the UPLMUC would find essential to its endorsement of a bill. The UPLMUC states that it "would not oppose a limited acreage BLM wilderness designation" that included hard release language, prohibition of grazing reductions, and prohibition of federal reserved water rights claims, and that preserved access to school trust lands (UPLMUC 1997, 6).

As the opposing coalitions jockey for political influence, the levels of rhetoric, tension, and mud-slinging have increased. It is well known by environmental organizations, for example, that when the public perceives a threat to the environment, new members and broad public support are generated as the public turns to the organizations committed to neutralizing the perceived threat (Hjelmar 1996, 51). To this end, SUWA has targeted and demonized Utah Congressman Jim Hansen, chair of the House Subcommittee on Natural Resources and Public Lands.

On entering the SUWA offices in Salt Lake City, visitors are greeted with a bright yellow banner quoting Hansen: "Those folks from SUWA are tough bastards to fight." SUWA has repeatedly used quotes from Hansen to advance its own cause. Excerpting from *The Kentucky Journal Courier*, a SUWA newsletter states that "Representative Hansen said that the Kaiparowits Plateau did not qualify as wilderness and that 'They might as well make Temple Square in Salt Lake City wilderness.' Here is Mr. Hansen's chance to see for himself" (SUWA 1996, 19). The newsletter then juxtaposes photographs of the Kaiparowits Plateau and Temple Square captioned respectively, "Wilderness according to 70% of the people of Utah," and "Wilderness according to Jim Hansen" (SUWA 1996, 19). It appears that SUWA has successfully capitalized on this approach, with its membership increasing from 7,746 in 1990 to 24,144 in 1997. Over half of current SUWA members live outside of Utah, as do nine of the fifteen directors on SUWA's board. In 1996, new members alone increased SUWA's budget by nearly $250,000 (Cates 1997).

Jim Hansen has joked that the environmental groups should give him a commission for increasing their membership, but he simultaneously observes that when they give him the "eco-thug award" it increases his popularity with his own constituents (Hansen 1997). Both Hansen and the UWC perceive that they benefit from publicity over their enmity. The Sierra Club's Lawson LeGate asserted that Utah's congressional delegation was able to do something he has been trying to do for over eight years: nationalize the Utah wilderness debate.

The eight or nine years of effort referred to by LeGate have included a consistent push by the UWC to influence public and media opinion inside and outside Utah. In 1990, for example, UWC published a four-hundred-page book entitled *Wilderness at the Edge*, promoting its 5.7-million-acre wilderness proposal. The book included background information on the wilderness designation process, maps and descriptions of the areas identified by UWC, and a number of scenic color photographs.

One indication of the politically effective nature of this book is the positive reaction it received from the conservative Salt Lake City radio and television station KSL. In 1991, a spokesman for KSL's editorial board issued a broadcast praising the book as a "wonderful contribution to the State and its people" (Gale 1991). The editorial proceeded to say, "We have said before that five-plus million acres is too much for wilderness. We still hold that opinion. But the Coalition's new book makes a convincing argument the BLM's two million acre proposal is not enough. Compromise is necessary" (Gale 1991). The KSL editorial prompted a response from Bill Howell, Executive Director of the Southeastern Utah Association of Local Governments. Howell's five-page letter to KSL criticized the station for having been influenced by the UWC's publication, saying, "I cannot understand how KSL can represent that a publication from people who are decidedly one-sided on a given issue can even come close to a balanced portrayal" (Howell 1991). Howell's letter included maps and numerous attachments presenting an alternate viewpoint, but the UPLMUC has no equivalent publication portraying its side of the wilderness issue.

In addition to distributing *Wilderness at the Edge* nationwide, the UWC has promoted its message by undertaking an "editorial board" tour outside Utah. Both Eaton (1997) and Rait (1997) noted that this joint effort, spearheaded by the Wilderness Society, and including SUWA and the Sierra Club, consisted of contacting major newspapers and "educating" them on the Utah wilderness debate, in particular the pending Utah delegation's push to pass legislation (Rait 1997). In addition, full-page advertisements were purchased in *The New York Times* and other major national papers, as well as in Salt Lake City newspapers.

The UWC has used a variety of additional techniques to wage its pro-wilderness campaign, including lawn signs and bus boards with the "5.7 million" caption, public rallies, activist letter-writing and phone campaigns to key politicians, and group outings designed to combine vacation experience with wilderness education on the UWC's proposed acreage. Dick Carter of the former UWA criticizes the UWC for adhering to a "no compromise" position, which he feels has polarized the debate. Yet he concedes that the UWC's campaign to defeat H.R. 1745 / S. 884 was "one of the great political arguments of all time" (1997).

Multiple-use advocates, meanwhile, engaged in a blocking effort of their own in attempting to derail the "reinventory" described in chapter 3. The UWC responded by creating its own review and documentation of its Citizens' Proposal, which was the basis for H.R. 1500. Over ten years have passed since the UWC's proposal was originally developed, and the group is concerned that some areas have been degraded, that some lands were previously overlooked due to time constraints or subsequent land exchanges, and that wilderness opponents will challenge any weaknesses in the original proposal (such as R.S. 2477 road claims). Since 1996 UWC volunteers have been engaged in a detailed review of road claims and in a biological analysis inventory known as the Wildlands Project. This process culminated with public meetings in four Utah and six national venues in 1998, with an updated proposal of approximately 8.5–8.6 million acres (Matz 1998).

Through these efforts the UWC seeks to continuously update and strengthen H.R. 1500 while it awaits a change in congressional leadership and an accompanying change in leadership of the Natural Resources Subcommittee. According to UWC strategist Liz McCoy, "The idea is to make the bill as strong and responsible as possible so that when leadership changes take place H.R. 1500 can be brought out of committee and onto the floor" (McCoy 1997).

## CONCLUSION: BREAKING THE STALEMATE

Dick Carter summarizes the current status of Utah wilderness politics in this way: "It's easy to get a bill stopped, but nobody can get one passed." Grand Canyon Trust President Geoff Barnard cites President Clinton's creation of the Grand Staircase–Escalante National Monument as one consequence of the polarized, nationalized process. In Barnard's view, "The monument was a direct result of the adversarial process" surrounding the Utah delegation's wilderness bill and environmentalist opposition (Velush 1997). While environmental groups applaud the creation of the new monument, opposition to the monument was significant in Utah and there is a movement in Congress to block such moves in the future.

Utah Governor Mike Leavitt is now proposing an alternative process for local resolution of the wilderness debate, and it is not known to what extent these two coalitions will be willing to support or participate in the process. The governor's proposed Incremental Regional Wilderness Strategy would divide the state into seven regions and would attempt to achieve a consensus wilderness recommendation for one region at a time.

The current political climate may provide inadequate incentives for public-interest groups on either side to take interest in the incremental strategy. "The desire to solve the problem is not there," according to Dick Carter. Mark Walsh of the Utah Association of Counties makes this assessment:

> You look at the environmental community; what's their incentive? There is no incentive. We've got 5.7 million acres, and it's being managed that way. For them to come in and sit down sends the message that there's going to be a reduction. So what's their incentive, are they going to get more? Absolutely not. They're going to get less. For a county official to come in and sit down, what's their incentive? Is it because they're going to get less wilderness? Absolutely not, they're going to get more wilderness. We're already at 2.5 million, roughly. Their recommendation was 1.1, roughly, a little less than that amount, so what's their incentive to come? You got the governor sitting here in the middle who's saying "Y'all come, let's talk together, let's sit down at the table and reason together" and we're all saying thank you very much Governor but no thank you. (Walsh 1997)

There are, however, two considerations that may ultimately provide incentive for local resolution. The first factor is that each side incurs some risk in leaving the situation indefinitely unresolved, and these perceived risks may increase with time. On the issue of roads, for example, the UWC fears that counties will try to use road construction and maintenance to disqualify areas from wilderness status. In a May 1997 E-mail bulletin to environmental activists, UWC's Jim Catlin (1997) warned of the dangers of an R.S. 2477 rider attached to the Senate's emergency flood relief legislation; "The opposition has admitted the true purpose for the rider," Catlin wrote, quoting Emery Country Commissioner Dixie Thompson as saying

"We are going to try to eliminate wilderness in Emery County" through this legislation.

Conversely, the Utah Association of Counties fears that environmental activists will delay wilderness designation in an effort to allow former road claims to become restored into the landscape and therefore invalidated. "This is one of the rubs we're in right now," says Mark Walsh. "We're identifying lands that may not now meet the (wilderness) criteria, but if it's managed in a certain fashion for a while it very well may. . . . I think that's the intent with respect to roads."

The other factor that may promote participation in local resolution processes is each side's grounding in the concerns of Utah citizens and each side's abiding interest in the welfare of the land. Beneath the sometimes hostile rhetoric, these concerns reveal themselves. The Sierra Club's Lawson LeGate argues: "This [UWC] wilderness proposal is homemade, homespun, as in Utah. Utahns developed this proposal" (LeGate 1997). The Utah Association of Counties' Mark Walsh also argues for Utahns: "Those lands have become part of the local economy, and the fact of the matter is that wilderness designation does affect the local economy" (Walsh 1997). The UPLMUC's *Ten Wilderness Issues* position paper ends with a statement about its members that could easily have been used by the UWC to describe its constituency: "These are people who know and care deeply for public lands. They know their future depends upon properly caring for . . . these lands" (UPLMUC 1997, 6).

## ℂ NOTES TO CHAPTER 4

1. For a number of years the UWC advocated a 5.7-million-acre proposal. Recently they have expanded that acreage as a result of a more recent inventory conducted by UWC volunteers. See "The New Citizens' Proposal: More Comprehensive, More Challenging," *The Utah Wilderness Coalition Newsletter*, June 1, 1998, 1.

2. For a review of the relationship between UWA and SUWA, see Brennan 1998.

3. Section 8 of the 1866 Lode Mining Act, revised and renamed in 1873, became Revised Statute 2477 (R.S. 2477). This statute reads, "The right-of-way for the construction of highways over public lands, not reserved for public uses, is hereby granted."

## ℂ REFERENCES TO CHAPTER 4

Brennan, Amy. 1998. Grassroots of the desert: the roles of the Utah Wilderness Association and the Southern Utah Wilderness Alliance in the debate over wilderness designation of Bureau of Land Management lands in southern Utah. Thesis submitted in partial fulfillment of the requirements for the degree of Master of Science in Forest Resources, Utah State University.

Carter, Richard. 1997. Former director, Utah Wilderness Association. Public lecture at the University of Utah, Salt Lake City, May 14.

Cates, Karl. 1997. "SUWA Is Elbowing Its Way into Urban Utah Mainstream," *Deseret News*, February 9, A1 and A11.

Catlin, Jim. 1997. E-mail notice on May 8 to ses@burgoyne.com.

Cutler, M. 1995. Old players with new power: the nongovernmental organizations. In *A New Century for Natural Resources Management*, edited by R. L. Knight and S. F. Bates, 189–208. Washington, DC: Island Press.

Davis, Charles. 1997. Conclusion: public lands and policy change. In *Western Public Lands and Environmental Politic*, edited by C. Davis, 193–201. Boulder, CO: Westview Press.

Eaton, Pamela. 1977. Regional Director, Four Corners States, the Wilderness Society. Telephone interview by authors, May 7.

Gale, G. Donald. 1991. Editorial—Wilderness Proposal Useful. KSL-AM-TV. January 17.

Hansen, James. 1997. Utah Representative, U.S. Congress. Course lecture at the University of Utah, Salt Lake City, May 5.

Hjelmar, U. 1996. *The Political Practice of Environmental Organizations*. Aldershot, England: Avebury Ashgate Publishing, Limited.

Howell, W. D. 1991. Letter to G. Donald Gale, KSL Broadcast House, February 25.

LeGate, Lawson. 1997. Field Representative, Utah Public Lands Office of the Sierra Club. Personal interview by authors, February 27.

Matz, Mike. 1998. Executive Director, Southern Utah Wilderness Alliance. Telephone interview by authors, August 12.

McCoy, Liz. 1997. Organizer, Utah Wilderness Coalition. Personal interview by authors, April 24.

Rait, Ken. 1997. Issues Director, Southern Utah Wilderness Alliance. Personal interview by authors, February 10.

SUWA (Southern Utah Wilderness Alliance). 1996. Religious shrine to be added to H.R. 1500. *Southern Utah Wilderness Alliance Newsletter* IX (No. 1, Spring): 19.

———. 1997. Giving the land a voice. *Southern Utah Wilderness Alliance Newsletter* 9 (Spring): 16.

———. 1998. Utah wilderness timeline. *Southern Utah Wilderness Alliance Newsletter* 15 (Summer): 11.

———. N.d. *Imagine*. Salt Lake City: Southern Utah Wilderness Alliance.

UPLMUC (Utah Public Lands Multiple Use Coalition). 1997. "Ten Wilderness Issues." Unpublished paper.

U.S. District Court, District of Utah. 1996. *State of Utah, et al. v. Bruce Babbitt, et al. Order* (2:96-CV-870B). November 18.

Velush, L. 1997. "Canyon Clout: Grand Canyon Trust Vaults to Big Leagues," *Arizona Daily Sun*, January 5, 1.

Walsh, Mark. 1997. Utah Association of Counties. Personal interview by authors, March 5.

# CHAPTER 5

# Don't Cry Out Acreage Figures in a Crowded Theater

## Lucas Smart

## Amber Ayers

### INTRODUCTION

The United States is a representative democracy. This being the case, elected officials and their constituents should steer the Utah wilderness debate toward the most popularly supported proposal, draw the boundaries on a map, and go home. However, this simple plan is easier said than done. Popular public opinion on the issue is difficult to measure. Inconsistency in poll results, even within individual polls, and questions about the best way to aggregate poll data make it difficult to identify the most popular proposal.

In this chapter we examine the results of ten polls concerning Utah wilderness designation conducted between 1982 and 1998. In most cases the survey tool, or poll questionnaire, was not available for our review. For this reason we have limited the analysis of these polls to the results of each poll and the sample from which the poll was taken. Although not entirely revealing, these polls offer valuable insights into Utahns' preferences regarding Utah wilderness. We also discuss the perceptions of people who are well versed in the wilderness debate, and how they view public-opinion polls on the wilderness issue. Other forms of popular input, such as hearings, will also be discussed. And finally, we will examine how the level of awareness and understanding of the issue varies, and how popular opinion relates to major political events.

### POLLS AND THE POLITICAL PROCESS

Throughout the Utah wilderness debate, politicians have gradually accepted the idea of more than one million acres of wilderness. While it would be impossible to determine the exact cause of this shift, it is likely that public-opinion polls, which generally show that Utahns favor more than one million acres of wilderness, may have been a factor. The tendency for congressional wilderness proposals to increase in acreage over time seems to correlate with public opinion. However, on May 21, 1995, the *Salt Lake Tribune* published an article about wilderness polls that stated, "The June 1 deadline for introducing a Utah wilderness bill is rushing toward the state's congressional delegation. Not coincidentally, so too is a wave of conflicting poll numbers aimed at persuading the Congress that Utahns are either crazy about wilderness or livid about it."

*Acreage Proposals*

Although many public-opinion polls relevant to the Utah wilderness debate include various questions concerning wilderness issues, most focus on acreage. It is difficult to translate the abstract concept of several million acres into an understanding of how much land is actually being discussed. One approach is to think of the various acreage proposals in terms of a percentage of the state rather than a specific acreage. In these terms the 5.7-million-acre proposal works out to be about 10 percent of the state's total area, and the 1.2-million-acre proposal is 2 percent. Unfortunately, most of the surveys do not simplify the proposals into these kinds of terms. As Dan Jones, director of a Salt Lake City polling firm, put it, "When you start talking about one million acres versus five million acres people just don't have any idea what you are talking about" (Jones 1997). Another dilemma presented with the use of acreage figures is the fact that for many interest groups these figures become mantras rather than working numerical benchmarks. While this might portray the opinions of people committed to various acreage proposals, it may inhibit a careful analysis of those acreage proposals.

POLL RESULTS ON ACREAGE

One way to examine the various poll results on this subject is to consider the support, or lack thereof, for each of the acreage proposals in each poll. When considering these poll results it is important to keep in mind the impact of margin of error. Typically the margin of error for public polls is approximately plus or minus 4 percent. This means that the reported results of the poll are accurate only to within four percentage points in either direction. This variation alone may explain some of the differences in the poll results discussed in this chapter. (These data are summarized in table 5.1.)

One of the earliest polls that asked a question on wilderness was conducted by Dan Jones and Associates in 1982. The survey questioned

TABLE 5.1—Summary of Utah Wilderness Acreage Proposal Surveys

(* = most favored response)

| Poll | Acreage Results | | Sample |
|---|---|---|---|
| Deseret News<br>February 1982<br>Dan Jones | 3%<br>13%<br>20%<br>*28%<br>13%<br>14% | no wilderness<br>less than 900,000 acres<br>900,000 acres<br>2.6 million acres<br>3.5 million acres<br>have no opinion | 595 adults statewide |
| Deseret News/KSL Poll<br>1989<br>Dan Jones | 1%<br>16%<br>7%<br>19%<br>*24%<br>32% | no wilderness<br>less than 1 million acres<br>1–2 million acres<br>2–4 million acres<br>more than 4 million acres<br>don't know | statewide |
| Deseret News/KSL Poll<br>December 18, 1994<br>Dan Jones | 7%<br>12%<br>*24%<br>19%<br>22%<br>16% | no wilderness<br>less than 1 million acres<br>1–2 million acres<br>2–4 million acres<br>more than 4 million acres<br>don't know | statewide |
| Salt Lake Tribune Poll<br>February 19–25, 1995<br>Valley Research | *32%<br>27%<br>31% | no additional wilderness<br>1.2 million acres<br>5.7 million acres | 604 adults from Weber,<br>Davis, Salt Lake,<br>and Summit Counties |
| Waldholtz Survey<br>April 26, 1995<br>Dan Jones | *36%<br>24%<br>23%<br>17% | 1.2 million acres<br>2.0 million acres<br>5.7 million acres<br>results not reported | Second Congressional<br>District |
| KUTV / Coalition for<br>Utah's Future<br>May 5–17, 1995<br>Valley Research | 5%<br>12%<br>12%<br>10%<br>23%<br>*31%<br>8% | 0 acres<br>1 million acres<br>1.9 million acres<br>2.9 million acres<br>3.2 million acres<br>5.7 million acres<br>don't know | statewide<br>366 urban and<br>336 rural respondents |
| Wilderness Education<br>Project Poll<br>May 8–11, 1195<br>Dan Jones | *21%<br>16%<br>20%<br>15%<br>19%<br>8% | 1 million acres<br>1.2 million acres<br>1.9 million acres<br>2.8 million acres<br>5.7 million acres<br>don't know | statewide<br>607 telephone surveys |
| Deseret News/KSL<br>June 5–6, 1995<br>Dan Jones | 4%<br>18%<br>26%<br>*36%<br>7%<br>8% | none<br>1 million acres<br>1.8 million acres<br>5.7 million acres<br>other<br>don't know | statewide |

TABLE 5.1    (Continued)

| | | | |
|---|---|---|---|
| KBYU Utah Colleges | *30% | 3.2 million acres | statewide |
| Exit Poll | 27% | less than 3.2 million acres | |
| 1996 | 20% | more than 3.2 million acres | |
| | 8% | don't know | |
| Utah Wilderness | *74% | 9.25 million acres | 401 Utah adults |
| Coalition | | | |
| June 26–29, 1998 | | | |
| Wirthlin Worldwide | | | |

595 adults from six regions proportionate to each region's percentage of the overall state population. The most popular proposal was 2.6 million acres, with support from 28 percent of respondents, followed by 900,000 acres, with support from 20 percent of respondents. The next largest percentage of respondents, 14 percent, had no opinion, and proposals for both 3.5 million acres and "less than 900,000" were equally supported by 13 percent of respondents. Finally, the "no wilderness" proposal was the least popular proposal identified in this poll, with support from only 3 percent of respondents.

The next acreage poll was conducted seven years later, in 1989, by Dan Jones for *Deseret News* and KSL, a Salt Lake City television station. This statewide poll indicated that the largest percentage of respondents, 32 percent, had no opinion. However, of actual proposals, "more than 4 million acres" ranked first, with support from 24 percent of respondents, followed by "2–4 million acres," with support from 19 percent of respondents. A proposal for "less than one million acres" came in third, with support from 16 percent of those polled; the option of "1–2 million acres" finished second to last, with support from 7 percent of respondents. Finally, "no wilderness" was last, with support from only 1 percent of respondents.

Dan Jones conducted his next statewide wilderness poll for the *Deseret News* and KSL five years later, in December 1994. The most popular acreage proposal in this poll was "1–2 million acres," with support from 24 percent of respondents, followed by a "more-than-4-million-acre" proposal, which 22 percent of respondents favored. Third place went to a proposal for "2–4 million acres," followed by the 16 percent of respondents who "don't know." Once again "no wilderness" was the least popular proposal, with support from 7 percent of respondents.

A 1995 *Salt Lake Tribune* poll posed questions to 604 adults who lived on the Wasatch Front. The idea of using specific acreage numbers was replaced by asking respondents this question: "Do you support the concept of additional wilderness areas on BLM lands?" The answer was a definite yes; 73 percent were in favor of additional wilderness and only 19 percent were not. However, these results may be misleading. In the same poll respondents were asked this question: "Additional wilderness proposals range from 1.2 million acres to 5.7 million acres. What is your feeling?" 32 percent answered "No additional wilderness" while 27 percent wanted additional wilderness on the "low end" and 31 percent wanted additional acreage on the "high end."

In April 1995, Dan Jones conducted what is commonly referred to as the Waldholtz survey, because it was commissioned by Representative Enid Greene Waldholtz. The survey identified the 1.2-million-acre proposal as the most favored, with 36 percent of respondents indicating this was the acreage they believed would be most appropriate for Utah wilderness designation. The Waldholtz survey identified a 2.0-million-acre proposal as the runner-up, with support from 24 percent of respondents, and 5.7 million acres as the least favored proposal, with support from 23 percent of respondents.

The Waldholtz survey stands in sharp contrast to the KUTV/Coalition for Utah's Future survey conducted by Valley Research, another Salt Lake City consulting firm, May 5–17, 1995. This survey identified 5.7 million acres as the most favored proposal, with support from 31 percent of respondents. The runner-up in this survey was the 3.2-million-acre proposal, which 23 percent of survey respondents favored. Although this survey did not include a 1.2-million-acre proposal, it did have both a 1-million-acre proposal and a 1.9-million-acre proposal, both of which received support from 12 percent of respondents. This survey also included a "no wilderness" option, which 5 percent of respondents supported, followed by a "don't agree with any answer" that 8 percent of respondents chose.

In May 1995, Dan Jones conducted a poll for the Utah Wilderness Education Project (a multiple-use organization) that surveyed 607 adult Utahns. In this poll 21 percent of respondents favored 1 million acres, which was the most favored proposal; 1.9 million acres was the runner-up, with support from 20 percent of respondents, followed closely by the 5.7 proposal, with support from 19 percent of respondents. Both the 1.2-million-acre proposal and the 2.8-million-acre proposal came in close, with respective support from 16 percent and 15 percent of respondents, followed by 8 percent who answered "don't know."

Dan Jones and Associates conducted another statewide survey during the summer of 1995 for the *Deseret News* and KSL TV. In this poll the most favored acreage proposal was 5.7 million acres, which was supported by 36 percent of respondents. The next most popular proposal was 1.8 million acres, which was supported by 26 percent of respondents, followed by a 1-million-acre proposal that received support from 18 percent.

Finally, the least popular proposal identified in this poll was the "no wilderness" proposal, which 4 percent of respondents supported. Additionally, 8 percent of respondents chose the "don't know" response. We asked Dan Jones why there was such a large disparity between this poll and the Utah Wilderness Education Project poll he had conducted just a month before. He explained that he could not be sure but that the answer was probably based on the sample that was surveyed (Jones 1997).

Brigham Young University conducted a statewide exit poll during the 1996 elections. Several of the questions addressed wilderness proposals. The most favored proposal for this poll was 3.2 million acres, with support from 30 percent of respondents, followed by 27 percent of respondents who favored less than 3.2 million acres, and 20 percent of respondents who favored more than 3.2 million acres. Again a base line of 8 percent of respondents chose the "don't know" response, as in the previous three surveys.

Another poll was conducted by a polling firm called Wirthlin Worldwide for the Utah Wilderness Coalition during June 1998. The sample for the poll was 401 Utah adults. Unlike some other wilderness polls, the 401 respondents were informed by the poll-taker about what activities are permitted or banned in wilderness areas prior to being questioned about their opinions. Sixty-nine percent of respondents indicated that they did not believe Utah had enough wilderness. Eighty-nine percent said that wilderness was important to the state's economy. Thirty-six percent indicated that Utah must develop all its natural resources. Respondents were informed that 40 percent of BLM lands in Utah were being considered for wilderness designation; 74 percent indicated they were in favor of designating all of that as wilderness (*Salt Lake Tribune* 1998a).

In October 1998, Wirthlin Worldwide released the results of a second Utah wilderness poll, which appears to contradict their June 1998 poll. In the second poll, Wirthlin allowed respondents to choose alternative protective land-management designations as well as wilderness acreage designations. In this second poll, Wirthlin reported that the public would prefer 2.34 million acres of wilderness, 2.7 million acres of protected land with public access, 2 million acres managed for wildlife, and 1.9 million acres kept semi-primitive (*Salt Lake Tribune* 1998b). Wirthlin's second poll, which was conducted at the firm's own expense, met with criticism from wilderness advocates. SUWA claimed that Wirthlin, well known for his ties to conservative Republicans, revamped the poll at the behest of Utah's Republican leaders in order to "obfuscate the original findings" (*SUWA Newsletter* 1998, 4). Politics aside, the second Wirthlin poll is not considered further in this chapter because it employs alternative land designations that are not comparable to the wilderness acreage figures used in the other ten polls.

*Analysis*
Critically analyzing the results of these polls is difficult. Picking out evidence to support any given proposal is easy. For example, both of the following statements could be made:

(1) Based on the results of the Dan Jones/Deseret/KSL survey of June 5, 1995, more Utahns support 5.7 million acres of wilderness than any other proposal.

(2) Based on the results of the Dan Jones/Deseret/KSL survey of June 5, 1995, the majority of Utahns do not support the 5.7-million-acre wilderness proposal.

Both of these statements are absolutely true. The first statement refers to the fact that the 5.7 proposal is supported by a plurality, 36 percent, of respondents. Thus it was the most favored proposal presented in the survey. The second statement refers to the fact that the other three survey responses represent over fifty percent of the population.

Some trends in the surveys can be identified. For example, the surveys indicate that as time has passed, more people have developed an opinion about wilderness designation. During the first survey, in 1982, 14 percent of respondents indicated that they "didn't know" what acreage they supported. The number of respondents without an opinion was even greater for the 1989 survey, in which 32 percent responded "don't know." The numbers of disinterested, uninformed, or apathetic respondents began to taper off with the 1994 survey, when only 16 percent of respondents chose the "don't know" option. Those without opinions became a small minority in 1995. In three of the five 1995 surveys that offered a "don't know" or equivalent option, only 8 percent chose that response as their own. Considering the complexity of the issue, this result is fairly significant. These results indicate that, at any typical home, restaurant, or movie theater in Utah during 1995, nine out of ten people had an opinion about the desired number of acres of Utah wilderness.

Other generalizations can also be drawn from the survey data. Because the surveys were conducted using different methods and survey instruments, aggregating the results is problematic, but general trends can be observed across the data. We aggregated survey results by selecting only the most recent polls (conducted between 1995 and 1998), and eliminating all responses except the one that was most favored by the largest number of respondents. This provides a general picture of how many Utahns feel about wilderness.[1] (see table 5.2)

If the results shown in Table 5.2 are averaged, it appears that more Utahns support 4.9 million acres than any other individual proposal.

TABLE 5.2—Most Favored Responses in Recent Surveys (1995–1998)

| Poll | Most Favored |
|------|-------------|
| 1 | 5.7 million acres |
| 2 | 1.0 million acres |
| 3 | 5.7 million acres |
| 4 | 3.2 million acres |
| 5 | 9.2 million acres |
| Average | 4.9 million acres |

However, this does not mean that a majority of Utahns support that amount of wilderness; rather, it indicates that the largest block of respondents tends to favor the larger wilderness proposals. We cannot assume from the data available that there is a majority consensus; it is entirely possible that there is no single proposal that a majority of Utahns support.

## Discussion

One way to gain some insight into public opinion on Utah wilderness is to turn to people who have experience in the field. Dan Jones and Jim Woolf are two experts on the subject. The majority of wilderness polls reported in Utah newspapers were conducted by an independent consulting firm, Dan Jones and Associates. Private pollsters are professionals hired to conduct surveys by a variety of individuals or organizations. There are many reasons why someone may hire a professional to carry out a public-opinion poll. Some may be interested in reporting the facts. Elected officials may wish to find out how their constituents feel about an issue and pass legislation based on the findings of a poll. Other individuals or organizations who have a specific agenda may be trying to find data to support their goals. Rather than conducting polls themselves, an organization may hire a professional pollster. These experts are chosen to lend expertise and legitimacy to the results. By using techniques such as random-digit dialing, where a computer randomly chooses and dials telephone numbers, there is less likely to be a bias in the survey sample. The surveys themselves and the results of the surveys are considered privileged material and cannot be released by the firm conducting the poll, only by the client that has hired the firm to conduct it.

Dan Jones and Associates have conducted polls for groups with diverging motivations and interests, including the *Deseret News*, the Wilderness Education Project, and elected officials. Sometimes the results of these polls indicate that the 5.7-million-acre proposal is the most favored. Other times the results show that more people favor a 1.2-million-acre wilderness designation. Jones attributes these anomalies to definitional problems: "People have a different view of the word 'wilderness.' We need a strong definition of wilderness available to the public." He also said that public opinion surveys must communicate with the respondents and using "big words" does not accomplish this. The words chosen to implement a question are important (Jones 1997).

Jim Woolf, environmental editor for the *Salt Lake Tribune* and a veteran of the Utah wilderness debate, offered some interesting insights on how the public feels about wilderness (Woolf 1997). Woolf refers to 1995 as the year of "the poll wars." Five surveys were conducted during this year and many of them show drastically different results. He believes the differences in the polls may lie in the context of the questions and the amount of information presented within the questions. Also, the choice of words used by the pollsters causes opinions to waver. Woolf estimates that 20 percent of Utahns care intensely about wilderness and another 10–20 percent are adamantly opposed to wilderness designation. In his opinion, "There is a huge group in the middle, who are largely uninformed. This leaves them vulnerable to how the questions are worded. That's why the poll results are all over the map."

## WILDERNESS COMPREHENSION

In the heat of a political debate, facts can be less significant than opinions, and opinions can be easier to obtain than facts. One factor concerning public opinion among Utahns concerns how much the people holding those opinions actually know about wilderness. Some national surveys indicate that people generally do not understand what wilderness is. For example, one poll conducted by the National Forest Products Association and the American Forest Institute, which was published in the *Salt Lake Tribune* in 1978, asked respondents if they had visited a wilderness area during the last year. Those who answered "yes" were then asked which wilderness area they had visited. Many responded with answers like Yellowstone Park and New York City's Fire Island. This kind of common misconception can lead to opinions about wilderness that are based on ideology and perception rather than facts.

However, Utahns consider themselves to be fairly well informed about the wilderness issue. In the KBYU exit poll, respondents were asked this question: "How informed do you consider yourself to be on the wilderness issue in Utah?" Only 15 percent of respondents felt that they were "very informed." However, 57 percent believed that they were "somewhat informed," followed by 23 percent who answered "not very informed," and 5 percent who chose "not informed." By comparing these results to the results of a similar survey conducted in Arizona, we find that Utahns are just a bit more confident about their knowledge of wilderness than their Arizona neighbors. In the Arizona survey, which was conducted by BLM, respondents were asked to assess their own knowledge of wilderness by answering questions like "How much do you feel you know about federal wilderness areas?" Answers ranged from "Quite a bit" to "Very little." About 11 percent of Arizona respondents felt they knew quite a bit about wilderness, compared to 15 percent of Utahns who believed they were very informed. Most Arizonans, 40 percent, believed that they did not know very much about wilderness, compared to only 23 percent of Utahns who said they were not very informed. By a slight margin Utahns seem to be a little more comfortable with their knowledge of wilderness than Arizonans.

Even though Utahns feel fairly confident about their knowledge of wilderness, this does not necessarily mean that they have a true substantive knowledge of the issue. In a 1995 Valley Research poll, Utah residents from the Wasatch Front were asked very specific questions about what is allowed in wilderness areas. The questions were presented by providing a list of activities preceded by the question "Which of the following activities are allowed in a wilderness area?" The first category was "off-road vehicles," to which 29 percent incorrectly answered yes. However, 69 percent gave the correct answer. Next, respondents were asked about "cattle grazing." Again the majority, 65 percent, correctly answered yes, compared to only 31 percent who answered no. The third question was about "hunting," to which 67 percent of respondents knew that hunting is allowed in wilderness areas, compared to 28 percent who mistakenly thought it was not. The question on "mountain biking" had the largest percentage of incorrect answers: only 50 percent of respondents knew it is prohibited in wilderness areas, compared to 47 percent who thought it is legal. Utahns' best showing was in the question about "camping," which the large majority, 80 percent, knew is allowed.

Considering that many people do not know the difference between wilderness and national parks, the results of this poll indicate that the issue is close to the hearts and minds of many Utahns. The high level of publicity this issue has received for so many years has given it considerable visibility among individual Utahns. Perhaps one of the reasons why the debate over Utah wilderness has been so fierce and long-lived is that Utahns obviously care about the issue. Every election year Americans are chastised by the media for their low turnout on election day. Often in conjunction with this tongue-lashing we are offered the results of a poll in which a significant number of people were unable to locate the United States on a map or name their current senator. The inference is that ignorance and apathy go hand in hand. Perhaps the reverse of this is true regarding Utahns and the wilderness debate; rather than being ill informed, Utahns are not only aware of the issue, but also aware of the specific nuances of wilderness designation. This evidence, in view of the duration and intensity of the controversy, would seem to indicate that there is a correlation between familiarity with the wilderness issue and the intensity of the conflict.

## PUBLIC COMMENT

Another expression of public opinion on Utah wilderness is the public input during the BLM wilderness review. Scoping, or considering public opinion, is an integral part of the Environmental Impact Statement (EIS) process. For this reason the BLM recorded and classified all of the public comment it received during its review process (BLM Utah 1991). But unlike polls, public comment is non-random; respondents self-select. This limits the conclusions that can be drawn about public sentiment in general. For example, an aggressive interest group may be able to introduce an inordinate amount of comments supporting its position.

On the other hand, opportunities for public comment are posted and made available to everyone interested in a given planning process. The comment period for the BLM's initial Wilderness EIS draft lasted over six months, during which time the BLM received, recorded, and "considered" 4,496 comments or inputs under 6,213 different signatures. The disparity between comments and signatures is due to the fact that a person submitting an oral and a written comment is counted as having made two signed comments if their input discussed more than one issue. Of the 4,496 comments, 785 were oral and introduced during sixteen public hearings held in May 1986; 3,619 were written, and ninety-two were introduced as petitions or form letters. The BLM organized the comments into three categories:

 (a) Those who favored the no action or no wilderness alternative, which was 21 percent of the total comments.
 (b) People who did not express an opinion on the alternatives or on wilderness in general, which was 35 percent of the comments.
 (c) Those who favored at least some wilderness or the idea of wilderness in general, with 44 percent of the comments.

Like the poll results, these figures seem to indicate that public opinion generally favors wilderness. However, because the public comment is offered by choice rather than gathered over a random distribution, it is impossible to generalize from these results and make assumptions about the Utah population as a whole.

However, the BLM carefully recorded and reproduced this public input in the BLM's Environmental Impact Statement (EIS). The EIS is required by the National Environmental Policy Act (NEPA) for any major federal action significantly affecting the environment. Although NEPA does not require any specific level of environmental protection, it does require periods of public notice and comment and the consideration of that comment when choosing between several alternatives.

The public comments ranged from innocuous and indifferent to passionate and irate. However, most of the letters were written by concerned individuals who sought to offer a constructive point of view on wilderness designation. For example, in a letter that is typical of those opposing wilderness, one respondent wrote: "Public lands are for the entire population so that all can enjoy the beauties of these areas. By locking up vast acreage, this will only allow a very few to do this." Another respondent reflected a favorable attitude toward wilderness: "I have spent considerable time in the last decade in the back country of Utah, especially southern Utah, and have gone into many of the areas proposed for wilderness and later rejected by the BLM. I feel that wilderness is one of the most important legacies we can leave our children . . . thus I would like to urge you and Congress to adopt the Utah Wilderness Coalition's 5.7-million-acre proposal for wilderness in Utah" (BLM Utah, Public Comment Section).

It is difficult to determine how much this public comment affected the BLM's proposed designations. Like that of poll results, the interpretation of public comments can be used to support or to attack any particular point of view on wilderness.

### DISCUSSION

Americans clearly revel in their right to speak their mind. As a nation we try to make decisions democratically, so gauging and accurately assessing public opinion has become an important part of the political process. The goal of public-opinion surveys is to find out what the people think, and then utilize that information in a way that serves the democratic process (Erikson and Tedin 1995).

Establishing a direct link between public opinion and specific political activity is difficult. However, two things are clear. First, wilderness proposals for the state have grown in size over time. Second, public awareness about the wilderness debate has grown as well. Changing public preferences for specific wilderness acreage is more difficult to assess, but it seems to follow a general trend of favoring more wilderness in recent years than in the very early years.

We have also considered the inherent challenge of measuring what people think is an appropriate number of acres to be designated wilderness when the amount itself, millions of acres, is such a difficult concept to grasp. According to University of Utah professor Matthew Burbank, who researches polls and public-opinion surveys, "It is more helpful to consider acreage figures as symbols rather than as actual physical tracts of land. Individuals who choose to support 5.7 million acres of wilderness are probably choosing environmental protection, and people who are opposed to wilderness or support smaller designations are airing their beliefs about use/conservation conflicts" (Burbank 1997).

Essentially the wilderness debate has become too big to grasp. Each of the wilderness proposals includes scores of acres of land with varying wilderness qualities. When parties argue over millions of acres, they are not typically arguing about the application of FLPMA dictates to specific areas. Rather, acreage figures have become intangible icons that identify general beliefs, not preferences to specific sites.

Our review of poll results has indicated wide disparities between individual polls. These disparities could be explained in several ways. It is possible that some or all of the polls have been tailored to produce a certain result in order to buttress the position of an interested party. It is also possible that public opinion on the issue actually went through dramatic shifts during the course of the debate. Another explanation is that polling is just too uncertain to produce replicable results. In actuality all of these explanations are part of the reason that Utah wilderness polls do not clearly point to simple answers regarding how many acres should be protected as wilderness.

## CONCLUSION

In an effort to come to a conclusion about the number of acres Utahns would like to see protected as wilderness, we aggregated the results of the five most recent statewide polls. Our analysis indicates that 4.9 million acres would probably suit more Utahns than any other individual proposal. Interestingly, 4.9 million acres is just short of the mid-point between the current WSAs and the 5.7-million-acre proposal that was, until recently, espoused by the UWC. The UWC's latest proposal has not yet been the subject of a public-opinion poll.

Next we asked the question: How much do Utahns really know about wilderness? The answer, we discovered, is quite a bit. Confidence levels for Utahns on this subject are consistently higher than those for Arizonans. Furthermore, this confidence seems to be well founded in view of the results of the February 1995 *Salt Lake Tribune* poll. These results indicated that more Utahns knew the right answer to each of the questions about things that were allowed in wilderness areas than those who did not. These results are particularly impressive when you consider that the questions are not entirely obvious or simple. For example, it is not obvious that cattle are allowed in a wilderness area but mountain bikes are not. As the wilderness debate continues, Utahns should take pride in the fact that they are part of the controversy. Utahns, both for and against various wilderness proposals, have taken the time to learn about the issue and form an opinion.

Governor Leavitt described the situation in an October 1996 memo to his Cabinet: "Utahns share a common love of the land. There is a disagreement on how to protect sensitive lands but a common desire to preserve them. For decades our efforts have revolved around our conflicts. It is time to build on what unites us."

## NOTES TO CHAPTER 5

1. In one poll, specific acreage figures were not used, so we estimated the results. We used "4.4 million acres" for "more than 3.2 million acres" because 4.4 million is midway between 3.2 million and the 5.7-million-acre proposal that was being touted by the UWC at the time of the polls, the largest acreage proposal then being discussed in the media and in politics.

## REFERENCES TO CHAPTER 5

BLM (Bureau of Land Management of the U.S. Department of the Interior). 1983. *Arizona Wilderness Public Opinion Survey.* Phoenix, AZ: Arizona State Office.

BLM Utah (Utah State Office, Bureau of Land Management of the U.S. Department of the Interior). 1991. *Utah Statewide Wilderness Study Report.*

Burbank, Matthew. 1997. Personal interview by authors, July 23.

Erickson, Robert S., and Kent L. Tedin. 1995. *American Public Opinion.* 5th ed. Needham Heights, MA: Allyn and Bacon.

Jones, Dan. 1997. Personal interview by authors, May 7.

*Salt Lake Tribune.* 1998a. "Utahns Want More Wilderness, Survey Shows," July 7, B1.

———. 1998b. "Pollster Recasts Results of Wilderness Survey," October 10, B1.

State of Utah. Governor's Office of Planning and Budget. 1995. *Review of Selected Wilderness Public Opinion Surveys.* Salt Lake City, UT: State of Utah, Governor's Office of Planning and Budget.

*SUWA Newsletter.* 1998. Fall/Winter issue, vol. 15, no. 3.

Woolf, Jim. 1997. Personal interview by authors, June 6.

# CHAPTER 6

# Babel in the Wilderness

*The Rhetoric of Sufficiency/Release*
*and Excepted Activities*

## Meredith McKell Graff

### OVERVIEW

Since the passage of the Wilderness Act, probably no other wilderness issues have created more controversy than the current decade's fight over sufficiency/release language and excepted activities. While this debate has swirled throughout western states with wilderness proposals before Congress, much of the focus has been on Utah. Because of increasingly polarized discourse, Utah has not passed any wilderness legislation since the Utah Wilderness Act of 1984, which established wilderness in several national forests. Although several wilderness bills have been introduced since then, none have passed.

The Wilderness Act provided very few criteria that could serve as guidelines in today's wilderness debate. According to R. W. Gorte, the logic behind the imprecision was to allow for "differing perceptions of what constitutes wilderness" (1994, 6). To compound the ambiguity, public perception of what constitutes wilderness has changed. Dick Carter, former Coordinator of the Utah Wilderness Association (UWA), asserted that "The idea of 'wilderness as recreation' is almost a thing of the past—to maintain some sort of aesthetic is doomed. Wilderness has shifted from its primary recreation focus to that of bio-diversity and ecosystem functions" (1997). It is because of society's changing values and the shrinking available land from which to designate wilderness that the debate over the release language and excepted activities has grown fierce.

This chapter will examine the purpose of release language as it has been used since its creation in 1980, and will explore whether the release language created for forest lands is still relevant in BLM wilderness proposals where no regular review process is mandated by the management statute. Release language refers to language in wilderness bills that establishes limitations on the further consideration of lands in a given state or area for wilderness designation. This chapter will also analyze the issue of excepted activities in wilderness lands. The Wilderness Act permits certain exceptions, such as mineral prospecting and surveys, in order to provide information on mineral resources; water development projects with presidential approval; livestock grazing; fire, disease, and insect control; and aircraft landings and motorboat use where previously established. Wilderness laws since 1964 have also provided specific, additional exceptions to prohibited activities. What should be excepted and the scope of exception reached a fever pitch in Utah with the past decade's legislation.

In 1989 Congressman Wayne Owens (D-Utah), introduced H.R. 1500, the Utah BLM Wilderness Act. In response, Congressman James Hansen (R-Utah), introduced H.R. 1501. Neither bill passed. Both bills are significant in that each has reappeared in the same or similar form in subsequent years. In 1995 Representative Hansen's bill was reintroduced as H.R. 1745 (and in the Senate as S. 884). This bill, in addition to controversial release language and sweeping exceptions, explicitly excepted projects unusual to wilderness legislation. In 1997 a reincarnation of Representative Owens's H.R. 1500, known as "America's Red Rock Wilderness Act," was introduced in the House. By then Representative Owens was no longer part of Utah's congressional delegation, and the bill was introduced by Congressman Maurice Hinchey (D-New York). Hansen's H.R. 1745 created controversy over its explicit release and exception provisions; the Owens/Hinchey bill contains no release or exception language.

These bills highlight the spectrum of viewpoints regarding the evolution of release language as it applies to BLM wilderness lands, and the types of permissible excepted wilderness activities, particularly in Utah. Excepted activities will be reviewed in wilderness laws since the passage of the original Wilderness Act, in conjunction with the exceptions expressed in 1995's H.R. 1745, and its final version, as amended by the Senate in S. 884. These activities are summarized in table 6.1, which appears at the end of the chapter.

To a great extent the political fate of future wilderness legislation depends on how BLM wilderness study-area lands not included in a wilderness act are treated following passage of that law, and what activities will be excepted within the new wilderness areas. Until the particular language of release and exception intersects with the language of communication and agreement, the possibility of designating additional wilderness lands in Utah hangs in limbo.

## SUFFICIENCY/RELEASE LANGUAGE DEFINITIONS

*Inception.* Sufficiency/release language was constructed by Congress in response to *California v. Block* (1982), which invalidated the RARE II Final Environmental Impact Statement (FEIS) for California wilderness and prevented development on those roadless lands recommended for non-wilderness uses. Block's District Court case, *California v. Bergland* (1980), held that the RARE II FEIS violated NEPA, and the court enjoined the U.S. Forest Service (USFS) from developing any of the disputed areas prior to considering the wilderness values in compliance with NEPA. In their Congressional Research Service report, Gorte and Baldwin explain that "Congress responded to [*California v. Block*], and the potential for additional wilderness studies by developing release language that (1) prevent[ed] judicial review of the first round of Forest Service analysis of wilderness potential; (2) guide[d] the timing of Forest Service wilderness reviews; (3) provide[d] for managing undesignated, potential national forest wilderness areas prior to such future reviews" (1993, summary page).

Following the appellate sanction, John Crowell, Assistant Secretary of Agriculture for Natural Resources and Environment, directed the USFS in 1983 to re-evaluate *all* RARE II recommendations, but provided for state exemption from re-evaluation "if Congress enacted a state-wide bill with language that (1) precluded judicial review of the RARE II recommendations; (2) addressed the timing of future wilderness reviews; (3) guided management of the areas in the interim" (Gorte and Baldwin 1993, 5).

Following Crowell's exemption provision, Congressmen Phil Burton (D-California), "Buzz" Johnson (D-California), and John Seiberling (D-Ohio), chairman of the House Subcommittee on Public Lands, called together representatives from government, environmental interests, and business to craft language that could be included in states' wilderness proposals to avoid future lawsuits like the two in California (Hendee, Stankey, and Lucas 1990, 141).

Initially *sufficiency* meant that the RARE II study was enough—no further study was needed for NEPA's purposes. *Release* meant that the lands not included in a wilderness proposal would be taken out of consideration as wilderness at least until the next National Forest Management Act (NFMA) review cycle. Whether lands not included in wilderness are subsequently reviewed for wilderness characteristics and future designation depends on the type of sufficiency/release language employed in a particular wilderness proposal. Release language has splintered into three types. The type of sufficiency/release language one supports tends to define one's position on wilderness in the political debate.

*"Soft" release language* began as the only release language. It simply took out of consideration as wilderness lands not included in a particular wilderness proposal, but left the door open for future consideration following a NFMA review, if the released lands retained wilderness characteristics. Soft release language appeared in six national forest wilderness laws, beginning with the 1980 Alaska National Interest Lands Conservation Act (P.L. 96-487), through 1983 (Browning, Hendee, and Roggenbuck 1988). This early release language was permissive in nature and was considered "soft" because the lands, while initially released, could be reconsidered after the initial forest plans were developed (Gorte and Baldwin 1993; see table 6.1).

*"Compromise" release language* was created as a result of "continued pressure from development interests" beginning in 1984 (Browning, Hendee, and Roggenbuck 1988). It differed from soft release language by providing that the lands released as non-wilderness would be managed for multiple use. Compromise release language sought to mediate between the competing interests of preservationists, environmentalists, eco-biologists, recreationists, resource users, and developers. Forest lands released under compromise language were to be managed for multiple use in accordance with NFMA. Non-forest wilderness was to be managed under FLPMA, which established wilderness review for BLM lands. While the USFS wilderness laws required ten- to fifteen-year review cycles, FLPMA contains no similar regular wilderness review requirement.

*Hard release language*, developed concurrently with soft release language, is proscriptive in nature. It ranges from strictly prohibiting *any and all* future review of wilderness potential to requiring that wilderness review be initiated or completed by a specified date. Hard release supporters argue that this type of release language provides the greatest certainty because it specifies how long wilderness characteristics must be protected (Gorte and Baldwin 1993). While hard release language has received attention and consideration in congressional debates and subcommittee sessions in the past fifteen years, this specific construction did not appear in a final wilderness proposal until 1995, when S. 884 and H.R. 1745, the Utah Public Lands Management Act, departed significantly from the prior decade's compromise release language, which had been used in over twenty wilderness laws passed between 1983 and 1995.

*Sufficiency language* has evolved as a means to resolve the question of which national forest roadless areas should be eligible for further review and which lands should be released for other uses. "Sufficiency" specifically refers to "Congress' view that RARE II was sufficient for congressional purposes" but has generally come to indicate a limit to judicial review (Browning, Hendee, and Roggenbuck 1988).

## RELEASE LANGUAGE: THE ISSUES

The future of release language in wilderness legislation was questioned by Gorte and Baldwin in their report to Congress on wilderness legislation. They saw little merit in continuing to use old release language since RARE II recommendations have been replaced by RPA/NFMA recommendations in forest land wilderness (Gorte and Baldwin 1993). While final adjudication of BLM wilderness recommendation lawsuits is still pending, the release language of the 1980s that was crafted to address forest wilderness lands is a poor fit for BLM/FLPMA wilderness lands.

Critics of soft and compromise release language assert that when these types of release language are applied to BLM lands, there is "no clear direction . . . provided as to future reviews of wilderness suitability" (Gorte and Baldwin 1993, 10). Even though FLPMA, Section 603, directs initial review of BLM lands for wilderness characteristics and requires land-use plans, FLPMA does not stipulate that the plans be cyclical or prepared on a finite time schedule as in RPA/NFMA plans.

In Utah, BLM protection of roadless areas as potential wilderness has been the source of debate and animosity. The problem, again, rests with the uncertainty provided by FLPMA, which requires the agency to protect the wilderness characteristics of study areas "so as not to impair the suitability of such areas for preservation of wilderness" (Sec. 603[c]). Without further recommendation to, or designation by, Congress, these lands could conceivably wait for generations before attaining wilderness status, if at all. Mining lease-holders and oil and gas companies would be effectively closed out of these lands by the *de facto* non-release. Advocates of hard release on BLM lands contend that WSAs not released and not designated, but protected as wilderness, would prevent economic development.

Opponents, however, suggest such claims are exaggerated. According to Robert Keiter, University of Utah law professor and director of the Wallace Stegner Center, management of the 3.2 million acres of BLM land in southern Utah that have been managed as *de facto* wilderness for more than ten years under the FLPMA "non-impairment" standard has had "little direct impact on local economic opportunities," suggesting that wilderness designation may not significantly affect this region's economy (1995).

The first wilderness legislation to address BLM wilderness lands was the 1983 Lee Metcalf Wilderness Act, Montana, which included lands

variously managed by the USFS, BLM, and U.S. Fish and Wildlife Service (USFWS) (see table 6.1). This act's release language specified that
> . . . certain national forest areas and three BLM areas that have been adequately studied for their wilderness values under provisions in RARE II or FLPMA no longer need to be managed to protect their suitability as wilderness. The Department of Agriculture shall not be required to review again the wilderness potential of the national forest plans prior to revision of its initial land management plans. (Browning, Hendee, and Roggenbuck 1988, 53)

This release construction addressed only the prohibition to review wilderness potential of *forest lands* during the initial planning cycle, however. This act ignores future review of BLM lands.

The 1984 Arizona Wilderness Act included some BLM lands (see table 6.1), and provided adequately for forest lands, but it did not provide the same level of specificity for BLM lands. For example, the Arizona act required the Secretary of Agriculture to review three national forest areas for possible classification as wilderness, with the recommendation due date set at January 1986. However, this act directed the Secretary to manage the BLM wilderness study areas to preserve their wilderness quality and potential for wilderness designation, without setting any future date or cycle for review. In addition, as with other forest lands wilderness acts, this act released forest areas not designated as wilderness for multiple-use management, stating they "need not be managed to protect their suitability for wilderness designation prior to or during revision of the initial land management plans" (Browning, Hendee, and Roggenbuck 1988, 60). The only BLM lands permanently released to multiple-use management in this act were specified by name; the other BLM lands remain subject to further wilderness review, but without the periodic review cycle afforded forest lands through NFMA.

Relying upon the language of these wilderness laws, and several others that address USFS/BLM lands, the Arizona Desert Wilderness Act of 1990 designated BLM and USFS wilderness lands as wilderness (see table 6.1). The 1990 Arizona Act applied the forest lands NFMA release language, which requires ten- to fifteen-year cyclical reviews, to FLPMA lands not subject to review cycles or future review deadlines. Furthermore, the 1990 Arizona act did not specify how potential wilderness areas not designated are to be managed in the interim.

The California Desert Protection Act (1994), repeats the old compromise language developed for forest lands that was used in the 1990 Arizona act (see table 6.1). Because of its ambiguity and failure to address future management or release/review, it is now considered by some in

Congress as a "monumental headache" due to the volume of litigation it has generated (Freemeyer 1997).

Proponents of soft or compromise release language contend that it works just as well in BLM wilderness lands as it did in USFS forest lands. According to these advocates, FLPMA allows for multiple-use management, but leaves open the opportunity for protection of wilderness characteristics, under the Section 603(c) standard of protecting "natural scenic, scientific, and historical values" (Arthur 1997). Since BLM must manage its lands according to FLPMA, and since Congress may consider any land for wilderness designation, even land "released" by prior wilderness act, soft and compromise release proponents, such as Congressman Maurice Hinchey (D-New York), believe that no express release language is necessary in future wilderness bills (Arthur 1997).

Hard release advocates point to the failure of 1980s-crafted release language, intended for forest lands, to adequately resolve BLM wilderness lands review and management issues. This position was reflected in the failed Utah Public Lands Management Act of 1995, H.R. 1745, sponsored by Congressman Hansen (R-Utah), which states:

Except [for specified Continuing Wilderness Study Areas], any public lands administered by the [BLM] in the State of Utah not designated wilderness by this Act shall not be subject to §603 of the [FLPMA] but shall be managed for the full range of non-wilderness multiple uses in accordance with land management plans adopted pursuant to §202 of [FLPMA]. Such lands shall not be managed for the purpose of protecting suitability for wilderness designation or their wilderness character and shall remain available for non-wilderness multiple uses, subject to the requirements of other federal laws. (H.R. 1745, Sec. 10[a] and [b])

Regarding release, the Utah Public Lands Multiple Use Coalition's *Wilderness Position Paper* recommends that "Federal lands not formally designated as wilderness must be released from current wilderness management into management for multiple use. Such lands should not be reconsidered for possible wilderness designation or management during the next planning cycle" (1995). A problem with this approach is that, under FLPMA, there is no planning cycle. This group's Wilderness Position Paper, and the Utah Farm Bureau Federation's Position Paper entitled "Ten Wilderness Issues," make the point that the BLM has the authority to create "Areas of Critical Environmental Concern" to protect sensitive environmental landmarks without the *de facto* wilderness created by soft or compromise release when applied to FLPMA lands, where there is no review cycle in place.

Not everyone is supportive of this view, however. Congressman John Seiberling (D-Ohio), speaking at a hearing of the House Subcommittee on Public Lands and National Parks, stated: "The release language in H.R. 1745 is unprecedented and unacceptable. All prior wilderness bills have released undesignated lands to multiple-use management but have expressly permitted federal land managers to review the wilderness qualities of released lands. . . . The language of H.R. 1745 deviates from that rational approach" (quoted in O'Connell 1995, 11).

When this bill was considered by the Senate, the section on release language was amended. Hard release advocates insist that the release language amendment was a major step toward compromise because it softened release from "non-wilderness multiple use" to "multiple use." However, the compromise was greater than those simple changes. A close look at the amendment reveals additional special management provisions to protect areas under multiple-use management. Section 9 in the amended bill adds protection to new areas that it designates as "Areas of Critical Environmental Concern, Outstanding Natural Areas, National Natural Landmarks, Research Natural Areas, Primitive Areas, [and] Visual Resource Management Class I areas" (S. 884). These additions, an expansion of the additions advocated by the Utah Public Lands Multiple Use Coalition/Utah Farm Bureau Federation, provide special protection authority to the BLM in its non-wilderness management of the released lands, which is not provided under FLPMA. In his report to Congress concerning H.R. 1745 / S. 884, Ross Gorte suggested that the BLM would be required to "develop some type of active or developmental land management for the released areas" (1995, 2).

Not all participants in the debate saw the release amendment as productive, however. Some saw even the revised release language of the Senate version as too broad in its approach, which would set inappropriate precedents for future wilderness bills and current management of wilderness lands. In her report to the Senate, Sylvia Baca, Deputy Interior Assistant Secretary for Land and Minerals Management, said:

> [T]he precedent that would be established by hard release of lands with wilderness potential extends far beyond Utah. The majority of BLM lands with wilderness potential have yet to be considered by Congress. The elimination of wilderness consideration in future BLM land management plans throughout the West could have major impacts. Mandated "non-wilderness multiple use" on all of these lands could severely and inappropriately constrain future management options. Finally, the BLM is not alone in managing wilderness on the Federal lands. Land managers in other Federal and State land management agencies could also be affected if this precedent were to be followed. (U.S. Congress, Senate 1995)

In contrast, the most recent resolution, H.R. 1500, which mirrors its predecessors, does not contain any release language. According to Christopher Arthur, Minority Staff Director of the House Public Lands and National Parks Subcommittee, the intent of the drafters was to allow for future review of non-wilderness lands not designated under the act (Arthur 1997). FLPMA uses multiple use as a standard, but it does not *mandate* multiple use. Instead, it leaves such decisions up to the managing agency, which has the option of managing for wilderness values if it deems appropriate. This position is supported by Professor Robert Keiter (1995), who finds several problems with the hard release language in H.R. 1745:

> It has not been used in other state wilderness bills; it will foreclose future options and management flexibility; it is not necessary to open undesignated lands to multiple-use management and, in any event, cannot entirely preclude future wilderness designations; and it unwisely discounts the potential future importance of wilderness as a scarce resource. (Keiter 1995, 7)

With most potential forest wilderness lands already designated wilderness or under other federal management, the future of wilderness legislation points to the "forgotten lands" of the BLM. The resolution of the release issue is critical for the passage of future wilderness legislation. The solution, according to Subcommittee Staff Director Arthur, is to have no release language at all (1997). His counterpart on the Majority Staff, Allen D. Freemeyer, contends that silence will only invite more litigation, and opts for clarity and specificity (1997). Others, like Environmental and Natural Resources Policy Specialist Gorte and Attorney Baldwin, suggest that a new version of release language is needed to address the particular needs of BLM/FLPMA lands in future legislation (1993, 10). The old language was written in response to issues that had relevance to forest lands, but it is a poor fit to the public lands managed by the BLM.

## EXCEPTED ACTIVITIES

Excepted activity permits have been used in wilderness bills since the original 1964 act to allow for reasonable prior uses, such as motorboat use on certain designated waterways; to protect the public's health and safety, such as vault toilets in critical watersheds; and special mining allowances in areas where mineral resource extraction was crucial to local and national needs. Table 6.1 shows that excepted activities have specifically included the following:

> The 1978 Boundary Waters Canoe Area ("BWCA") Wilderness Act, which permitted aircraft flyovers according to controls set by an earlier Presidential directive;

The 1980 Central Idaho Wilderness Act, which established a special mining management zone in the Frank Church–River of No Return Wilderness to allow for cobalt exploration and mining;

The Utah Wilderness Act of 1984 and the Wyoming Wilderness Act of 1984, both of which permitted helicopter use to service vault toilets in wilderness watersheds;

The 1982 C. C. Deam Wilderness Act, which permitted access to families who had relatives buried in historic cemeteries on the wilderness land; and

The Texas Wilderness Act of 1984, which classified the Indian Mounds Wilderness Area despite active oil and gas drilling, leaving the Forest Service to mitigate the damage to wilderness characteristics caused by the activities. (Browning, Hendee, and Roggenbuck 1988)

Excepted activities appear in wilderness bills during the drafting and subcommittee hearings stage in order to address critical environmental issues, such as toilet permits in mountainous wilderness areas where the water flows into public water supplies in valleys below. Another example is permits that allow families to visit grave sites in historic cemeteries within wilderness areas; the impetus for this exception is sensitivity and concern for the families, and interest in continued historical research. Exception for public cabins in the 1980 ANILCA clearly had safety in mind, where winter temperatures drop into double digits below freezing, catching hunters without shelter. Such exceptions, and others like these, are clearly in keeping with the spirit of the Act.

Other exceptions are perhaps less essential. The 1980 Colorado Wilderness Act allows construction of a water development project on wilderness-designated lands. The California Wilderness Act of 1984 excepts construction of a power line within the San Jacinto Wilderness Area, and allows construction of a hydroelectric project in the San Joaquin Wilderness Area. It additionally allows mineral exploration and development and mining within the North Fork Roadless Area. Some exceptions, such as projects tacked on to legitimate legislation, have no precedent within the Act for their presence within particular wilderness acts. For example, the 1983 Monongahela Wilderness Act (West Virginia) not only allows exploration and core drilling, but also permits use of mechanized equipment within the Cranberry Wilderness Area.

Exceptions tend to follow prior uses and needs of the region. Some exceptions that could be considered "outside the spirit of the Wilderness Act" are justifiable in the context of a particular wilderness act or a substantive area within the act. In the 1989 Nevada Wilderness Protection

Act, low-level military overflights are not precluded. While such an exception could be criticized in a more populous region, Nevada is a state of vast open and unoccupied spaces, some of which are used by the military for land and air exercises. In the 1990 Arizona Desert Wilderness Act, Immigration and Naturalization Service border operations, including low-level overflights, are not precluded. In both instances, the low-level overflights are specific to type of use and have precedent.

Some excepted uses correlate with and fall within permitted Act activities, such as grazing, fish and wildlife protection and management, and recreation. The 1984 Vermont Wilderness Act allows for maintenance of the Appalachian Long Trail and other associated trails and structures. In Alabama, the Sipsey Wild and Scenic River Act of 1988 designated that existing roads could be converted to recreational use by hikers and/or horse riders. In the same spirit of historic, recreational, and scientific activities on wilderness lands, the 1996 Omnibus Parks and Public Lands Management Act allows mushroom gathering in the Opal Creek (Oregon) Wilderness Area, where morel mushrooms flourish. The same act also allows for gathering basket materials, a nod to the preservation of indigenous crafts.

In every instance in past wilderness acts, excepted activities have rationales that either are in keeping with the intent of the Wilderness Act or are necessary for the maintenance of life for humans or wildlife. Other times, the exceptions take precedence from prior uses in those areas. Much of the criticism of Representative Hansen's bill, H.R. 1745, is leveled at exceptions unlike past wilderness acts. Exceptions are specific to a particular area, lake, waterway, or location. Hansen's bill contains generalized and unprecedented exceptions that apply to all areas within the bill.

Regarding access, Hansen's bill permits "reasonable access" (Sec. 3[I][4]), which it defines as "motorized access where necessary and customarily or historically employed on routes in existence as of the date of enactment of this Act and where necessary to meet the reasonable purposes for development and use. . . ." Further on in the bill, this definition of access is applied to irrigation, pumping, and transmission facilities (Sec. 4[d]). These provisions did not sit well with Senators Bumpers, Bradley, Bingaman, and Wellstone, who argued that the bill includes "provisions that allow unprecedented and almost unfettered motorized access to . . . places 'untrammeled by man' protected and managed so as to preserve their natural conditions. In this bill, access is granted to all wilderness areas rather than on an area-by-area basis as is usually the case" (Senate Report 104-192). Law Professor Robert Keiter, in his *Comments on Utah Public Lands Management Act of 1995*, contends that the access provision "goes beyond related provisions in other state wilderness bills, which have provided for limited access that is either necessary or reasonable" (1995, 4). Hansen's staff hinted that the next incarnation of this bill will specify where motorized access should be permitted, rather than take an all-inclusive approach (Freemeyer 1997).

Low-level overflights were another contentious excepted activity in the bill. Where, in other wilderness bills, permitted overflights were limited to military exercises, and then only in areas of prior use, H.R. 1745 states that "Nothing in this Act shall be construed to restrict or preclude low-level overflights over the areas designated as wilderness by this Act . . ." (Sec. 7[a]). This is much broader language than the overflight provisions of other wilderness bills. For example, the 1989 Nevada Act permitted civilian or military low-level overflights only where these had been routine in the past.

The Hansen legislation also provides exceptions for water project construction within the wilderness areas and construction of wilderness-adjacent industrial power facilities, exception language that is not common, but not without precedent, in wilderness laws. In Section 3, the bill allows construction of water diversion, carriage and storage facilities, including dams, and access routes to operate, maintain, repair, modify, and replace such facilities (Sec. 3[I][1]). Section 8 allows construction, operation, or expansion of industrial facilities adjacent to wilderness areas, with the caveat in Section 3(e) that "[t]he fact that non-wilderness activities or uses can be seen, heard, or smelled from areas within a wilderness shall not preclude such activities or uses up to the boundary of the wilderness area." While other wilderness acts have included exceptions for power facilities, dams, mining, and other non-wilderness uses, none have applied to all wilderness lands within the particular acts, but have been specific to wilderness areas within the acts in order to comply with the 1964 Act. For example, the 1980 Colorado Wilderness Act permitted the "construction, maintenance, and/or expansion of the Homestake Water Development Project in the cities of Aurora and Colorado Springs, in the Holy Cross Wilderness" and allowed "motorized access and the use of motorized equipment of the McGuire Water Transmission Line ditch in the Rawah Wilderness." In 1995, the Congressional Research Service reported:

> precedents for . . . special management provisions exist in other wilderness legislation. Specific provisions allowing what might otherwise be considered a 'nonconforming use' of a wilderness area have been authorized in numerous wilderness areas, but exceptions are typically for a specific area, rather than for all areas or groups of areas. To date, no single wilderness statute has contained as many special management provisions as are contained in H.R. 1745/S. 884. (Gorte 1995, 4)

According to Freemeyer, Majority Staff Director of the House Subcommittee for Public Lands and National Parks, "If we were to rewrite the bill now, knowing the greater information we have about the land, we could except activities to particular areas" (1997).

The Owens/Hinchey Act is notable for its absence of exceptions. Where the Hansen Act sought to spell out its excepted uses, in order to avoid the mass of litigation that has followed the California Desert Protection Act of 1990 (Freemeyer 1997), the Owens/Hinchey Act is silent on issues common to the majority of wilderness acts. Minority Staff Director Arthur contends that H.R. 1500's silence is appropriate because the 1964 act and FLPMA provide the necessary direction for excepted activities (1997). However, reliance on these two statutes for direction may not be enough. Environment and Natural Resources Policy Specialist Ross Gorte contends that, while the Wilderness Act prohibits commercial activities and motorized access, as well as roads, structures, and facilities in wilderness areas, Congress has had to grant general and specific exceptions to the general standards and prohibitions (1994). Where the Hansen bill has been perceived by many as having "gone too far" (Arthur 1997), the Owens/Hinchey bill may not go far enough. It will be a great day for Utah when legislators can come together to craft a new Utah wilderness bill that will take the best ideas and craft a bill that everyone—or at least a majority—can endorse.

## CONCLUSION

The wilderness debate in Utah and some other states has been polarized by special interests, misinformation, and an almost religious fervor that is preventing well-meaning leaders, both local and national, from enacting wilderness protection for critical lands. Without more information and accurate information, bills with provisions viewed as inflammatory by some will continue to be promulgated, creating a greater rift and no resolution. One reason the debate over language continues is that our perception of the purpose of wilderness has evolved from a recreational focus to one of "protecting natural ecological processes" (Keiter 1996, 1).

Another reason we don't seem to be speaking the same language is that many people misunderstand the limitations of wilderness designation, believing the access permitted to wilderness areas is similar to the access we have to national parks and recreation areas. With greater public education, wilderness bills could be written that provide legitimate and reasonable exceptions for established prior uses, necessary activities to preserve the health and welfare of all living things, and special activities that are limited to designated areas.

WSAs that are currently protected by the BLM, but do not become part of a particular wilderness act, should be reviewed periodically for their continued protection as wilderness, just as NFMA requires periodic review of forest lands. The antiquated release language crafted in 1980 for USFS lands to avoid further litigation does not have clear application to non-USFS lands. The most recent wilderness bills have addressed BLM lands, rather than USFS lands. The regular review cycles required by NFMA do not apply to BLM lands. Congress should write new release language that includes periodic review of BLM wilderness lands. Landowners, commercial enterprises, and state trust lands administrators would not have to wait indefinitely for final decisions by Congress on inholdings within WSAs. With new periodic release reviews established for particular wilderness legislation, or general periodic release reviews mandated by an amendment to FLPMA, there would be a proven, acceptable method of treating lands in question. All sides of the debate could achieve satisfaction from the performance of appropriate and adequate review before any WSAs were released. Congress would still be able to reconsider released BLM lands, just as it has been able to revisit USFS lands released in prior wilderness bills. With release language similar to that crafted in 1980 for USFS lands, release of BLM lands would cease being the political "hot potato" that it has become today.

TABLE 6.1—Wilderness Legislation 1980–1997
Involving Release Language and Excepted Activities

KEY:

| | | | |
|---|---|---|---|
| PL | Public Law | MM | Mining and Mineral Leasing |
| NF | National Forest Service | MU | Motorized Use |
| BLM | Bureau of Land Management | FW | Fish and Wildlife |
| R/S | Type of Release / Suficiency Language | GR | Grazing |
| F/S | Facilities and Structures | FID | Fire, Insect & Disease |
| Misc. | Act-Specific Excepted Activities | | |
| | S=Soft Release | | |
| | C=Compromise Release | | |
| | H=Hard Release | | |
| | s=sufficiency language included | | |

| PL | Title | Yr. | NF | BLM | R/S | MM | MU | FW | GR | F/S | FID | Misc |
|---|---|---|---|---|---|---|---|---|---|---|---|---|
| 96-487 | ANILCA | 1980 | x | | S/s | x | x | x | | | x | Public cabins maintained for safety |
| 96-560 | Colorado Wilderness Act | 1980 | x | | S/s | | x | x | x | | x | Construction of water development project |
| 97-384 | C. C. Deam Wilderness | 1982 | x | | S/s | | | | | | | Access to public cemeteries |
| 97-407 | Paddy Creek Wilderness Act | 1982 | x | | S/s | | | | | | | |
| 97-466 | Monongahela W. Virginia Wilderness Act | 1983 | x | | S/s | x | | | | | | Exploration and core drilling. Use of mech. equip. allowed in Cranberry Wilderness |
| 98-140 | Lee Metcalf Wilderness Act | 1983 | x | x | C/no | | | | | | | Bear Trap Canyon managed by BLM |
| 98-321 | Wisconsin Wilderness Act | 1984 | x | | C/s | | | | | x | | |
| 98-322 | Vermont Wilderness Act | 1984 | x | | C/s | | | | | | | Appalachian Trail, Long Trail, and associated trails and structures within wilderness maintained |
| 98-323 | New Hampshire Wilderness Act | 1984 | x | | C/s | x | | | | | | |
| 98-324 | North Carolina Wilderness Act | 1984 | x | | C/s | | | | | | | |
| 98-328 | Oregon Wilderness Act | 1984 | x | | C/s | | | | | | | |

TABLE 6.1 (Continued)

| PL | Title | Yr. | NF | BLM | R/S | MM | MU | FW | GR | F/S | FID | Misc |
|---|---|---|---|---|---|---|---|---|---|---|---|---|
| 98-339 | Washington State | 1984 | x | x | C/s | | | | | | | |
| 98-406 | Arizona Wilderness Act | 1984 | x | x | C/s | | x | | x | x | | Installation and maintenance of hydrologic, meteorological, or telecommunications facilities, and limited motorized access to facilities when necessary for flood warning, flood control, and reservoir operation. |
| 98-425 | California Wilderness Act | 1984 | x | | C/s | x | x | | | x | | 1) Non-motorized dispersed recreation at Dinkey Lakes at level no less than that of 1979; 2) Continued motorized access to facilities related to grazing in San Joaquin and Wolf Creek; 3) Construction of powerline within San Jacinto Wilderness; 4) Act does not affect right to use, divert, or construct and maintain hydroelectric project in San Joaquin; 5) Mineral exploration, development, and mining permitted in North Fork Roadless Area; 6) Operation and maintenance of existing cabin for grazing purposes in Ansel Adams Wilderness to continue. |
| 98-428 | Utah Wilderness Act | 1984 | x | | C/s | | x | | x | x | | Sanitary facilities, including vault toilets, to protect watersheds; limited motorized access to watershed facilities; flood control, flood warning, and water reservoir operations permitted in Mount Naomi, Wellsville Mountain, Mount Olympus, Mount Nebo, Twin Peaks, High Uintas, Pine Valley Mountain, Mount Timpanogas, and Deseret Peak, which may |

TABLE 6.1 (Continued)

| PL | Title | Yr. | NF | BLM | R/S | MM | MU | FW | GR | F/S | FID | Misc |
|----|-------|-----|----|-----|-----|----|----|----|----|-----|-----|------|
| | | | | | | | | | | | | include hydrologic, meteorologic, climatological, or telecommunications facilities with limited motorized access. |
| 98-430 | Florida Wilderness Act | 1984 | x | | C/s | x | x | | | | | Phosphate leasing not permitted in Osceola National Forest unless presidential approval; motorboat use not prohibited in Alexander Springs. |
| 98-508 | Arkansas Wilderness Act | 1984 | x | | C/s | | | | | | | |
| 98-514 | Georgia Wilderness Act | 1984 | x | | C/s | | | | | | | |
| 98-515 | Mississippi National Forest Wilderness Act | 1984 | x | | C/s | | | | | | | |
| 98-550 | Wyoming Wilderness Act | 1984 | x | | C/s | x | x | x | x | x | | Secretary of Agriculture to identify, protect, and interpret archeological sites within Wyoming Wilderness; Act shall not prevent, impair, or affect water rights for construction, operation, or maintenance of water development projects in Huston Park, Encampment River, Platte River, and Savage Run areas. |
| 98-574 | Texas Wilderness Act | 1984 | x | | C/s | | | | | | | |
| 98-578 | Tennessee Wilderness Act | 1984 | x | | C/s | | | | | | | |
| 98-585 | Pennsylvania Wilderness Act | 1984 | x | | C/s | | | | | | | |
| 98-586 | Virginia Wilderness Act | 1984 | x | | C/s | | | | | | | |
| 99-197 | Kentucky Wilderness Act | 1985 | x | | C/s | | | | | | | |
| 99-490 | Tennessee Wilderness Act | 1986 | x | | C/s | | | | | | | |
| 99-504 | Nebraska Wilderness Act | 1986 | x | | C/s | | | | x | | | |
| 100-184 | Michigan Wilderness Act | 1987 | x | | C/s | | | | | | | |
| 100-225 | El Malpais, N.M., Wilderness Act | 1987 | | x | No R/s lang. | | | | x | | | Secretary of Agriculture to develop cultural resources management plans for long-term scientific use or archeological resources. |

TABLE 6.1 (Continued)

| PL | Title | Yr. | NF | BLM | R/S | MM | MU | FW | GR | F/S | FID | Misc |
|---|---|---|---|---|---|---|---|---|---|---|---|---|
| 100-91 | Overflight altitude for NPS | 1987 | x | | | | | | | | | Assessment to determine any adverse impacts to wilderness resources associated with overflights. |
| 100-547 | Sipsey Wild and Scenic River, Alabama Act | 1988 | | x | | | | | | | x | Existing roads may be converted into hiking and/or horse trails. |
| 100-195 | Nevada Wilderness Protection Act | 1989 | | x | | | | | | | | Installation and maintenance of flood warning and flood control devices; low-level overflights not precluded. |
| 100-628 | Arizona Desert Wilderness Act | 1990 | | x | | | | | | | | Low-level overflights. INS border operations shall continue without restriction. |
| 101-633 | Illinois Wilderness Act | 1990 | x | | | | | | | | | Access to cemeteries by relatives unrestricted. |
| 102-301 | Los Padres Act | 1992 | | x | | | | | | | x | Access to restore and maintain fish and condor populations. |
| 103-77 | Colorado Wilderness Act | 1993 | | x | | | | | | | | Access to water resource facilities for maintenance and repair. |
| 103-433 | California Desert Protection Act | 1994 | | x | C/no suff. lang. | | x | x | x | | | Motorized vehicles permitted for fish and wildlife management and law enforcement (incl. INS border patrol). |
| 104-333 | Omnibus Parks and Public Lands Management Act | 1996 | x | x | H*/s | | | | x | | | Ratifies easements in Gates of the Arctic Wilderness (ANICLA) allowing ATV access by residents of the Village of Anaktuvuk Pass; expands Bisti/De-Na-Zin Wilderness (N.M.); establishes Opal Creek Wilderness (OR), which provides for mushroom gathering, and basket materials collection, access for disabled. |

*hard rel. of proposed not incl. wild. only

## ℂ REFERENCES TO CHAPTER 6

Arthur, Christopher. 1997. Minority Staff Director, House Subcommittee on Public Lands and National Parks. Personal interview by author, May 21.

Browning, James A., John C. Hendee, and Joe W. Roggenbuck. 1988. *103 Wilderness Laws: Milestones and Management Direction in Wilderness Legislation, 1964–1987.* Moscow, ID: University of Idaho Press.

————. 1993. *Supplement to Appendix B Wilderness Laws 104 to 118: Wilderness Legislation, 1988–1993.* Moscow, ID: University of Idaho Press.

*California v. Bergland.* 1980. 483 F. Supp. 465 (E.D. Calif. 1980).

*California v. Block.* 1982. 690 F.2d 753 (9th Cir. 1982).

Congressional Green Sheets Weekly Bulletin. 1995. Week of December 4, 1995: B3–B4.

Freemeyer, Allen D. 1997. Majority Staff Director, House Subcommittee on Public Lands and National Parks. Personal interview by author. May 16.

Gorte, Ross W. 1994. *Wilderness: Overview and Statistics.* CRS: 94-976 ENR.

————. 1995. *Utah Wilderness Legislation in the 104th Congress.* CRS: 95-1191 ENR.

Gorte, Ross W., and Pamela Baldwin. 1993. *Wilderness Legislation: History of Release Language, 1979–1992.* CRS: 93-280 ENR.

Hendee, John C., George H. Stankey, and Robert C. Lucas. 1990. *Wilderness Management.* Golden, CO: North American Press (an imprint of Fulcrum Publishing).

Hinchey, Maurice. 1997. *America's Red Rock Wilderness Act of 1997: A bill to designate certain federal lands in the State of Utah as wilderness, and for other purposes.* 105th Cong., 1st sess. 1997 H.R. 1500; 105 H.R. 1500.

Keiter, Robert B. 1995. *Comments on Utah Public Land Management.* University of Utah College of Law: Private distribution (available from the author).

————. 1996. *Legal Perspectives on Ecosystem Management.* Letter to Louise Milkman, U.S. Department of Justice, Environment and Natural Resources Division, Washington, DC 20530.

Lilieholm, Robert J. 1995. Wilderness and adjacent land issues. In Donald L. Snyder, Christopher Fawson, E. Bruce Godfrey, John Keith, and Robert J. Lilieholm, *Wilderness Designation in Utah: Issues and Potential Economic Impacts.* Logan, UT: Utah Agricultural Experiment Station, Utah State University. Research Report 151:49–69.

O'Connell, Kim A. 1995. Minimalist measure imperils Utah lands: delegation ignores citizen's proposal for redrock wilderness; congressmen push the Utah Public Lands Management Act. *National Parks* 69 (September): 11.

Owens, Wayne. 1991. *Reintroduction of the Utah BLM Wilderness Act.* Floor speech by legislative sponsor. 104th Cong., 1st sess. 137 *Congressional Record, House,* 1762, vol. 137, no. 44.

U.S. Congress, Senate. 1995. *Report from the Committee on Energy and Natural Resources.* Amendment to S. 884. 104th Cong., 1st sess. 104 Senate Report 192. Testimony of Sylvia Baca.

### WILDERNESS LEGISLATION CITED

*Alaska National Interest Lands Conservation Act* (ANILCA). 1980. P.L. 96-487.

*Arizona Desert Wilderness Act.* 1990. P.L. 101-628.

*Arizona Wilderness Act.* 1984. P.L. 98-406.

*Arkansas Wilderness Act.* 1984. P.L. 98-508.

*California Desert Protection Act.* 1994. P.L. 103-433.
*California Wilderness Act.* 1984. P.L. 98-425.
*C. C. Deam Wilderness Act.* P.L. 97-384.
*Colorado Wilderness Act.* 1980. P.L. 96-560.
*Colorado Wilderness Act.* 1993. P.L. 103-77.
El Malpais: *To Establish the El Malpais National Monument and El Malpais National Conservation Area in the State of New Mexico, To Authorize the Masau Trail, and for other Purposes Wilderness Act.* 1987. P.L. 100-225.
*Florida Wilderness Act.* 1984. P.L. 98-430.
*Georgia Wilderness Act.* 1984. P.L. 98-514.
*Illinois Wilderness Act.* 1990. P.L. 101-633.
*Kentucky Wilderness Act.* 1985. P.L. 99-197.
*Lee Metcalf Wilderness Act.* 1983. P.L. 98-140.
*Los Padres Condor Range and River Protection Act.* 1992. P.L. 102–301.
*Michigan Wilderness Act.* 1987. P.L. 100-184.
*Mississippi National Forest Wilderness Act.* 1984. P.L. 98-515.
*Monongahala, West Virginia, Wilderness Act.* 1983. P.L. 97-466.
*Nebraska Wilderness Act.* 1986. P.L. 99-490.
*Nevada Wilderness Protection Act.* 1989. P.L. 100-195.
*New Hampshire Wilderness Act.* 1984. P.L. 98-323.
*North Carolina Wilderness Act.* 1984. P.L. 98-324.
*Omnibus Parks and Public Lands Management Act.* 1996. P.L. 104-333.
*Oregon Wilderness Act.* 1984. P.L. 98-328.
*Overflight Altitude for National Parks Service.* 1987. P.L. 100-91.
*Paddy Creek Wilderness Act.* 1982. P.L. 97-407.
*Pennsylvania Wilderness Act.* P.L. 98-585.
*Sipsey Wild and Scenic River, Alabama, Act.* 1988. P.L. 100-547.
*Tennessee Wilderness Act.* 1984. P.L. 98-578.
*Tennessee Wilderness Act.* 1986. P.L. 99-490.
*Texas Wilderness Act.* 1984. P.L. 98-574.
*Utah Wilderness Act.* 1984. P.L. 98-428.
*Vermont Wilderness Act.* 1984. P.L. 98-322.
*Virginia Wilderness Act.* 1984. P.L. 98-586.
*Washington State Wilderness Act.* 1984. P.L. 98-339.
*Wisconsin Wilderness Act.* 1984. P.L. 98-321.
*Wyoming Wilderness Act.* 1984. P.L. 98-550.

# Competition for Resources

We fight over undeveloped public lands because they offer so much to the public: solitude, open space, recreation, scenery, habitat preservation, biodiversity, archaeological protection, clean air and water, and—an increasingly rare commodity in America—silence. These are resources derived from wilderness that are available to everyone. Some of them, such as recreation, require the user to visit a wilderness area. Others, such as clean air and water, are enjoyed by everyone who lives in regional proximity to a wilderness area.

But this list of resources is only part of the story. Public lands also offer a storehouse of commercial wealth that can provide jobs, sustain local economies, generate tax revenue, and produce goods that all of us use. For many people who live in the rural West, the resources found on public lands are the foundation of their livelihood. These resources range from the extraction of specific resources via private, profit-making activity, such as ranching and mining, to recreation-based businesses that depend on the availability of scenery, free-running rivers, hiking trails, equestrian access, or four-wheel-drive roads.

This section of the book analyzes the political efforts of individuals and groups to secure access to this great variety of public lands resources. Chapter 7, by Joshua Footer and J. T. VonLunen, examines the long and sometimes bitter conflict between mining interests and wilderness advocates. In chapter 8 Cyrus McKell and David Harward explain the role of school trust lands in the wilderness debate. This is followed by a chapter on grazing by Christopher Krueger, Christian Senf, and Janelle Eurick. Chapter 10, by

Christa Powell and Buck Swaney, explores the complex and critically important relationship between wilderness designation and roads, especially the controversial R.S. 2477 county roads. Following that, R. Kelly Beck examines how wilderness designation affects archaeological resources. The final chapter in this section, written by Chris Perri, provides a broad overview of the relationship between wilderness and economic activity.

Viewed as a whole, this section of the book catalogues the various uses of public lands—uses that often are mutually exclusive, or at least viewed that way by partisans of the debate. This debate has, at times, made it difficult to assess the actual extent of resource use and potential. Consider, for example, these statistics culled from the following chapters: only 0.9 percent of employment in Utah is in mining; only 3 percent of the state's livestock operators have grazing leases in WSAs; and only 0.03 percent of the state's budget for schools comes from trust lands.

Why all the fuss? There are two answers. First, while wilderness designation will have a negligible impact on the state's economy and budget as a whole, the impact of wilderness designation on specific rural areas can be quite significant. Rural western economies tend to be fragile, isolated, and vulnerable to sudden change. We should not be surprised that the people who live in these areas want to maintain whatever opportunities public lands might present to them.

The second reason is purely political. It is said that, in politics, perception is reality. A significant number of people *believe* that large-scale wilderness designation will destroy the rancher's way of life, throw thousands of miners out of work, and harm an already notoriously underfunded school system. Others *believe* that every acre of BLM land not protected as wilderness will soon fall prey to the bulldozer. In politics, people act on their beliefs, not according to some abstract notion of rationality or scientific ideal.

The unequal economic impact of wilderness designation and the perceptions of harm described above form a kind of thematic refrain that can be heard throughout the following chapters.

—The Editors

# CHAPTER 7

# A Legacy of Conflict
## Mining and Wilderness

Joshua Footer

J. T. VonLunen

### INTRODUCTION

There is a long history of conflict between mining and wilderness. For an area to be designated as wilderness, it must be roadless, have an acreage of five thousand acres or more, be natural and without the imprint of man, and provide the opportunity for solitude and/or primitive recreation (Haugrud 1985, 13–27). For mining to take place there must be roads or train tracks to move in equipment and remove the mined mineral. Secondly, mining operations imprint the land with the human signature. And for some people it is difficult for solitude to be attained if a mine is operating. Without making a value judgment about whether or not mining should occur in wilderness areas, it is obvious that an inherent conflict exists between mining and wilderness. It is nearly impossible to allow mining and still preserve the qualities of wilderness. However, the debate and conflict rage over what to do if public land has both wilderness characteristics and resource potential that can be realized through mineral exploration.

Scott Groene, former Issues Director for the Southern Utah Wilderness Alliance (SUWA), said that "mining in wilderness areas is absurd. The practice of mining goes against the definition and spirit of wilderness" (Groene 1997). This viewpoint is echoed in SUWA's wilderness proposal, H.R. 1500, which advocated 5.7 million acres of wilderness in Utah. Mark Walsh, director of the Utah Association of Counties, believes that those areas with mining claims should not be designated as wilderness, therefore avoiding the conflict. Walsh's sentiments are reflected in the Utah Association of Counties' wilderness proposal of 1.1 million acres of designated wilderness in Utah.

## BACKGROUND

During most of the history of the United States, its citizens were encouraged by the federal government to explore and develop the public lands. This was especially true during the "frontier" days of the nineteenth century. In order to tap the vast natural wealth of the West, Congress set out to "tame" the land with laws designed to promote expansion. Out of this desire to expand and use America's natural resources, Congress enacted the General Mining Law of 1872. The crux of the Mining Law of 1872 holds that any United States citizen has the right to explore for and extract minerals on public lands if certain procedures are followed. After a valid claim is located, the prospector has the right to develop and mine the minerals. Under the claim, the prospector holds the right to possess the land and extract the minerals without incurring a charge from the government. In order to "patent," or gain title to, the claim, the prospector incurs a nominal charge (Haugrud 1985, 87).

The assumption behind the Mining Law of 1872 was that mineral exploration on federal lands was beneficial to the nation as a whole. Therefore, the law was designed to "promote the development of the mining resources of the United States" (Leshy 1987, 17). It should be pointed out that Congress did not take an environmentally friendly position when it adopted the Mining Law; back then, extraction rather than protection was the sole objective of national policy. Thus, Congress granted large amounts of power and autonomy to the mining industry, relying on a vision of mining as an old-time treasure hunt. Their sole focus was to develop the rugged yet promising West. John Leshy accurately described Congress's vision: "That activity was stridently frontier and democratic in character—individualistic, egalitarian, distrustful of speculation and monopoly. The land's mineral riches would be made available to every citizen, and the efforts of each would be protected only to [the] extent that a discovery was made and pursued, and even then within limits designed to prevent monopolization of large deposits" (Leshy 1987, 17-18). Charles Wilkinson called the 1872 Mining Law "a faithful reflection of the needs of the western mining industry" (Wilkinson 1992, 43). What is clear from looking at the Mining Law of 1872 is that Congress's intention was to promote mineral exploration of the wild, frontier, western federal lands.

Regardless of where one stands on mining in wilderness areas, one thing is clear; the 1872 Mining Law is confusing, with a framework that complicates its application. Leshy writes:

> The Law is at once highly specific, wondrously vague, and maddeningly terse;
> for example, though it makes discovery of a valuable mineral the touchstone

for the miner's right to mine and purchase lands, it nowhere defines either concept. It draws certain distinctions between lode and placer claims, yet lacks precision on how the two differ. The Law contains a fairly elaborate procedural code for applying for title (patent), yet is silent on the evidence required to justify title. With few exceptions, it gives the federal government little direction about its responsibilities in administering the Law. Finally, it contains only oblique reference to the role of the courts in answering questions arising in its administration. (Leshy 1987, 19–20)

The result of the law's imprecise framework is that the courts have weighed heavily in the law's interpretation and application. There have been numerous judicial attempts to clarify the original 1872 law, but most have been adjudicated on a case-by-case basis without additional legislative guidance.

It is not only federal courts that have added their own interpretation to the law, but state courts as well. Most of the interpretive case law occurred in the first fifty years of the law's existence, a fact that dramatically shaped the law of the West—a law dominated by mining interests (Leshy 1987, 19–20). While the mining law has primarily been modified by court decisions, thousands of interpretations and applications have also been made by the various federal agencies that have the daunting task of implementing its myriad regulations and directives. Therefore, the mining law is a statute whose true function cannot be wholly discerned from its text. Rather, the layers of interpretation and adjustments that have been made by the courts and the implementing agencies have metamorphosed the mining law into a statute that is substantially different from Congress's original intention (Leshy 1987, 22–23).

Mining in wilderness is covered by Section 4(d) of the Wilderness Act. This section holds that prospecting and mining may continue to occur in national forest wilderness until December 31, 1983. After that date, mining may continue only on lands that had valid existing claims prior to that date (Hendee, Stankey, and Lucas 1978, 71). In other words, one could not file a claim for mining after December 31, 1983 (in a wilderness area), but could continue mining a claim that existed prior to that date. A patent conveying both surface and mineral rights may be taken on a valid claim located prior to the Wilderness Act; for a valid claim located after the date of the Wilderness Act, the patent conveys title to mineral rights only (Hendee, Stankey, and Lucas 1978, 71).

Even after the passage of the Wilderness Act in 1964, there was still a twenty-year window that allowed for mining in wilderness areas. It was only after January 1, 1984, that wilderness lands were withdrawn from mineral development, except those with valid existing rights. This meant not only that new mining claims could be located until January 1, 1984, but also that hardrock mineral development on claims that were valid in 1984 could occur in wilderness areas even after 1984 (Leshy 1987, 232).

The most notable example was the Forest Service's 1995 decision to settle a claim filed in federal court by Robert Steele and Jack Dansie. The two wanted to operate a gypsum mine and use a road that bisected land located within the Mount Nebo Wilderness Area. Under the terms of a settlement, the Forest Service agreed to pay the claimants $120,000 and to allow development of the patented site. Currently, Steele and Dansie's gypsum mine is the only open-pit mine operating in any federal wilderness area, and the only wilderness mine to allow year-round motorized access. The key issue in this settlement was the fact that Steele and Dansie owned patented claims before Congress designated the Mount Nebo area as a wilderness (Associated Press 1997).

Even though loopholes existed that permitted exploration and development within wilderness, the tide was turning toward wilderness preservation. The Wilderness Act had a chilling effect on mining in wilderness (Leshy 1987, 232). According to the Rocky Mountain Mineral Law Foundation, "Mere designation of land as wilderness has chilled exploration in those areas and been almost a totally effective barrier to mineral development and production" (Leshy 1987, 232). Leshy explains three reasons for the "chilling effect" that has occurred. First, most of the designated wilderness areas have been open for development for the last one hundred years. Usually, any significant mineral development would have disqualified these lands from wilderness consideration. This suggests that these areas do not contain easily discoverable or readily extractable deposits with current technologies and market prices (Leshy 1987, 232). In reference to the Kaiparowits Plateau, Scott Groene made a similar point; "There must have been a reason that such a vast coal reserve was never developed. They (mineral developers) knew about the coal in the ground for the last thirty years" (Groene 1997). Of course it is potential future extraction that is at issue.

Second, because of the roadless requirement of wilderness, the costs of extracting minerals make extraction unprofitable. The remoteness and rugged terrain of the areas usually deter exploration since they may be open to mining for only a few months a year (Leshy 1987, 233). And third, Congress usually excludes areas with known mineral deposits from wilderness areas by drawing the boundaries around the deposit (Leshy 1987, 233). This point will be illustrated by maps of the various wilderness proposals and mining claims later in the chapter.

Another factor is the political implication of mining in a proposed wilderness area. Congress, with its powers to regulate and control, has taken the extraordinary step of singling out an area for preservation because of remarkable natural characteristics. Therefore, it is politically costly for a mining company to damage such lands that Congress believed to be worthy of protection. Sometimes, the bad publicity a mining company receives when mineral development occurs in a wilderness area is not worth the potential profits.[1]

## THE ECONOMICS OF MINING IN WILDERNESS

One of the most contentious issues in the mining and wilderness debate is the economic reality of wilderness designation and its effect on mining production. The issue can be boiled down to perceived worth: what is valued more? Is the aesthetic beauty, naturalness, and wildness of the land worth more than the economic infusion that mining could provide to communities surrounded by land that could be designated as wilderness? The issues examined in the following section are related to the economic realities of mining and wilderness designation. We will look at how rural, urban, and state economies are affected by mining. Then we will explore how these economies would be affected by the various wilderness proposals.

One of the reasons that many rural Utahns reject vast tracts of wilderness designation in Utah is that they are fearful of a large-scale loss of employment and the resulting economic loss. But the actual number of jobs in mining is quite modest. In 1995 the mining sector accounted for 0.9 percent of the total employment in Utah (State of Utah 1997, 80). According to the 1991 Power study, the number of Utah jobs in the mineral extraction sector has rapidly declined since 1980 (Power 1991, 2). The mineral (especially uranium) sector, oil and gas, and coal have all experienced a sharp decline in employee numbers. For example, the mineral (uranium) sector had approximately 9,000 employees in 1980, but by 1989, the numbers were down to around 3,000 statewide (Power 1991, 4). This decrease in employment within the mining sector indicates a wholesale transformation of Utah's economy. According to economist Thomas Power,

> The transformation of the Utah economy from heavy reliance upon extractive natural resource use is well underway and it will continue. The important point from a public policy point of view is not whether this trend will continue or whether it can or should be stopped. It cannot and should not be. The important issue is whether public economic policy will recognize where the Utah economy is now and where it will almost certainly be in the future and focus public economic policy upon obtaining the most benefit for

Utahns from the new economy that is emerging. To do this, Utah has to resist the natural tendency to guide public policy by the "view through the rear-view mirror." (Power 1991, 2)

Directly contradicting Power's study is the Leaming Study. George Leaming holds that, of the negative economic impacts associated with wilderness designation, over 99.5 percent of such impacts would be absorbed by the mining industry (Rait n.d. 246). Leaming arrived at his mining impact assessment by making the assumption that any mineral that is present or has yet to be found will be developed in Utah within the next twenty-five years. Ken Rait, former Issues Director for SUWA, criticizes Leaming's analysis of the economic impacts of wilderness designation on the mining industry. Rait believes that Leaming used methods for mineral accountability that contradict the BLM's process of utilizing favorability and certainty rankings to determine potential forgone losses from wilderness designation (Rait n.d. 246). He writes:

> What we find is that the losses to the mining sector, as calculated by Leaming over 25 years, are 8 times the total income earned by all Utahns. The losses are overstated by 70 to 250 times, and the losses predicted are 26 times the total annual earnings from mining, forestry, agriculture, and fisheries in the state. In southern Utah's Garfield County, Leaming actually predicts losses on an order of magnitude higher than the total personal income in the county. Leaming calculates that the statewide impacts from wilderness designation would total $13.2 billion annually. (Rait n.d., 246)

In 1995, less than 1 percent of Utah's employment came from the mining sector. The Utah Office of Planning and Budget has projected that number to remain constant through the early part of the next century (State of Utah 1997, 80). As well, during the last ten years, the percentage of Utah's economy that was mining-related dropped from 5 to 2 percent due to the fluctuations in the global energy market (Rait n.d., 247). SUWA believes that the drop in mineral contributions to the statewide economy of Utah is due to its unique geography. Utah has the second highest cost per barrel of oil of any state containing significant oil and gas reserves—costs are greatly escalated due to the remote access and complex geology of Utah's landscape (Rait n.d., 247). SUWA argues that it simply does not make great financial sense to mine in Utah in many areas. The remoteness of many of the sites increases production costs, making it difficult to sell a competitive product in the global mineral marketplace.

Conversely, there are some who believe that it is wilderness designation and the BLM's management of WSAs that inhibit mineral exploration and rural economic development and thus global marketplace competitiveness. And while mining is only a small part of the state's overall economy, it is a significant economic activity in some areas of the state; in some counties it accounts for nearly a fourth of the county economy.

Mark Walsh, director of the Utah Association of Counties, believes that wilderness designation will handicap the economy of Utah by not allowing rural communities to use the inherent natural resources to their economic benefit. He cites the new national monument, one-third of which rests upon the Kaiparowits Plateau, which is known to have one-half of Utah's coal reserves. The designation by the Clinton administration of the Grand Staircase–Escalante National Monument was a "deliberate attempt to shut down an industry (the coal industry). That designation was not a good way to make public policy." Walsh believes that the National Monument designation damaged the ability of many southern Utahns to make a living: "It was designated with arrogance and cynicism."

Thomas W. Bachtell, director of the public lands commission for the Utah Mining Association, president of Buenaventura Resources Corporation, and member of the Board of Directors of the Rocky Mountain Oil and Gas Association, believes that large-scale designation of wilderness in southern Utah will radically harm the economy. "The new national monument will in the long term prove my point," says Bachtell. He cites the example of a job in the tourism industry versus a job in the mineral development industry. Natural-resource extraction jobs pay three to five times more than tourist industry jobs. In 1995, the average monthly wage for an employee in the mining industry was $3,484; compare that with the average wage in the service/tourism industry at $1,798 (State of Utah 1997, 89). He asks, "How will the families be supported if mining is prohibited?" The question, according to Bachtell, is value. "What produces the most value? Mineral development produces tangible benefits, while tourism only allows the community to 'put its eggs all in one basket.' Mineral development will allow for a diverse economy with tourism being melded around the mine sites" (Bachtell 1997).

The Utah Public Lands Multiple Use Coalition, in their wilderness position paper, rejects claims for wilderness designation on the grounds that the mineral worth of Utah's lands has not yet been fully grasped:

> The production of energy, strategic minerals and other minerals is an important element of the Utah economy and critical to the national economy. Energy and mineral potential on public lands in Utah has not yet been adequately nor scientifically inventoried and explored. Wilderness designation could preclude such activities altogether, thereby permanently precluding access to potentially significant critical mineral and other resources. (Utah Public Lands Multiple Use Coalition 1995, 5)

Although the mining industry plays a rather minor role in Utah's economy as a whole, it plays a much bigger role in the economies of many rural areas. In 1980, one-third of all non-agricultural jobs in many southern Utah counties (Kane, Garfield, San Juan) were in the mining sector. But by 1989, half of these jobs had been lost (Power 1991, 5). However, although there was a wide-scale loss of jobs in the mining sector, overall employment numbers were higher in 1989 than in 1980 (Power 1991, 5). It is also noteworthy that the rural economies of Kane, Garfield, and San Juan counties did not experience a wholesale collapse due to the loss of mining jobs. According to economist Thomas Power, "Even here, the rest of the economy has a life independent of the extractive industry. . . . Given the rather minor role that mineral extraction plays as a source of employment and income in the Utah economy, it is unlikely that any modest impact that wilderness designation might have on this industry could have a significant impact on the overall economy" (Power 1991, 5).

In the largest sense, the mining-in-wilderness issue boils down to dollars. If there are dollars to be made, there will always be someone who wants to mine. We come back to the question of worth. What is worth more? Is preserving the natural, pristine environment worth more than developing such lands for their mineral and other economic potential? Or should the economic interests of rural families be more important than lands whose value can be measured only in abstract notions of beauty and ecology? Wilderness advocates believe the land is priceless and once it is developed, it is lost forever. Development advocates believe in multiple use, including extractive development. They feel that those pristine lands hold natural resource value that should be developed first and foremost for the good of both the local and larger economies. Then the land can be reclaimed and returned back to the earth and no one would know the difference. For the time being, uncertainty defines the economic future of mining in wilderness. The 1997 Economic Report to the Governor aptly defines the current economic situation of mining in wilderness: "Uncertainty by mining companies about the status of the 1872 Mining Law and the future of wilderness study areas (WSAs) continues to affect mineral exploration in Utah. Many companies are taking a wait-and-see attitude until these issues are resolved" (State of Utah 1997, 200).

*LAND EXCHANGING*

What is the value of a section of land in the Burning Hills WSA (located on the Kaiparowits Plateau)? Six hundred billion? Nothing? Priceless? Answers vary depending upon whom you ask. Some value the land for its possible resource value, while others value the land for recreation and soli-tude. Resource value, represented in mineral extraction profits, compels mining interests to place a dollar figure on such lands. Environmental groups, on the other hand, believe the land is priceless and should never be sold, no matter how much mineral wealth is contained in its soils. Even so, the Utah Geological Survey (UGS), the Multiple-Use Coalition, and SUWA have had to put a value on the land.

Dollar amounts have been assigned to lands as part of an effort to exchange lands (see chapter 8 for more discussion of land exchanges). The objective is to trade out lands that have valid mining patents and wilder-ness characteristics for other land of "equal value." This is done to ensure the holder of the mining patent that profits will not be lost due to wilder-ness designation. Section 603(c) of FLPMA refers to Sections 4 and 5 of the Wilderness Act for guidance and management practices related to land trading. Section 5(a) of the Wilderness Act reads:

> In any case where State-owned or privately owned land is completely sur-rounded by national forest lands within areas designated by this Act as wilderness, such state or private owner shall be given such rights as may be necessary to assure adequate access to such State-owned or privately owned land by such State or private owner and their successors in interest, or the State-owned land or privately owned land *shall be exchanged for federally owned land in the same State of approximately equal value* under authorities available to the Secretary of Agriculture . . . Provided, however, that the United States shall not transfer to a State or private owner any mineral inter-ests unless the State or private owner relinquishes or causes to be relinquished to the United States the mineral interests in the surrounded land [emphasis added]. (Wilderness Act; Hendee, Stankey, and Lucas 1978, 82)

This section of the Wilderness Act provides the basis for land swap-ping. It is important to note the italicized portion of the Act, which states that land shall be exchanged for federally owned land in the same state of approximately equal value. As stated earlier, land values vary due to a num-ber of factors: deposit location, market value, and who assesses the land.

People on both sides of this debate agree that many areas in southern Utah are so remote that it is not economically feasible to mine them under current market conditions. There simply is not the infrastructure necessary for the mining process. Roads and/or railroads would have to be built from the mine site to major thoroughfares in order to transport the raw materi-als to a processing plant. Additionally, the geomorphology of southern Utah deters most types of mining. Deep canyons and high plateaus make southern Utah very inaccessible. Construction of a transportation network and its inherent infrastructure would be very costly and time-consuming. Although a significant mineral deposit may exist, transportation, production, and extraction costs make many parts of southern Utah uneconomical to mine now or in the near future.

For the exchange rate on a possible land swap, the market value of the minerals in the contested lands has to be estimated. The market value is the price a consumer is willing to pay for a product. Market values fluctuate due to the needs of the consumer and types of extractive technologies used in the mining process. An estimate of equal value might be flawed because of the constant fluctuation of market values. Bryce Tripp, a Utah Geological Survey (UGS) economic geologist, cites as an example a change in cement production that calls for higher calcium limestone deposits. Patented claims that have this type of higher calcium deposit have had their market value increase due to the heightened demand.

Scientists and economists who assess land values have different estimates of the amount of mineral deposits located in the Burning Hills WSA. Lee Allison, Utah's state geologist, claims the Utah Geological Survey provides a conservative analysis. The UGS estimates that there are 11.36 billion tons of technologically recoverable coal in the Kaiparowits field. This estimate is 30 percent lower than United States Geological Survey estimates and 50 percent lower than mining industry estimates (Allison 1997). Again, it is painfully clear that estimates vary depending on who is evaluating the land.

In order to make land exchanging "fair," Allison suggests a unit for unit exchange. This unit for unit exchange will leave out the dollar value and focus on what actually is in place. This technique is much more reliable with coal because tonnage estimates are more certain due to drill hole estimates and outcroppings. Oil, gas, and hardrock minerals are more difficult to estimate precisely, so an agreement on the amount in place will be more difficult to determine.

## MINING AND THE WILDERNESS PROPOSALS

Throughout this chapter, we have pointed out the inherent conflict between mining and wilderness. The three best-known wilderness proposals, 5.7 million acres (H.R. 1500), 1.9 million acres (H.R. 1745), and 3.2 million acres (WSAs currently in existence), will have different degrees of impact on Utah's mining potential. We have taken these three wilderness proposals and overlaid them with coal and mineral claims. On each map are the total number of coal and mining claims that are located in and out of the proposed wilderness areas. The maps and statistics illustrate how mining claims would be affected by the various wilderness proposals.

*Map 7.1: 1.9 million acres: H.R. 1745:*
A wilderness proposal for 1.9 million acres was introduced by Representative Jim Hansen (R-Utah). Representative Hansen, along with the rest of Utah's congressional delegation, the Utah Farm Bureau, the Utah Mining Association, and other mining interests, drew the wilderness boundaries to exclude coal and mineral claims that were deemed to have the highest certainty (c) and favorability (f) ratings. This is especially obvious in the Book Cliffs region of eastern Utah in parts of Carbon, Uintah, Emery, and Grand counties, along with the Burning Hills WSA and the Kaiparowits Plateau in Kane and Garfield counties.

*Map 7.2: 5.7 million acres: H.R. 1500:*
House bill 1500 advocated approximately 5.7 million acres of wilderness designation in Utah. In contrast to H.R. 1745, which chose to draw its wilderness boundaries around coal and mineral claims, H.R. 1500 purposely includes those claims so as to protect those lands from the environmental impact of mining. In regard to the Book Cliffs region and the Kaiparowits Plateau, H.R. 1500 contrasts starkly with H.R. 1745. All the coal and mining claims excluded from protection under 1745 would be protected as wilderness areas under H.R. 1500.

*Map 7.3: WSAs currently in existence*
This map displays the Wilderness Study Areas that currently exist under the management of the BLM. The total acreage of WSAs is approximately 3.2 million acres in Utah. While not offering as much protection as H.R. 1500 in terms of wilderness designation, a bill designating all WSA acreage approximates the middle ground, in terms of acreage, in the debate over wilderness designation and mining claims in Utah.

These three maps illustrate the disparity between the three wilderness acreages and their impact on mining. Mining interests favor 1.9 million acres or less, while environmentalists demand 5.7 million acres, or perhaps 9.1 million acres according to the latest proposal. Neither side seems to be willing to compromise. Standing in between the two proposals are the 3.2 million acres of WSAs currently in existence. The disparity between the 1.9-million-acre proposal and the 5.7-million-acre proposal can be seen in the non-protected and protected areas of the Book Cliffs region of eastern Utah and in the Kaiparowits Plateau. The statistics on mineral and coal leases further clarify just how much is involved in the different wilderness proposals.

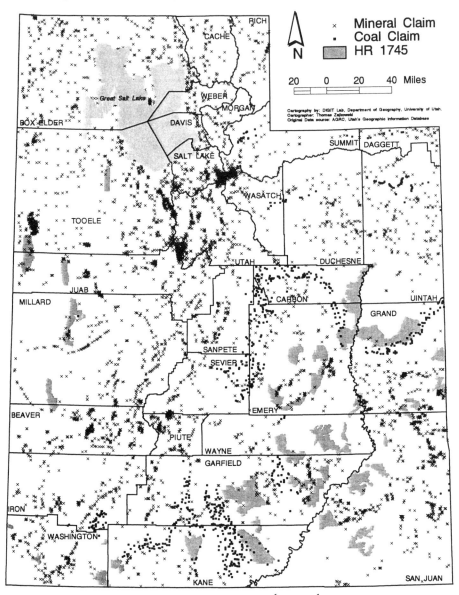

Map 7.1—H.R. 1745 Land in Utah
(with mineral and coal claims)

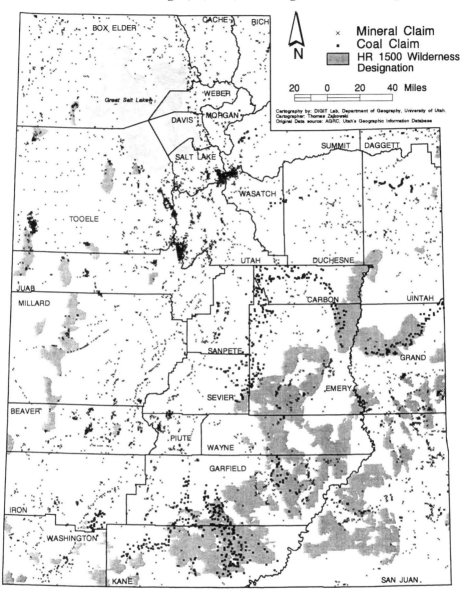

Map 7.2—H.R. 1500 Land in Utah
(with mineral and coal claims)

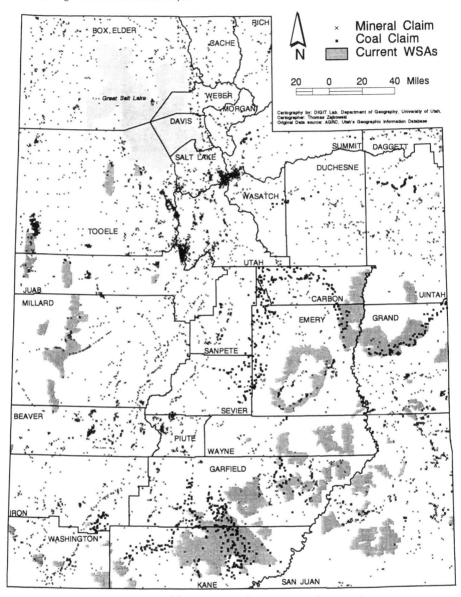

Map 7.3—Wilderness Study Area Land in Utah
(with mineral and coal claims)

*Statistics on Mineral and Coal Claims in Utah*

The exact number of filed claims and leases for both minerals and coal, and their relationship to the three acreage totals, are detailed below:

A. 1.9 Million Acres (H.R. 1745)

Minerals: Out of 6,326 total claims, 44 would be located within a wilderness area. This is .6 percent of mineral claims that would be located in a wilderness area if this bill became law.

Coal: Out of 829 total claims, 16 would be located within a wilderness area. This is 1.9 percent of coal leases that would be located in a wilderness area if this bill became law.

B. 5.7 Million Acres (H.R. 1500)

Minerals: Out of 6,326 total claims, 247 would be located within a wilderness area. This is 3.9 percent of mineral claims that would be located in a wilderness area if this bill became law.

Coal: Out of 829 total claims, 214 would be located within a wilderness area. This is 25.8 percent of coal leases that would be located in a wilderness area if this bill becomes law.

C. 3.2 Million Acres (WSAs currently in existence)

Minerals: Out of 6,326 total claims, 83 are located within WSA boundaries. Thus, 1.3 percent of all mineral claims are currently located within WSA boundaries.

Coal: Out of 829 total leases, 148 are located within WSA boundaries. Thus, 17.85 percent of all coal leases are currently located within WSA boundaries.

## THE FUTURE OF THE MINING-IN-WILDERNESS DEBATE

It has become apparent that the laws governing mining need to be amended. The main suggestion is to add a mining royalty for federal lands. Those supporting a royalty of some kind include Mark Walsh, Director of the Utah Association of Counties, Ted Stewart, former Director of the Utah Department of Natural Resources, Margaret Kelsey, Wilderness Coordinator for the Utah division of the BLM, Tom Bachtell, Director of the Public Lands Committee for the Utah Mining Association, and Scott Groene, former Issues Director for SUWA. When we speak of a royalty, we are talking about adding a fee or percentage onto the net proceeds from a successful mineral, coal, or oil find.

As far as mining in wilderness areas is concerned, the issue is basically settled. Unless a party has a claim that was grandfathered under the Wilderness Act, no new claim can be located, patented, and mined in wilderness areas or WSAs. But the future of the wilderness debate is still up in the air. Mark Walsh believes that government must step in and declare policy. Scott Groene believes that the "people's wishes" must be addressed, which SUWA defines as 5.7 million acres of wilderness, or perhaps 9.1 million acres. Either way, the wilderness debate rages.

Each individual must make a personal decision about how he or she feels about the issue of mining in wilderness. In this chapter, we have attempted to provide accurate information from both sides of the debate. The maps and their corresponding data provide a tangible picture of how each of three wilderness proposals could affect mining in Utah. The 5.7-million-acre proposal would protect the most wilderness, but have the greatest impact on mining. The 1.9-million-acre proposal would protect the least wilderness, but allow the greatest potential for future mining activity. Look at the maps, read the statistics, take in both sides of the issue, and then decide how much of Utah should be designated as wilderness.

## ⊄ APPENDIX TO CHAPTER 7

The following definitions will aid the reader's understanding of the various laws and leasing arrangements relevant to mining in wilderness areas.

### DEFINITIONS

*Mineral Leasing Act of 1920 as amended (30 U.S.C. 18 et seq.)*
This act provides that "deposits of coal, phosphate, sodium, potassium, oil, oil shale, native asphalt, solid and semi-solid bitumen, and bituminous rock or gas, and lands containing such deposits owned by the United States" may be acquired only through a leasing system (Maley 1990, 137).

### Oil and Gas Leasing
Oil and gas leasing on federal lands is administered by the BLM through a competitive and non-competitive leasing system. Oil and gas leases are issued for public-domain lands under authority of the Mineral Leasing Act of February 25, 1920 (Maley 1990, 138).

### Competitive Leasing
All lands available for leasing are to be offered for competitive oral bidding.
Each BLM state office is required to hold sales for such lands at least quarterly.

The length of competitive leases shall not exceed five years with a maximum acreage of 2,560 acres per lease. However, in Alaska, the acreage may extend up to 5,760 acres per lease (Maley 1990, 138).

### Non-Competitive Leasing
These leases are available only on lands that were offered out to competitive bidding, but received no such bid. These lands are available for two years after the first business day following the last day of the competitive bid auction (Maley 1990, 138–39).

### Coal Leasing
Coal leasing applies to coal acquired under the Coal Lands Act of 1873.

Coal has never fallen under the domain of the Mining Law of 1872. Acquisition of fee title to lands known to be valuable for coal, or the development of coal deposits, has fallen under the domain of the Coal Lands Act of 1873.

The Mineral Leasing Act of 1920 governs coal as a leasing act mineral.

Coal is now leased through a competitive leasing system with the major elements of the coal leasing system being land-use planning, setting leasing targets, coal activity planning, and coal-lease sale scheduling.

Bids for coal must be of fair market value (Maley 1990, 143).

### Non-Impairment Mandate
Section 603(c) of FLPMA says to manage wilderness study areas so as "not to impair the suitability of such areas for preservation as wilderness. . . ." This section also provides for exceptions from the non-impairment mandate with "grandfathered uses." Under "grandfathered uses," all mining activities are to continue with the same "manner and degree." These activities are regulated to prevent impairment and unnecessary and undue degradation. The use (mining) is "grandfathered," not the claim in and of itself. A "grandfathered" mineral use outside the boundary of a WSA may extend into the area as long as the activity follows the logical pace and progression of development (Maley 1990, 394).

### Valid Existing Rights
The BLM cannot regulate valid existing rights to the non-impairment standard.

### Mining Claims
Mining claims have valid existing rights if a discovery was made on the claim before October 21, 1976, and the claim was supported by discovery activity.

A mining claim would be grandfathered if it was worked before October 21, 1976.

Activities to use and develop a claim must satisfy the non-impairment criteria unless it would unreasonably interfere with the claimant's right to use and enjoyment of the claim. If so, the claimant may proceed while regulated to prevent unnecessary or undue degradation.

*Mineral leases*
Mineral leases have valid existing rights if they were issued before October 21, 1976. Pre-FLPMA leases are not applicable to the grandfathered uses because of their more liberal nature. Activities must satisfy the non-impairment criteria unless this would unreasonably interfere with the rights provided by the lease. If rights can be exercised only through activities that permanently impair wilderness suitability, such activities will be regulated to prevent unnecessary and undue regulation (Maley 1990, 393).

## MINERAL AND RESOURCE ASSESSMENT

At present, prospecting and mining continue throughout Utah. Valuable metal deposits include lead, iron, uranium, copper, gold, and silver. Coal, oil, natural gas, oil shale, and tar sands are hydrocarbon deposits found in Utah. Industrial materials such as limestone, dolomite, clay, and gravel are abundant (Stokes 1986, 7).

The BLM had each WSA in Utah independently assessed for its energy and mineral resources by Science Applications, Inc. (BLM Utah 1990a, Appendix 6, 317–21). Science Applications Incorporated (SAI) set up a dual rating system for each resource. The first rating estimates the geologic favorability (f) and the second estimates the degree of certainty (c). These are both rated on a scale of one to four with four being the highest rating. For instance, the Burning Hills WSA on the Kaiparowits Plateau received a rating of $f4$ and $c4$. This indicates there is a potential for large tonnages of coal and there is a certainty of finding coal (BLM Utah 1990b, III, 1–24). This rating system is applied for each natural resource located in Wilderness Study Areas. We have listed the WSAs that have received high favorability (f3-f4) and certainty (c3-c4) ratings.

*A. Oil and Gas*

| | |
|---|---|
| Behind the Rocks | Papoose Canyon |
| Coal Canyon | Flume Canyon |
| Desolation Canyon | Winter Ridge |
| Phipps–Death Hollow | Spruce Canyon |

Jack Canyon

Turtle Canyon

Floy Canyon

*B. Coal*

The Blues

Mud Spring Canyon

Wahweap

Burning Hills

Death Ridge

Turtle Hills

Desolation Canyon

Mount Ellen–Blue Hills

Fifty Mile Mountain

Carcass Canyon

*C. Tar Sands*

French Spring–Happy Canyon

Fiddler Butte

Winter Ridge

*D. Uranium/Vanadium*

Mount Hillers

Little Rockies

Bridger Jack Mesa

Horseshoe Canyon (North)

San Rafael Reef

Mexican Mountain

Sids Mountain

Muddy Creek

Crack Canyon

*E. Copper/Silver/Gold*

North Stansbury Mountain

Deep Creek Mountains

Mount Pennell

Little Rockies

Mount Hillers

*F. Mineral and Energy Resources*

The crux of the debate over mining in wilderness study areas can be summarized by the following issues, which the BLM believes are central to the mining-in-wilderness debate. The key concerned interests are the Rocky Mountain Oil and Gas Association, the Utah Mining Association, the Utah Oil and Gas Association, and environmental groups, with SUWA heading the list (BLM internal memo).

The potential to develop oil, gas, and hydrocarbon resources in eleven WSAs.

The potential to develop tar sand resources in three WSAs.

The potential to develop the coal resources in ten WSAs.

The potential to develop unknown but likely locatable mineral deposits in nine WSAs.

The number of existing claims has decreased.

The number of existing oil and gas leases has decreased.

The number of existing coal leases has decreased.

## ₵ NOTES TO CHAPTER 7

1. Editors' note: One of the most dramatic and prolonged controversies involving proposed wilderness and mining in Utah is the proposal for a mine in Westwater Canyon. See *Salt Lake Tribune*, March 16, 1998, and April 7, 1998, and *High Country News*, October 16, 1995 and April 12, 1999.

## ₵ REFERENCES TO CHAPTER 7

Allison, Lee. 1997. Personal interview by authors, April 17.

Associated Press. 1997. "Will Gypsum Mine in the Wilderness Set a Precedent?" *Salt Lake Tribune*, On-Line (http://www.sltrib.com/97/aug/080597/utah/30491.htm), August 5.

Bachtell, Thomas. 1997. Personal interview by authors, April.

Bateman, Alan M. 1950. *Economic Mineral Deposits.* New York: John Wiley & Sons.

BLM Utah (Utah State Office, Bureau of Land Management of the U.S. Department of the Interior). 1990a. *Utah BLM Statewide Wilderness Environmental Impact Statement, Overview, Final.* Washington, DC.

———. 1990b. *Utah BLM Statewide Wilderness Environmental Impact Statement, vol. III, Part B, South-West Region, Final.* Washington, DC.

Groene, Scott. 1997. Personal interview by authors, March.

Haugrud, K. Jack. 1985. *Wilderness Preservation: A Guide to Wilderness Selection on the BLM Lands.* Palo Alto, CA: Stanford University Press.

Hendee, John C., George H. Stankey, and Robert C. Lucas. 1978. *Wilderness Management.* Washington, DC: U.S. GPO.

Kelsey, Margaret. 1997. Personal interview by authors, April.

Leshy, John D. 1987. *The Mining Law: A Study in Perpetual Motion.* Washington, DC: Resources for the Future.

Magill, Frank N. 1990. *Magill's Survey of Science: Earth Science Series, vol. 4.* Princeton, NJ: Salem Press.

Maley, Terry S. 1990. *Handbook of Mineral Law.* Boise, ID: Mineral Land Publications.

Power, Thomas Michael. 1991. *Wildland Preservation and the Economy of Utah.* SUWA publication. April.

Rait, Ken. N.d. *The Use and Abuse of Economics in Utah's Wilderness Debate.* SUWA publication.

State of Utah. Governor's Office of Planning and Budget. 1997. *1997 Economic Report to the Governor.* Salt Lake City, UT.

Stewart, Ted. 1997. Personal interview by authors, April.

Stokes, William. 1986. *Geology of Utah.* Salt Lake City, UT: Utah Geological Survey, Department of Natural Resources.

Tripp, Bryce. 1997. Personal interview by authors, April 10.

Utah Petroleum Association. *Horizontal Drilling Brochure.*

Utah Public Lands Multiple Use Coalition. 1995. *Wilderness Position Paper.*

Walsh, Mark. 1997. Personal interview by authors, March.

Wilkinson, Charles. 1992. *Crossing the Next Meridian: Land, Water, and the Future of the West.* Washington, DC: Island Press.

# CHAPTER 8

# State Trust Lands

## A Problem in Wilderness Designation

Cyrus McKell

Dave Harward

### INTRODUCTION

Utah ranks last in the United States for expenditure per pupil for public education. Many citizens have expressed support for increasing public school funding to improve the quality of education. One possibility is for the state to increase the revenue from its 3.7 million acres of public school trust lands. These lands were granted to Utah at statehood from the federal government with a mandate to manage them for revenue production to support public education (Utah State Constitution 1895). However, many thousands of acres of trust lands are isolated in WSAs and are not producing revenues according to their potential (Bird 1997), and they haven't made much money for the schools (Groene 1997).

Under provisions of the 1964 Wilderness Act, Section 5(a), adequate access must be given to trust lands and private lands within wilderness areas. If fully implemented to increase revenues, this could create serious problems for wilderness management and endanger wilderness quality. However, most proposed wilderness legislation calls for solving the problem of trust land inclusions by trading them out for other federal lands or some type of value-for-value exchange, similar to the recently completed federal-state trust land exchange described below.

*School Trust Lands Are in Isolated Locations*
Management of school trust lands for maximum revenue is not an easy task because over five thousand land parcels are remotely isolated in a checkerboard pattern in Sections 2, 16, 32, and 36 of each township in most of Utah's public lands. Although some trust lands have been "traded out" of military reservations and sensitive areas, many thousands of acres

presently exist in national parks and monuments, national forests, Indian tribal lands, and on lands administered by the BLM. In these federally administered lands, school trust lands exist in a pattern that disregards topography, accessibility by roads, scenic value, proximity of rivers and streams, and potential for multiple uses.

According to the Utah BLM Statewide Wilderness Final EIS, most of the state trust land sections are used under state permits for livestock grazing, energy development, or mineral exploration (BLM Utah 1990). Management of federal lands surrounding trust lands generally dictates how they are used. Thus, if these trust lands were to remain in wilderness areas on a *de facto* basis, could they be managed any differently than the adjacent lands? If previous delays in dealing with isolated state school trust lands are a forecast for the future, wilderness designation would further complicate the problem of improving or even sustaining revenues from the isolated trust lands.

### Difficulties of Trading Out Trust Lands

Trading out the isolated trust lands for other federal lands of equal value seems like a reasonable approach and has been the subject of numerous legislative proposals. Developing a strategy for exchange of trust lands in wilderness areas for other federal lands seems a simple task, but for numerous reasons state and federal officials have not been able to develop politically acceptable arrangements. As the previous chapter pointed out, determining equal value for trading lands is extremely difficult. A recently completed settlement (described in greater detail below) between the Department of the Interior and the State of Utah has set a new strategy in motion for exchanging school trust lands surrounded by WSAs.

### Determining Value of Trust Lands

Determining the value of trust lands is difficult because there is little agreement as to the basis of value. What is scenic value or a remote location worth? Should land value reflect actual or potential revenues, or should value be influenced by philosophical criteria? In a statement supporting land exchange legislation that would resolve the problem of trust lands in wilderness areas, Jane Leeson of the Wilderness Society argued that the value of trust lands in national parks had been overestimated (U.S. Congress 1992). Conversely, if financial returns are to be the basis for value determination, the school trust lands have a history of limited use and low value. The Director of the Utah Geological Survey indicates that some trust lands have a high potential for minerals, oil, or gas (Allison 1997), which could be used to assess a high value in contrast to their low non-market wilderness value, yet Scott Groene of SUWA says that school officials are exaggerating the potential value of the trust lands (1997).

Utah citizens and public officials are left with the very difficult issue of how to increase revenue from state trust lands to provide support for public schools. Most wilderness legislation, as well as public discussions, calls for dealing appropriately with trust lands included in wilderness areas, but no satisfactory solution has received decisive political action.

To provide background information for the questions raised above, in this chapter we will discuss how Utah received its school trust lands, how they are managed, and what they yield in revenue, and then identify possible strategies to effect equitable land trades, including the land exchange recently authorized by Congress. Finally, we will discuss possible options for the future.

## ORIGIN OF SCHOOL TRUST LANDS AND THEIR PURPOSE

### Land Grants from Congress

Land grants to the states from the federal government date back to the beginning of the nation. The Land Ordinance of 1785 provided for a rectangular system of public land surveying and disposal (Matheson and Becker 1988). The Land Ordinance provided for the division of the public lands into townships of thirty-six square miles, which in turn were divided into one-square-mile sections containing 640 acres. The Land Ordinance also initiated a program of land grants for schools, providing that lot number 16 in every township would be reserved "for the maintenance of public schools within the said township" (Souder and Fairfax 1996, 18). Beginning with Ohio in 1803 and ending with Alaska in 1959, school trust lands were granted by Congress to a state at statehood. The main purpose was to support common schools and similar public institutions. When Ohio was given statehood it received Section 16 for the public schools and in return the state gave up any rights to other federal lands within its boundaries and waived its right to interfere with any disposal of federal lands within its boundaries by the federal government (Matheson and Becker 1988).

When Oregon gained statehood in 1884, the land grant standard was increased to two sections per township, "because of the additional land in the West," and with the acceptance of Utah to the Union, the land grant was increased to four sections per township because of the perception that "these arid lands had little value" (Bassett 1989, 197). When Utah's Enabling Act was finally passed by Congress in 1895, the state received Sections 2, 16, 32, and 36 in each township, which created the familiar "checkerboard" pattern of land ownership (Souder and Fairfax 1996). This systematic scattering of trust lands in Utah has also been called the "blue rash" by many individuals involved in the debate over school trust land and federal ownership of surrounding lands, due to the blue coloration of the isolated state trust land sections on land ownership maps.

## Purpose of Trust Lands

The state school trust lands were established to provide a source of funds for the common schools. In the 1894 Utah Enabling Act, Congress mandated that "the proceeds of lands herein granted for educational purposes, except as hereinafter otherwise provided, shall constitute a permanent school fund, the interest of which only shall be expended for the support of said schools." A trust would be created for each state's beneficiaries and "must meet two criteria: (1) School trust lands must be managed for the exclusive benefit of the public school system, and (2) school trust lands must be managed to obtain full value" (Utah Enabling Act 1894). Trust management would lead to a permanent fund where interest revenue from the state lands would serve the trust beneficiaries. The grant and acceptance of the Utah school trust lands created a trust relationship with the State of Utah as the trustee, the public school system as the beneficiary, and the school trust land as the trust corpus (Bassett 1989).

David Terry, Director of School and Institutional Trust Lands Administration (SITLA), states that "As trustee, the Trust Lands Administration must, by law, optimize revenues" (SITLA 1996). This purpose is recognized in the BLM Statewide Wilderness Study Report (BLM Utah 1991) by the statement "Trust lands are administered by the Utah Division of State Lands [now SITLA] for the purpose of economic gain in support of the State public schools and other institutional trust funds."

## Legal Challenges of Use and Revenues from Trust Lands

Combined with historical mandates for management of trust lands to produce revenues, there are numerous legal precedents driving the management of state school trust lands. Among the most important court decisions surrounding the issue of trust land management and wilderness designation are *Utah v. Andrus*, which is known as the Cotter decision, *Lassen v. Arizona Highway Department*, and *National Parks and Conservation Association (NPCA) v. Board of State Lands*. The Cotter decision concerns access to state trust lands surrounded by federal lands designated as WSAs. According to Fairfax, Souder, and Goldenmann, the Cotter decision is one of the most restrictive court decisions; it holds that "the BLM must grant a holder of a state oil and gas lease access to a school land parcel wholly surrounded by federal land in a WSA" (1992).

The *Lassen* ruling dealt with the question of full compensation for trust land use. In that case Arizona attempted to construct a road through state school trust lands. The U.S. Supreme Court ruled that "the State of Arizona must compensate the trust in money for the full appraised value of any material sites or rights of way which it obtains on or over trust lands" (Souder and Fairfax 1996).

An important Utah decision regarding managing revenues from school trust lands was rendered in *NPCA v. Board of State Lands* (1993). The Utah Supreme Court held that the state's duty of undivided loyalty toward the school trust requires maximum economic returns. In that ruling, economic optimization of school trust lands takes precedence over non-economic values (Rawson 1994).

## UTAH'S TRUST LAND MANAGEMENT ACT OF 1988: A REORGANIZATION

Trust lands administration has been the responsibility of several state agencies. From statehood in 1896, to 1967, school trust lands were administered under the Board of Land Commissioners in the State Land Office with the charge to manage the lands "for the exclusive benefit of the common schools" (Utah Enabling Act 1896). In 1967 the State Land Office was renamed the Division of State Lands in the Department of Natural Resources. In a move to streamline land management functions, trust lands administration was combined with sovereign lands and forestry in the Division of State Lands and Forestry in 1978. In 1994 the legislature recognized that managing school trust lands had unique requirements and established a separate agency, the School and Institutional Trust Lands Administration (SITLA).

The objective of SITLA is to manage trust lands as effectively as possible through the use of improved computer systems, planning rules, and better coordination with the federal agencies. Twelve permanent trust funds benefit from the revenues generated by SITLA (table 8.1). The major beneficiary is public schools. From 1990 to 1996, the total trust fund grew from $36.8 million to the current balance of $108.5 million, of which 95 percent is in the Public School Trust (SITLA 1996, 8). In 1996, SITLA contributed over $5.7 million to the beneficiaries, most of which was generated from mineral-gas-oil leases. If any trust lands are considered for sale, the sale must create a substantial amount of funds for the educational trusts. SITLA is

TABLE 8.1—Beneficiaries of State Trust Funds in Trust Acres,
Contributions to Trust Fund, and Trust Balances

| Beneficiary | Number of Surface Acres | Contributions to Funds, 1996 | FY 1996 Fund Balances |
|---|---|---|---|
| Public Schools | 3,573,978.27 | $5,354,482 | $105,932,115 |
| Reservoirs | 52,248.84 | $30,280 | $243,769 |
| Utah State University | 26,909.30 | $53,490 | $374,973 |
| School for the Blind | 19,141.47 | $18,299 | $157,405 |
| University of Utah | 15,294.88 | $78,048 | $452,414 |
| Miner's Hospital | 7,253.59 | $85,475 | $522,459 |
| Normal School | 6,977.24 | $32,298 | $199,158 |
| School of Mines | 6,722.07 | ($2,111) | $136,669 |
| School for the Deaf | 6,212.82 | $8,701 | $152,676 |
| Utah State Hospital | 3,381.26 | $27,551 | $181,419 |
| Public Buildings | 3,359.35 | $3,190 | $32,432 |
| Youth Development Center | 1,593.23 | $7,036 | $124,865 |
| Totals | 3,723,072.32 | $5,696,739 | $108,510,354 |

Source: Utah SITLA 1996, 8.

currently working with private developers who are constructing housing projects and an industrial park.

## MANAGEMENT PROBLEMS OF UTAH'S SCHOOL TRUST LANDS

### Financial Considerations of Trust Land Revenues

Trust land revenues provide a permanent fund for the beneficiaries of the trust, the schoolchildren of Utah. Revenues come from several sources: leases for surface use, leases and royalties for extraction of minerals, oil, and gas, and land sales. However, the major revenue from school trust lands comes from surface and mineral uses. Table 8.2 shows all sources of revenue from the lands and the expenditure figures of SITLA for fiscal years 1995 and 1996.

Wilderness designation could have a negative effect on the revenue possibilities of SITLA if the trades are not made promptly. Table 8.3 shows acreage totals from the BLM wilderness proposal, the acreage totals of the Wilderness Study Areas, and the acreage totals of H.R. 1500, as well as the acreage of inheld trust lands. Clearly a large number of acres are involved.

Wilderness designation could have a damaging effect on the options SITLA uses to administer those lands. As previously discussed, SITLA has an obligation to maximize revenue on the trust lands. However, with

TABLE 8.2—Trust Land Administration Revenues and Expenditures, FY 1995 and 1996

| Revenues | 1995 | 1996 |
|---|---|---|
| Land Sales | $603,557 | $3,269,755 |
| Investments | $5,758,669 | $7,663,801 |
| Minerals | $12,197,763 | $10,082,763 |
| Surface | $1,801,157 | $1,855,198 |
| Other | $4,924 | $17,771 |
| Total Revenue | $20,366,070 | $22,889,288 |
| Total Expenditures | $3,341,037 | $5,084,547 |
| Net Revenue | $17,025,033 | $17,804,741 |

Source: Utah SITLA 1996, 7.

TABLE 8.3—Wilderness Proposal Acreage

Total Proposal Acreage and 1988 State Trust Land Inholdings Acreage

| | BLM Proposal | WSAs | UWC Proposal (a) |
|---|---|---|---|
| Total Proposal Acreage | 1,975,219 | 3,235,834 | 5,700,000 |
| State Inholdings | 104,261 | 183,248 | 630,000 |
| % of All State Trust Lands | 2.8% | 4.92% | 16.92% |

(a) UWC trust land acreage estimated. No exact figures are available. Estimate made by taking 11.1 percent of the total acreage of the proposal. State trust lands are approximately 11.1 percent of all BLM lands in question.

Source: USDI—BLM 1990, 45.

wilderness designation, many of the activities SITLA manages would not be allowed by wilderness legislation. For example, the largest source of revenue on state lands comes from mineral revenue, an activity that would not occur after designation. Even now, the isolated trust lands that have potential mineral, oil, or coal reserves have constraints on them that reduce the opportunity for new exploration or development activities.

The amount of revenue at stake may be determined by calculating the average amount of revenue received per each acre of state trust lands. SITLA posted $22.9 million in revenue for fiscal 1996. These revenues were generated from the 3,723,072 acres of trust land that year. On average, each acre of school trust land generated revenues of $6.15. Applying this average revenue per acre to the amount of trust lands in each of the three major wilderness proposals provides dollar amounts that help to explain the financial management problem of SITLA. Table 8.4 shows the potential risk in lost revenues for the school trust if any one of the three wilderness proposals were enacted.

TABLE 8.4—Potential Revenue Lost to Wilderness Designation
State Trust Land Acreage Inside Three Wilderness Proposals
(based on a $6.15 average revenue per acre)

|  | BLM Proposal | WSAs | UWC Proposal (a) |
|---|---|---|---|
| Trust Land Acreage | 104,261 | 183,248 | 630,000 |
| Potential Revenue Lost | $641,205.15 | $1,126,975.20 | $3,874,500.00 |
| % of Total Trust Land Revenue | 2.80% | 4.92% | 16.93% |

(a) UWC trust land acreage estimated. No exact figures are available. Estimate made by taking 11.1 percent of the total acreage of the proposal. State trust lands are approximately 11.1 percent of all BLM lands in question.

The stance SITLA takes on wilderness designation is an obvious result of the threat of lost revenue from potentially productive lands; they argue that any wilderness designation must concurrently address the needs of the school trust. The SITLA statement on wilderness designation declares that purchase or exchange of the inheld lands for fair market value is the only satisfactory solution (SITLA 1996). By not being able to gain revenue from the lands within the various proposals, the school trust is losing money, and SITLA views this as an obstacle in maximizing revenue from the trust lands. "The Trust Lands Administration will oppose proposals for creating wilderness which do not compensate the beneficiaries—at fair-market value—for all trust lands affected by wilderness," according to the 1996 annual report (SITLA 1996, 17).

As it presently stands, the Institutional Trusts have a reserve of over $127 million dollars, with the major amount, $105 million, in the public school trust account. In 1996 the SITLA distribution to the public school budget was $5.4 million. This may seem a large sum but is only a small portion, about .03 percent of the actual spending on public schools, which amounted to $1.72 billion. Even so, it is important in the overall support of schools and needs to be increased (Liston 1997). According to Patricia Bowles, economist for the State Office of Education, the 1998 appropriation for public schools is $1.906 billion, a slight increase from the fiscal year 1997 authorization of $1.88 billion (Bowles 1997). Distributions to beneficiaries from the permanent fund will certainly increase in the future. However, the trust fund will continue to contribute only a very small percentage of the overall spending for education in the years to come. There will certainly be a need to increase spending on education; from 1966 to 1996, Utah's population doubled from one million to two million, which places a great burden on revenue sources to provide adequate schools, supplies, and teachers (Donner 1997).

*Management for Value Maximization of Trust Lands Conflicts with Criteria for Wilderness Preservation*

In determining the use of school trust lands, SITLA is constrained by its operating criteria of maximizing financial returns to the educational trust funds (SITLA 1995; Utah Enabling Act 1894). Uses such as recreation that return little or no revenues must therefore receive a secondary priority. With a higher priority on revenue than on wilderness criteria, there are many conflicts in position between those interested in wilderness values that emphasize preservation, solitude, and absence of human impacts, and those who advocate use of trust lands to maximize revenues for school trust funds. These conflicting positions appear to have been used to delay resolution of the larger question of wilderness legislation.

The Sierra Club claims that county officials have resisted trading out trust lands because their county might lose them to another county or they would miss an opportunity for a future project on trust lands traded out of their county (LeGate 1997). In contrast, wilderness advocates have publicly expressed opposition to measures that would increase access to trust lands. In response to a request by Conoco Oil Company to conduct an exploratory drilling for oil on a state trust section in the Grand Staircase–Escalante Monument, Scott Groene of the Southern Utah Wilderness Alliance said that "Americans will not stand for oil wells, pipelines, or roads being built in the 1.7-million-acre monument" (Groene 1997). Yet there are many existing leases by oil, gas, and mining companies in state trust lands, and the lessees have legal rights to access their properties.[1]

BLM Interim Management Policy (BLM 1995) specifies that lands shall be managed in a manner so as "not to impair the suitability of such areas for preservation as wilderness." Under the non-impairment principle, uses of BLM lands in WSAs that require access roads for mining or mineral leasing are being restricted and made difficult by intensive study requirements and bureaucratic delays, according to Allen Freemeyer (1997), administrative assistant to Congressman Hansen. Mr. Freemeyer stated that there has been a reduction in land use in WSAs, which he attributed to frustrating delays in obtaining leases and access. Previous uses can be continued if "grandfathered," but only if they do not cause unnecessary or undue degradation of the lands. Any proposed modification of the environment to enhance management, such as constructing a drift fence, repairing a stock watering pond to improve control of livestock movement, or use of motorized vehicles to control a fire, may be seen as a violation of the non-impairment principle.

Because trust lands are usually surrounded entirely by WSA lands, the principle of non-impairment comes into conflict with the objective of maximizing revenue through increased uses. In a list of Ten Wilderness Issues, the Utah Public Lands Multiple Use Coalition and Utah Farm Bureau Federation declared: "Restrictive management of the surrounding federal land makes trust sections captured within WSAs economically useless to the state" (Utah Public Lands Multiple Use Coalition n.d.).

A recent example of trust land use coming into conflict with BLM management is seen in statements regarding the intention of Conoco Oil Company to initiate drilling for oil on a lease of state trust land located in the new Grand Staircase–Escalante National Monument (Woolf 1997a). This area is not a WSA, but it demonstrates the difficulties that arise when the federal government wants to preserve an area and the state wants to maximize trust fund revenues. According to BLM guidelines, access must be granted to non-federal lands. However, the mission of the new national monument appears to conflict with this. Exploratory drilling by Conoco in the state trust land section that is adjacent to a county road could be in conflict with other management objectives of the monument. Environmental advocates have expressed concern that if the well is successful, Conoco would request permission to drill on adjacent federal lands where they have valid oil and gas leases.

Thus, for the long term, management of isolated state trust lands under a policy of maximum revenue return may be expected to conflict with the principles of preservation and minimum human impact that are specified in the Wilderness Act, FLPMA, and BLM management guidelines for WSA lands (BLM 1995). Inasmuch as BLM actually controls the land through on-site management but returns to the state a portion of the revenues received according to the relative amount of state land contained in the federal management unit, the dominant management policy may be expected to prevail unless directed otherwise by appeal or court action. Given that 44 percent of SITLA revenues come from mineral and oil/gas leases, the impact of the non-impairment regulations of FLPMA for WSAs could result in the inability of SITLA to increase or even maintain revenue from trust land inholdings.

### Trade Out for Equal Value Lands
The original intent of the Wilderness Act of 1964 was that state or private lands held in designated wilderness areas would be traded out. The law stated that inheld lands would be exchanged for federally owned land of approximately equal value in the same state. A major problem is finding other lands of agreed-upon equal value that could be blocked up into a manageable unit. Merely making a trade for lands that are also scattered and isolated would not materially improve the opportunities

for management of surface uses or for development of petroleum and mineral resources.

In commercial situations, the market determines land values on the basis of willing buyers and sellers. In wilderness land valuation, there are only managers and users who do not have to face the burden of paying a purchase price. If land condemnation approaches are followed, arrival at a fair valuation would be based on the value of adjacent land and the revenues generated, which is inadequate in the trust land valuation process. Another strategy is to conduct a "cost-benefit analysis," but the benefits are mostly intangible and costs are general. Opinion studies conducted in Utah showed that supporters of wilderness were willing to pay from about $50 to over $90 per acre for wilderness, which amounts to a value of $27 to $47 million to have from 5 to 30 percent of Utah designated as wilderness (Keith, Fawson, and Johnson 1996). In contrast, ranchers were willing to pay from $2 to $10 million per year for grazing their cows on all public lands. But applying these values to actual land valuation does not necessarily reveal the true long-range value of the land.

*1997 SITLA Policy Statement on Protection of Trust Assets*
In response to the establishment of the Grand Staircase–Escalante National Monument in September 1996, the SITLA Board of Trustees wrote a nine-page policy statement that focused on issues dealing with the 176,000 surface acres and 200,700 mineral acres of school trust lands in the monument (SITLA 1997). The policy reaffirmed the position of SITLA to manage all trust lands for maximum return of revenues and to seek a fair exchange for trust lands. The statement emphasized protection of trust land values during the period before exchange by working with existing lessees of state lands, and affirmed using all necessary activities and information that will result in fair assessments of land values. Any appraisal of land to determine value must guarantee fair valuation *or* full development of the surface or mineral resources. This strong statement may reflect the attitude toward land valuation that has made exchanges of trust lands difficult.

As chapter 7 indicates, the issue of equal mineral value has often been a stumbling block to land exchange because little or no information may be available regarding mineral value or because of unrealistic expectations of mineral values. Utah has a long history of developing mineral and petroleum resources and there are expectations for more development in the future. Other factors such as distance to processing facilities and current-market versus long-term market values also affect land value. An example of future expectations influencing present land value can be seen in the controversy over present versus long-term value of coal under the Kaiparowits Plateau in the Grand Staircase–Escalante National Monument. A Utah Department of Natural Resources report calculated that 876 million tons of coal reserves worth between $17 and $25 billion are in the Kaiparowits Plateau (Allison 1997). If they were mined, the royalties to the school trust fund would have been from $1.7 to over $2 billion. Long-term trends for an increase in coal markets would have made this coal attractive for export and thus influence a high valuation of the trust lands in the plateau (Jahanbani 1996). On the other hand, a BLM report indicated that coal from the Kaiparowits Plateau may have a low BTU energy content that would be less desirable in the market (Woolf 1997c).

Critical issues mentioned in the SITLA policy statement include receiving continued exercise of rights and obligations for trust land use, guarantee of multiple use of trust lands, obtaining equitable compensation for lost opportunities in determining land value, and receiving appropriations to cover costs of working with the BLM in developing the planning process for future management of the monument. Each of these issues has counterparts in relation to trust land use and management in WSAs. The message is clear that SITLA is trying to establish some new procedures for management of trust lands in its relations and strengthen its position *vis à vis* the management of the new monument.

Governor Leavitt said that "the issue of state trust lands must be addressed in order to meet the needs of school children. We must deal with the value of trust lands in the monument and value those lands for their coal content or in other ways" (1997). In the same interview, Secretary of the Interior Bruce Babbitt suggested swapping them out for other lands that have coal in them.

## ATTEMPTED SOLUTIONS FOR RESOLUTION OF WILDERNESS DESIGNATION AND REALIZATION OF TRUST LAND VALUES

### Project BOLD

In the late 1970s, Governor Scott Matheson's administration began formulating an innovative plan to exchange isolated state lands. Subsequently Project BOLD was formalized in 1983–84 as a strategy to "exchange school lands for Federal lands to consolidate State lands to resolve in a rational and equitable manner some of the problems caused by the checkerboard pattern of land ownership" (Utah Department of Natural Resources 1985). Project BOLD was designed as a separate state proposal and was not tied to the wilderness review process, but would require congressional approval of the proposed land exchanges. The unique objective of Project BOLD was to remove the state inholdings from WSAs without the burden of discussions on other issues involved in wilderness designation.

Initially, Project BOLD received considerable support from many quarters, and benefited from the leadership of Governor Matheson. Accompanied by a formal resolution from the Utah Legislature, legislation based on Project BOLD was introduced by both Utah Senators and Congressman Hansen in the U.S. House and Senate. The legislation was reviewed by Congress but not acted upon before the end of the 98th session in 1984. In 1984 Norman Bangerter succeeded Scott Matheson as governor, and support for Project BOLD began to wane. In a congressional field hearing in Salt Lake City in 1988, Governor Bangerter testified that he had "found little support for such a large statewide land exchange" (U.S. Congress 1992).

Although Project BOLD was innovative and ambitious, and held the promise of resolving a major public lands dilemma, it still failed. According to Brad Barber, who was involved in developing Project BOLD and is currently the Associate Director of the State Office of Planning and Budget, the reason for failure was lack of continued political support (1997). When Governor Bangerter was elected he failed to continue support for the project, partly because of declining support by county commissioners. Looking back we might wish that more support had been given to making Project BOLD a success in order to have the exchange problem resolved.

*Coalition for Utah's Future/Project 2000: Honest Broker Wilderness/Land-Use Project*

Another attempt at resolving the trust land issue began during 1990. A Coalition for Utah's Future (CUF)/Project 2000 task force on wilderness issues started to discuss the divisiveness of the wilderness debate in Utah. While there are considerable differences of opinion on wilderness among Utahns in general, the land itself is important to most Utahns. At a CUF/Project 2000 wilderness task force meeting in 1990, Terry Tempest Williams, a board member, stated that "all Utahns share a common love for the land" (Coalition for Utah's Future/Project 2000 1995, 2). Spurred by task-force interest in the wilderness debate and the comments by Williams, CUF/Project 2000 initiated a meeting of stakeholders in the wilderness debate. The purpose of gathering the involved parties was to go beyond the ideological arguments and address the particular issues of individual stakeholders. CUF agreed to act as a neutral party in the consensus-building process.

Deborah Callister, former wilderness issues coordinator for CUF/Project 2000, stated that the stakeholder group realized the immensity of the wilderness debate and the need to focus on issues within the debate (Callister 1997). The issue of school trust lands within wilderness designations became the first issue the task force attempted to resolve. However, it soon became apparent, according to Callister, that consensus-building and dispute resolution would not be a simple process. Following the 1992 elections, the next spring saw the withdrawal of the national environmental groups from the CUF/Project 2000 process even though resolving the school trust land issue was in their interest. According to Callister, the national groups did not participate beyond the school trust issue because they felt they would have better success dealing with the issue at the national level.

While there was some consensus among the remaining stakeholders, the state trust land issue was not resolved by this process. Many excellent ideas were laid out by the stakeholders in a CUF/Project 2000 document, including proposals ranging from allowing the state to maintain all rights to the land, to an acre-for-acre exchange. Any future effort to resolve the issue of state trust land inholdings could benefit from this document.

Participants from both sides of the issue lay blame for the breakdown of the process. Mark Walsh of the Utah Association of Counties stated that "the stakeholders didn't trust each other. There was no give, all take, on that issue" (Walsh 1997). Lawson LeGate of the Sierra Club said that the CUF/Project 2000 process failed to reach a workable consensus on this issue because the local-versus-national split interfered with reaching a resolution (LeGate 1997).

### Proposed Federal Legislation to Exchange Utah Trust Lands
In recent years, several attempts have been made to legislate the exchange of Utah trust lands held in national parks, Indian reservations, and lands managed by the BLM. In the 102nd Congress hearings were held before the House Subcommittee on National Parks and Public Lands on three bills, H.R. 4769, H.R. 4770, and H.R. 5118 (U.S. Congress 1992). Although similar in some respects, each bill presented a different approach to exchange and payment.

H.R. 4769 was introduced by Representative Hansen and called for acquisition of 32,000 acres of state inholdings in the Navajo reservation, and about 1,000 acres in the Goshute reservation. In return, the state would receive federal lands to be designated by the end of December 1994. In addition, H.R. 4769 would require the acquisition of all state inholdings in national parks in Utah. Compensation would be in the form of 25 percent additional receipts from mineral lease funds paid to the uniform School Trust Fund for twenty-five years, which was estimated to total over $662.5 million. No appraisal of land value would be required.

A similar bill, H.R. 4770, also introduced by Representative Hansen, called for the exchange of state trust lands in national forests for 80,000 acres of unspecified federal mining interests in Utah. The bill would prohibit the offering of lands in any designated wilderness area, a WSA, national park, Indian reservation, or defense withdrawal area. As with H.R. 4769, the deadline for action was December 1994. The basis for exchange was to be on an equal value-for-value basis.

The third land exchange bill, H.R. 5118, was introduced by Congressman Orton and covered all land exchanges mentioned in H.R. 4769 and H.R. 4770. The main difference was the requirement for acquiring 38,500 acres in fee and also an additional 1,000 acres of state mineral interests within the Navajo reservation. In the Goshute reservation, 1,000 surface and mineral rights to 1,500 subsurface acres would be acquired in exchange for specific federal lands. Lands to go to the state included a communications site in Uintah County and 1,364 acres of land in Emery County that have coal values. Other local exchanges were mentioned, but after extensive hearings no further action took place on the bills, apparently for lack of support and conflict over the payments and exchange stipulations.

In 1995, H.R. 1745 and S.B. 884 were introduced as the Utah Public Lands Management Act of 1995 with the purpose of designating wilderness areas. State trust lands were dealt with in a direct manner by declaring that 142,041 acres of trust lands located within or *adjacent to* areas designated as wilderness were to be exchanged for specific "Federal Exchange Lands" depicted on an accompanying map. An exchange of lands between the State of Utah and the Secretary of the Interior was to take place no later than two years after enactment of the act. The land exchange would involve each party offering to transfer all rights, title, and interest in the exchanged lands and to list all encumbrances such as leases, permits, etc. If the encumbrances would cause an imbalance in the exchange value, the Secretary of the Interior would transfer additional federal lands to the state. Considerable staff work would be required in state and federal agencies to identify lands for exchange and make an assessment of their value. No mention was made of a public review mechanism on the contentious value issue.

### Previous Trust Land Exchanges and Consolidation
A review of documents and maps showing land ownership in Utah and other western states indicates that land exchanges and consolidation have been successfully negotiated in the past. There are some examples in Utah

and other states where large blocks of lands have been created via exchange. One example is an area of over five thousand acres south of St. George, Utah, along the border with Arizona. Here the desert lands appear to have little else than surface use for grazing, but they have the potential for being used in the future growth of St. George. A larger tract of consolidated state trust land directly across the border in Arizona appears to have only grazing value but has the advantage of being leased as a unit for grazing rather than being in isolated tracts (Arizona State Lands Administration 1992). Other examples are the Parker Mountain wildlife management unit southeast of Fish Lake, which resulted from exchange and consolidation of state lands into a manageable unit, and a large tract in the Book Cliffs area for wildlife management. A trade-out of state land within the Aneth Extension of the Navajo Indian Reservation created a large block of state land just north of Bluff, Utah.

New hope for solving the school trust lands exchange problem was raised when Governor Leavitt and Secretary Babbitt signed an agreement on May 9, 1998. The agreement called for the exchange of 176,739 acres of trust lands in the Grand Staircase–Escalante National Monument, plus 200,000 acres of isolated trust lands in national parks, Indian reservations, national forests, and other federal lands. In return, Utah would receive $50 million in cash, 145,000 acres of federal lands with development potential or valuable oil, gas, and mineral resources, plus mineral rights and royalties from federal lands containing coal.

The agreement brought optimistic praise from individuals who have worked hard to formulate a land exchange agreement. Brad Barber, Deputy Director of the Utah Planning and Budget Office (who had been a prime mover in Governor Matheson's Project BOLD), said, "They [Governor Leavitt and Secretary Babbitt] did not want us spending any time revisiting the past—they only wanted us talking about finding solutions to problems." Geoff Webb, Special Assistant to Secretary Babbitt, said, "We both wanted the environment protected, we both wanted the school trust taken care of and we both wanted to resolve this thing" (Spangler 1998).

In June, Senator Hatch introduced the "Utah Schools and Lands Exchange Act of 1998," to complete the land exchange, stating, "This is a historic opportunity to resolve the decades-old problem of competing federal and state management objectives. It is not possible for school trust lands to generate money when isolated by park land" (Washington News Bureau, *Deseret News* 1998). In the House, Congressman Jim Hansen sponsored school trust land legislation in the Subcommittee on National Parks and Public Lands, which was later passed by the Resources

Committee. Subsequently the House approved the bill on June 24. Congressman Hansen said, "This is an equal value exchange that is fair and equitable to all parties involved" (Davidson 1998). David Terry, director of SITLA, was quoted in an editorial as saying that the land swap and the increased money flowing into the trust because of the swap will forever change the way the trust does business. In the same editorial, Wilderness Society President William Meadows praised the land exchange agreement: "We do believe that this legislation is a good deal for all concerned" (Bernick 1998).

In October 1998, during the harried conclusion of the 1998 legislative session, Congress approved Public Law 105-335, which provided for the exchange of certain lands in the State of Utah. President Clinton signed it into law on October 31, 1998. This act provided Utah with a cash payment of $50 million and 139,000 acres of federal land rich in natural resources, which now become part of the state's school trust lands. In exchange, the federal government received 376,739 acres of isolated state trust lands in the Grand Staircase–Escalante National Monument, as well as the Jacob Hamlin Arch on Lake Powell, the Eye of the Whale Arch in Arches National Park, and rock art in Dinosaur National Monument (Associated Press 1998). Thus, Utah and the United States have a new model for solving future problems of isolated school trust lands in areas that may be designated wilderness.

## ANALYSIS AND IMPLICATIONS FOR THE FUTURE

### Strategies for Compromise: Meeting The Needs of All Parties
The success of the national monument exchange is a hopeful precedent.[2] Additional acreage of trust lands would be affected if larger areas of wilderness are accepted. A great deal is at stake, for reasons which are discussed throughout this book, so the impact on state lands is considerable. Leaving state trust lands in their present status only compounds revenue and management problems. Perhaps a lesson can be learned from the example of Coalition for Utah's Future/Project 2000, which brought people together to exchange ideas and principles, find areas of common interest, and examine options on which agreement could be reached without focusing on the number of acres involved. The pilot project in Emery County in 1995 can serve as a model for ways to find solutions to disputes through inclusive community and interest group participation. Keeping score, and creating winners and losers, must give way to scoring for compromises to solve problems and provide additional revenues to benefit the schools of Utah.

*Incremental Designation with Trust Lands Included*
Finding consensus in legislation that deals with school trust lands in all of Utah may present too many difficulties in finding a "one size that fits all" solution. Blocking up exchanged trust lands in one region for exchanged trust lands located in another region may create political difficulties for county officials in the "losing region." An incremental, regional solution may be appropriate to keep exchanges within each region, and complete each region as local consensus is obtained. This approach may have some advantages that parallel the incremental approach suggested by Governor Leavitt (Brad Barber 1997). If all current proposals fail, this may be the most likely fallback strategy.

*A Trade-Out Forcing Mechanism in Legislation*
In addition to strategies contained in previous legislative attempts to exchange trust lands, there may be a place for a forcing mechanism in wilderness legislation to ensure that trust lands are given priority treatment and not just a promise to be addressed after designation. Otherwise trust lands may remain in wilderness areas for an extended time during negotiations. Unreleased studies have already been done to identify and prepare maps of potential areas for exchange of trust lands traded out of wilderness areas as indicated by the language in H.R. 1745. Future legislation could be more specific as to time and location and require that an exchange take place before legislation becomes effective.

*Management Difficulties of SITLA in Present Arrangements*
Professional managers in SITLA find management of the isolated sections of trust lands very difficult. Hands-on management, such as BLM's Allotment Management Planning (BLM 1995), is not possible for SITLA. As a result they limit their management to the execution of leases, interfacing with federal managers on a problem-by-problem basis, and keeping track of lease funds forwarded by BLM for the trust lands included in allotments. While 81 percent of all the trust lands are permitted for grazing, not all of the trust lands in WSAs are under grazing leases, primarily because of unsuitability and lack of interest by livestock operators who run cattle on nearby BLM lands (SITLA 1996, 12).

*Adverse Impacts of Inaction to Trust Fund Administration*
There is a legitimate concern in Utah for maintaining or increasing the revenues from trust lands to benefit school children. Many people, including Governor Leavitt, the SITLA Board of Directors, various public officials, and environmental leaders, support the effective management of trust

lands for revenue production. Revenue from grazing on all state trust lands has always been minimal, and it could be impacted even more by wilderness designation (see chapter 9). However, a consolidation of state trust lands could make grazing easier to administer. Also, when trust lands are isolated deep within wilderness areas, access is more difficult for oil, gas, and mineral lessees. These management problems may become more severe if a wilderness bill becomes law without solving the trust lands problems. Thus we may expect that use of trust lands will become even less desirable and the revenue stream from them will diminish. Resolution of the trust land dilemma must be given high priority by all participants in the wilderness debate, particularly the elected officials and public managers.

Inaction must not be used as a strategy in the wilderness chess-match. The proposed land trade and monetary compensation for state lands in the Grand Staircase–Escalante National Monument could serve as a model for resolution of inholding problems in wilderness and other federal lands. The management of isolated trust lands must be made more effective, and action must be taken to make a fair exchange of trust lands for federal lands. Wilderness legislation could also mandate a means to make payments for lands that would bring a fair return to the trusts. Further inaction is not fair or in the best interests of Utah schoolchildren.

## ₵ NOTES TO CHAPTER 8

1. Editors' note: Conoco was granted permission for exploratory drilling, using an existing road and drill pad. The results were disappointing to the company. More recently another company, 3-R Minerals, received permission to explore for minerals on school trust lands within the new monument. Their permit was approved just prior to the implementation of the land exchange legislation. See the *Salt Lake Tribune,* November 8, 1998, C7.

2. This was not the first success in regard to land exchanges outside of WSAs. In September 1997, a trade was negotiated for 120 acres of trust land near St. George in exchange for 200 acres of land in Summit and Salt Lake counties (*Deseret News,* September 13, 1997).

## ₵ REFERENCES TO CHAPTER 8

Allison, Lee. 1997. Director, Utah Geological Survey. Personal communication.

Arizona State Lands Administration. 1992. Personal communication with administrator.

Associated Press. 1998. "A Great Day All Around as Clinton Signs Massive Utah Land-Swap Deal," *Salt Lake Tribune,* October 31.

Babbitt, Bruce. 1997. Secretary of the Interior. Quote from an interview with Ted Koppel on NBC Television, May 15.

Bachtell, Thomas. 1997. Remarks made at the 2nd Annual Wallace Stegner Symposium. University of Utah, College of Law. May 15.

Barber, Brad, Governor's Office of Planning and Budget. 1997. State of Utah. Personal communication, May 6.

Bassett, Kedric A. 1989. Utah's school trust lands: dilemma in land use management & the possible effect on Utah's trust land management act. *Journal of Energy Law and Policy* 9 (2).

Bernick, Bob, 1998. "Land Swap Changing Way Trust Does Business," *Deseret News*, June 19.

Bird, Margaret. 1997. Member of Advisory Board, Utah Office of Education. Personal communication.

BLM (Bureau of Land Management of the U.S. Department of the Interior). 1995. H-8550.1. *Interim Management Policy and Guidelines for Lands Under Wilderness Review*. Supersedes Handbook 8550.1. November 10, 1987.

BLM Utah (Utah State Office, Bureau of Land Management of the U.S. Department of the Interior). 1990. *Utah BLM Statewide Wilderness Final Environmental Impact Statement*, vol. I. Overview. Washington, DC.

Bowles, Patricia. 1997. Economist, State Office of Education. Personal communication.

Callister, Deborah. 1997. Former wilderness issues coordinator of the Coalition for Utah's Future/Project 2000. Personal communication.

Coalition for Utah's Future/Project 2000. 1995. *Community and Wild Lands Futures, a Pilot Project in Emery County, Utah.*

Davidson, Lee. 1998. "House Oks Utah's Land-Swap Deal," *Deseret News*, June 24.

*Deseret News.* 1997. "Have Utah and Feds Found Peace at Last?" September 13, B1.

Donner, Peter. 1997. *1966–96 Population estimates for Utah.* Utah Economic and Business Review. David Eccles School of Business, Bureau of Economic and Business Research, University of Utah.

Fairfax, Sally, and Carolyn E. Yale. 1987. *Federal Lands.* Washington, DC: Island Press.

Fairfax, Sally, Jon A. Souder, and Gretta Goldenmann. 1992. School trust lands: a fresh look at conventional wisdom. *Environmental Law* 22 (3).

Freemeyer, Allen. 1997. Staff Director, Committee on Energy, Lands and Resources, U.S. Congress, House. Personal communication.

Groene, Scott. 1997. Issues Director of the Southern Utah Wilderness Alliance. Personal communication.

Jahanbani, F. R. 1996. *1995 Annual Review and Forecast of Utah Coal Production and Distribution.* State of Utah, Natural Resources, Office of Energy and Resource Planning.

Keith, John E., Christopher Fawson, and Van Johnson. 1996. "Wilderness Designation in Utah: Urban and Rural Willingness to Pay." Paper presented at Western Regional Science Meetings, Napa, CA.

*Lassen v. Arizona Highway Department.* 1967. 385 U.S. 458.

Leavitt, Governor Michael. 1997. Comment from television interview on ABC with Ted Koppel, May 15.

LeGate, Lawson. 1997. Sierra Club representative. Personal communication.

Liston, Louise. 1997. Chair, Garfield County Commission, and Member, SITLA Board of Trustees. Personal communication.

Matheson, Scott M., and Ralph E. Becker. 1988. *Improving Public Land Management Through Land Exchange: Opportunities and Pitfalls of the Utah Experience.* Rocky Mountain Mineral Law Institute, 33.

*National Parks and Conservation Association v. Board of State Lands.* 1993. 215 Utah Adv. Rep. 21.

Rawson, Eldred Blaine. 1994. Economic values take top priority on Utah's trust lands. *Journal of Energy, Natural Resources and Environment* 14 (1): 231–42.

*Salt Lake Tribune.* 1998. November 8, C7.

SITLA (State of Utah, Utah School and Institutional Trust Lands Administration). 1995. *First Annual Report.* State of Utah.

———. 1996. *Second Annual Report.* State of Utah.

———. 1997. Policy Statement 97-04, Cause No. 1. Subject: Grand Staircase Escalante, January 16.

Snyder, Donald L., et al. 1995. *Wilderness Designation in Utah: Issues and Potential Economic Impacts.* Logan, UT: Utah Agricultural Experiment Station, Utah State University.

Souder, Jon A., and Sally K. Fairfax. 1996. *State Trust Lands: History, Management and Sustainable Uses.* Lawrence: University Press of Kansas.

Spangler, Jerry. 1998. "Historic Land Deal with U.S. Hailed as Huge Win for Utah," *Deseret News,* May 9.

U.S. Congress. 1964. *The Wilderness Act of 1964.* P.L. 88-577. Washington, DC.

———. 1992. *Utah Land Exchange Legislation.* Hearing before the Subcommittee on National Parks and Public Lands, Committee on Interior and Insular Affairs, House of Representatives. Serial No. 102–97.

———. 1998. *Utah Schools and Land Exchange Act of 1998.* P.L. 105-335, 112 Stat. 3139, October 31.

Utah Department of Natural Resources and Energy. 1985. *Project BOLD Proposal for Utah Land Consolidation and Exchange.* Prepared by the Utah State Lands and Forestry Division, Salt Lake City, UT.

*Utah Enabling Act.* 1894. Enabling Act between the United States of America and the State of Utah.

Utah Public Lands Multiple-Use Coalition and Utah Farm Bureau Federation. N.d. *Ten Wilderness Issues.*

Utah State Constitution. 1895. Utah State Constitution, Article X. State of Utah Archives.

*Utah v. Andrus.* 1979. 486 F. Supp. 995 (D. Utah 1979).

Utah Wilderness Association. N.d. *Defend the Desert, Wilderness Proposals for Utah's BLM Lands.* Brochure published by UWA.

Walsh, Mark. 1997. Executive Director, Utah Association of Counties. Personal communication.

Washington News Bureau. 1998. "Hatch Introduces Bill to Formalize State Trust Lands Exchange," *Deseret News,* June 10.

Woolf, Jim. 1997a. "Conoco Wants to Drill for Oil in Escalante Monument," *Salt Lake Tribune,* February 12, A2.

———. 1997b. "Monument Site Isn't Unique Say Backers of Oil Drilling," *Salt Lake Tribune,* April 23, A4.

———. 1997c. "Kaiparowits Coal Is Poor-Quality, BLM Report Says," *Salt Lake Tribune,* May 14, B2.

# CHAPTER 9

# Beef and Backpackers

*Grazing in Wilderness*

Christopher Krueger

Christian Senf

Janelle Eurick

## CONFLICTING PARADIGMS

It is difficult to overstate the contentiousness of the language used by wilderness advocates and their multiple-use adversaries with regard to grazing—and strange, perhaps, that they are "adversaries" at all. Livestock grazing is guaranteed by many statutes as a protected economic activity in designated wilderness areas. However, the legal status of grazing does nothing to prevent the perception—by many wilderness advocates—that livestock destroy the aesthetic and "natural" qualities of wilderness. On the opposite side, a strong undercurrent of fear now permeates Utah ranching communities. They perceive that regulations and limitations, which can only increase with wilderness designation, will end their generations-old way of life. Contributing to the rancor of the debate is the ambiguity of laws and customs derived from a 150-year tradition of grazing on public lands.

At the heart of this debate lies a fundamental difference of opinion on the value of land. Ranchers maintain that the value of land is found in its utilization. The ranching community believes that well-managed grazing enhances the land's value. Wilderness advocates find inherent value in the landscape that is best preserved by limiting impacts. They see wilderness grazing as unnecessarily intrusive and degrading. This incompatibility of paradigms creates a difficult starting point for compromise.

Historically, America defined its land by use. Rangeland existed solely to provide forage for livestock and income for the rancher.[1] The advent of range science and the later passage of multiple-use laws promulgated a second definition, based on multiple use, which values the land in terms of biological, economic, and recreational resources (Heady and Child 1994, 2). This modern definition conforms to the multiple-use definition of FLPMA, and is used by professional range managers. Therefore, it will be the one used in this chapter.

With this definition in mind, we can examine the conflict between BLM policy, wilderness advocates, and traditional ranching interests. We will begin by briefly tracing the long history of public-lands grazing.

## GRAZING HISTORY

Grazing has long held an important and influential position on western lands. Even before these lands were officially acquired by purchase or force from Mexico and indigenous peoples, ranchers were moving cattle and sheep onto them. It was, by most accounts, a stockman's dream. Ranchers had little incentive to buy full title to the land; they usually owned small plots of private land near water, which made grazing possible, and had unlimited access to surrounding grazing lands. There were no regulations, and little competition for the bountiful forage.

The first attempts at livestock management were initiated by the Forest Service in 1906. In 1934, the Taylor Grazing Act created the Grazing Service, an independent agency within the Department of the Interior, which adopted regulations similar to those of the Forest Service. In 1946, the Grazing Service and the General Land Office were combined to create the Bureau of Land Management. The BLM was given the responsibility of managing all remaining "unreserved" public lands.

Grazing was permitted in the first BLM-administered wilderness areas despite limited attempts to banish livestock. The grazing lobbies were powerful. Western Senators—who served on the public-lands-related committees—were quite sympathetic. Many wilderness advocates, like Aldo Leopold, were tolerant and even supportive of cattle and sheep on wilderness lands. They did not see, as many in the ranching and environmental communities do today, an inherent conflict between the two uses. As Congress moved toward creating statutory wilderness in the late 1950s and early 1960s, the grazing and wilderness advocacy groups lobbied for and against wilderness grazing privileges. Proposals filtered through the lawmaking process, and the few legislators who opposed grazing finally consented to allow livestock in wilderness (McClaran 1990, 864–65). Grazing privileges were included in the 1964 bill that became law.

This uneasy alliance between wilderness advocates and grazing interests has faltered with recent attempts to remove livestock from all public lands, and from wilderness in particular. Ranching interests have resisted recent congressional and administrative interventions by exerting influence through western members of Congress, the BLM, and the Forest Service. Ranching interests argue that enough mechanisms exist to ensure healthy range for a variety of uses (Kinsel 1997). Livestock grazing continues to have far-reaching implications for the wilderness designation process.

When evaluating lands for inclusion into the Wilderness System, the BLM and Forest Service consider the existence of grazing permits and range improvements when designating a WSA and making wilderness recommendations to Congress. Although the BLM acknowledges that the existence of a valid grazing permit does not automatically exclude a WSA from inclusion into the National Wilderness Preservation System (NWPS), it certainly factors the existence of a permit into the final decision. If existing rights will "probably result in activities that destroy the wilderness, the BLM will exclude the affected area from recommendation for wilderness designation" (Haugrud 1985, 52). In question is the degree, if any, to which livestock alter the landscape and diminish statutory wilderness characteristics. Thus, the permit system that controls the extent of wilderness grazing privileges is at the forefront of the debate.

*THE GRAZING SYSTEM TODAY*

As drafted in 1906, and amended through statutes and administrative law many times, the permit systems of the Forest Service and BLM have become a complex and controversial method of utilizing the forage on public lands for economic production.

The permit system is a comprehensive plan that affects some 270 million acres of Forest Service and BLM land. Each Forest Service or BLM district is subdivided into a number of independently managed allotments. The agencies then "rent" the land out to the permittees (the individual ranchers) by requiring a use fee. On each allotment, the individual permittee is granted exclusive grazing use. The permittee almost always owns land and water rights adjacent to or within these allotments.

To calculate the grazing fee, both agencies now count each cow as one animal, and each sheep as a fifth of an animal. Permittees pay for each month they graze each animal on public lands. This is an Animal Unit Month (AUM). Western ranchers currently pay the federal government $1.35 per AUM. Grazing fees on private land, however, average $11.20 per AUM, and in some cases are considerably higher. Environmentalists contend the current federal grazing fee promotes overgrazing and degradation of the public land while allowing ranchers to sublease public lands for high profits (Gregg and Bumpers 1996). Ranchers argue that the actual cost of grazing public lands is considerably higher given the costs of necessary range improvements and the need to comply with numerous regulations. And, ranchers say, these costs may be even higher in wilderness areas. In contrast, private land leases generally include improvements, water, feed, and other essentials.

As part of their management plans, the Forest Service and the BLM have compiled and implemented a series of regulations to reduce damage to the land. Ranchers such as A. C. Ekker, whose grazing allotments contain several WSAs, maintain that the regulations within WSAs adversely impact their operations (Utah Wilderness Education Project 1995). The most important of these regulations is the number of AUMs. In the past, however, limiting AUMs was an ineffective means of regulation; until very recently, the permittees were granted as many AUMs as they requested (Wilkinson 1992, 111).

In addition to regulating AUMs, other federal and state agencies exist to control livestock losses to wild predators on both private and public lands. In Utah, predator control is carried out by the Animal and Plant Health Inspection Service–Animal Damage Control (APHIS-ADC), a division of the United States Department of Agriculture.[2] The ADC is authorized to find the best methods of controlling or suppressing predacious animal populations for the protection of livestock or other domestic animals (Animal Damage Control Act 1931, 426). Operating freely before the 1960s, the agency's involvement on public lands has since been restricted by several statutes, notably the National Environmental Protection Act (NEPA) and the Endangered Species Act (ESA).

## WILDERNESS IMPACTS

BLM and Forest Service range managers must evaluate the cumulative effects that shape the landscape. The implication that physical effects are by definition *damaging* is erroneous, as all animals—including humans—impact the land to some degree. Although the landscape is resilient and compensating factors may quickly mitigate physical effects, permanent changes in rangeland may result from animal impacts (Heady and Child 1994, 68–69).

Such permanent changes have profound implications for wilderness management, which strives to maintain the "primeval character and influence, without permanent improvements . . . which is protected and managed so as to preserve its natural conditions and which generally appears to have been affected primarily by the forces of nature. . ." (Wilderness

Act 1964, Sec. 2[c]). The tendency of livestock to transform the landscape seems—to environmental groups—fundamentally at odds with this definition. This incongruence is a principal argument of wilderness advocates, who worry about introduced species, soil degradation, riparian damage, and predator control. However, this "primeval character" definition is dismissed by ranching interests. Wilderness grazing advocates point to Section 4(d)(4)(2) of the Wilderness Act and the subsequent congressional interpretations that uphold livestock grazing as an important component of wilderness management (Utah Wilderness Education Project 1995). The ambiguous wording of the Act has confounded both the grazing and wilderness lobbies.

During the severe overgrazing of the late nineteenth and early twentieth centuries, native perennial grasses were eliminated and replaced by exotic or shallow-rooted vegetation types (Westbrooks 1993). Welsh et al. identify 310 plant species (not all considered weeds) that have been introduced into Utah alone (Heady and Child 1994, 302). Many of these non-indigenous plants threaten the biodiversity of natural areas and degrade the production of agricultural lands. A U.S. Office of Technology Assessment report documents losses of $97 billion caused by seventy-nine non-indigenous invasive species in the United States between 1909 and 1991 (Westbrooks 1993).

Environmentalists maintain that livestock are a primary contributor to soil degradation in arid landscapes. Arid land soils are more susceptible to degradation than soils found in humid environments. This is especially evident with cryptobiotic or cryptogamic soils (Murray 1997). Cryptogamic soils are very sensitive to physical impacts such as trampling, and grazed soils can have less than one-third the cryptogamic biomass of similar undisturbed soils. Extensive trampling by grazing livestock is also a primary cause of soil compaction. Soil compaction increases surface water flows and enhances susceptibility to erosion. Temperate arid and semi-arid precipitation events tend to be sudden and severe, further compounding erosion. The increased runoff erodes stream banks and cuts down streambeds, lowering water tables and drying out many intermittent and perennial streams that native species depend on (Chaney, Elmore, and Platts 1993). One study conducted in western Colorado found that grazed watersheds produce up to 76 percent more sediment than ungrazed areas (Murray 1997). Recovery from compaction and decreased soil stability may take several hundred years (Belnap 1995, 39).

Cattle are not the only cause of soil compaction and desertification, however. Substantial increases in off-road vehicle use and hiking have greatly increased human impact on desert ecosystems. The increased recreational use of these sensitive arid and semi-arid ecosystems has compounded the degradation initiated by overgrazing. This combination of uses has resulted in accelerating desertification processes (Belnap 1995, 39).

Trampling may have some desirable effect as well. The trampling action of livestock can break hardened soil crusts and help cover seeds. Livestock trampling reduces large accumulations of mulch and litter by stirring plant materials into the soil, thereby returning nutrients to the soil and hastening decomposition of dead material (Heady and Child 1994, 67). Livestock can also be used to disperse forage plants. By feeding livestock hay with desirable seeds attached, the animals can be used to reseed heavily impacted areas (Heady and Child 1994, 103). This passive transport technique must be used selectively, as undesirable species may be unintentionally introduced. Environmentalists contend that the introduction of non-indigenous species at the turn of the century was catalyzed by the importation of seeds carried by cattle (Murray 1997).

Of all potential impacts, however, the most contentious is the degradation of riparian areas. The riparian area is the single most important component of an arid land ecosystem. Although riparian zones comprise only 1 percent of the area of the western United States, they provide habitat for more species of birds than all western rangelands combined. In the Great Basin of southeastern Oregon, fully 75 percent of all wildlife species depend on riparian habitats (Chaney, Elmore, and Platts 1993). A healthy riparian zone possesses a tremendous variety of vegetation that serves to limit flood flows, stabilize stream channels, filter nutrients, protect soils, and form productive wet meadows and flood plains. A favorable micro-climate, the presence of water, and lush vegetation make these areas extremely attractive to domestic cattle as well as wildlife (Clary and Webster 1989, 209). Documentation shows that cattle may spend five to thirty times more of their lives in a riparian zone as opposed to an adjacent upland region, depending on the size and extent of the riparian area (Clary and Webster 1989, 7).

The complexity of riparian ecosystems adds to the difficulty of assessing impacts. Their ecological function is not completely understood, and the only point generally accepted by all range managers is that overuse has contributed to their "deterioration" (e.g., loss of native species, sedimentation of streams). Overgrazing is unquestionably responsible for the deterioration of some riparian areas, but increased recreational use, wildfires, and poorly planned roadways all contribute to the degradation of stream channels (Heady and Child 1994, 453). Many range managers argue that riparian areas can be safely grazed with proper management of all potentially degrading activities. Management strategies that include mechanical structures or intensive monitoring might conflict with other wilderness values, however. Furthermore, no single grazing management system has conclusively demonstrated sustained improvement for all riparian zones (Clary and Webster 1989, 2).

Although riparian areas are among the most resilient ecosystems in our arid lands, extensive field observations conducted by the U.S. Department of Agriculture in the late 1980s confirmed that western riparian areas are in their most degraded state in history (Chaney, Elmore, and Platts 1993). Utah's WSAs contain 23,775 acres of this invaluable commodity (BLM Utah 1990, 114).

Another significant impact of grazing operations involves predator control. ADC usually follows one of two strategies. The first, preventive control, is designed to prevent attacks on livestock before they happen. The underlying premise is that there is a correlation between the density of the coyote population and the rate of animal losses. Thus, if coyote numbers are reduced, the loss rate is reduced (Wagner 1988). The second strategy, called corrective control, is used in cases when ranchers have confirmed a kill by a certain animal and the offending animal is taken either by ADC agents or state specialists. This management strategy is used to stop or reduce current losses (Wagner 1988).

The Animal Damage Control Program in Utah uses several different methods to remove offending animals from private, public, and federal lands. The most effective methods are aerial hunting and M-44 cyanide devices. ADC agents can fly over an area, target predators, and shoot them from an aircraft with relative accuracy. M-44 cyanide devices kill predators, usually coyotes, with poisoned bait. Spring-activated foot snares are also commonly used by ADC officials when black bear and cougar problems arise. Another, more controversial method of predator control is denning, which involves ADC officials destroying young animals during the denning season by releasing a fumigant cartridge into the den and asphyxiating the young. This method is used on USFS and BLM lands where livestock killing can be attributed to food gathering by predators to feed their young (State of Utah 1997). Ground shooting is associated with target species and can involve the use of spotlights, decoy dogs, and predator calling. A final method is the livestock protection collar. This device, fitting under the throat of an animal, is designed to inject a lethal dose of sodium fluoroacetate into the mouth of an attacking coyote as it bites its prey in the throat region (State of Utah 1997, 1).

In Utah, the main predation problem associated with livestock growers is the coyote, but cougars and bears also pose a risk to ranchers. Although preventive hunting of coyotes commonly involves M-44 and aerial shooting, cougars and bears are state-protected predators and are taken only after their kills have been confirmed, which "ensures only offending animals are taken" (State of Utah 1997).

Animal control has come under a great deal of criticism from the environmental community, however, as a particularly significant nonconforming use of wilderness. Interactions among competitors, including predator and prey relationships, are important parts of natural ecosystems. Environmentalists believe predators should be free from human interference. The BLM also recognizes the importance of predators to ecological processes by stating that predacious animals "play an important role in the natural selection and survival processes, helping to maintain critical population balances of wild species" (BLM Utah 1990, 34).

## THE REGULATIONS BATTLE

During the 1970s, the Forest Service and BLM drafted Resource Management Plans (RMPs) in accordance with FLPMA. In some locations, grazing was phased out (Snyder and Godfrey 1991, 297–98). However, agencies maintain that these cutbacks were made to protect the land's resources[3] and not because of wilderness designation. However, some in the livestock industry noted that there seemed to be a disproportionate number of cuts made on WSAs or wilderness areas (Gerber 1997). Grazing advocates suggest that the BLM's manageability criterion has been used to discourage grazing in potential wilderness.

Both the BLM and Forest Service have also been criticized by wilderness advocates for WSA recommendations when such lands contain pre-designation uses, such as fences and motorized vehicle access, that appear to conflict with the statutory wilderness characteristics. The manageability criterion says "to find a WSA is manageable, the BLM must be reasonably certain the entire area can be managed in the long term to preserve its wilderness characteristics, based upon present knowledge of the WSAs resources and private development rights" (Haugrud 1985, 50). If an area does not meet this criterion, it is removed from consideration. Environmentalists contend that private rights should not be the only consideration for manageability, as Congress can annul private rights if it is in the public interest and due compensation is awarded (Haugrud 1985, 51–52). Satisfying the manageability criterion is perhaps the most difficult step for permanently protecting a WSA, as it is perceived as inadequate by both ranchers and the wilderness advocates.

Additional controversy is generated once an area *has* been set aside as a WSA or statutorily designated a wilderness. The broad language of the

Wilderness Act was intended to allow range managers a great degree of latitude in making decisions allowing for the maintenance of existing structures *and* construction of new improvements. The great diversity of lands that livestock graze within wilderness requires a degree of sight-specific interpretation and decision making that is incompatible with all-encompassing statutory regulations. But the varying and sometimes conflicting interpretations have led to pronouncements that "are simply not in accordance with section 4(d)(4)(2) of the Wilderness Act" (U.S. Congress 1978). Due to these inconsistent interpretations, grazing permittees demanded that Congress clarify the intentions of 4(d)(4)(2) (U.S. Congress 1978).

In response to these criticisms, Congress issued a report that attempted to clarify the intent and purpose of the Wilderness Act as it pertains to grazing (U.S. Congress 1978). Subsequently, special language to this effect has been incorporated into all wilderness legislation to ensure that congressional dictates concerning wilderness are followed irrespective of agency jurisdiction. These congressional guidelines were made available to all personnel responsible for administering grazing in wilderness to ensure that the intent of Congress was understood and implemented.

Additionally, Reports 95-620 and 95-1321, issued by the House Committee on Interior and Insular Affairs, specifically address the perceived resistance the U.S. Forest Service has toward maintaining wilderness grazing. These two reports provide guidance on how Section 4(d)(4)(2) of the Wilderness Act should be interpreted. The reports reiterate that grazing in wilderness areas

> . . . will be controlled under the general regulations governing the grazing of livestock on National Forests. . . . This includes the establishment of normal range allotments and allotment management plans. Furthermore, wilderness designation should not prevent the maintenance of existing fences or other livestock management improvements, nor the construction and maintenance of new fences and improvements which are consistent with allotment management plans and/or which are necessary for the protection of the range. (U.S. Congress 1977)

The conferees explicitly stated, "The maintenance of supporting facilities, existing in an area prior to its classification as wilderness (including fences, line cabins, water wells and lines, stock tanks, etc.) is permissible in wilderness" (U.S. Congress 1978). Finally, the conferees also maintain that AUMs on wilderness areas can be increased if no adverse impacts on wilderness values are anticipated (BLM Utah 1990).

Statutory implementation of H.R. 96-1126 in the various wilderness bills of the 1980s and 1990s has yielded detailed guidelines for managing grazing on wilderness lands. They attempt to protect simultaneously both the permittee and the wilderness values of the land. First, they explicitly state that the AUMs on the land shall not be affected solely by wilderness designation, but instead shall rest on the allotment management plan (U.S. Department of Agriculture 1981), which is determined by carrying capacity. Second, management of various range improvements is determined by a combination of economic hardship on the permittee and damage to wilderness values. For instance, the regulations call for consideration of "minimal threat to or loss of property" and "achievement of least amount of impact by non-conforming uses on wilderness values" (U.S. Department of Agriculture 1981). Regarding transportation, these regulations require range managers to consider such factors as the cost and availability of primitive (and hence conforming) transport when deciding whether to allow motorized access.

Both the BLM and Forest Service guidelines still leave a great deal of discretion to individual range managers. Consider the issue of water catchments—small reservoirs built by permittees—that serve as watering holes for roaming stock. The BLM regulations permit the existence of such basins if they existed prior to 1976 (BLM 1983).[4] In addition, the regulations even permit the construction of new basins. "New, permanent developments will be allowed," provided they do not "cause unnecessary degradation of the lands," including changes in "the visual condition of the lands and waters . . . [and] all wilderness values" (BLM 1983, 8560.37). However, it is still the subjective interpretation of the land manager as to what constitutes an "unnecessary degradation."

Exacerbating this situation are the limited staffing and budgetary constraints that prevent the agencies from accurately monitoring allotments. Range managers simply do not have the resources to consistently and effectively monitor allotments. In a May 1991 report, the General Accounting Office confirmed that three out of four Forest Service allotments were not being monitored despite having had 24 percent of all western allotments classified as overstocked and/or in declining condition. Forest Service officials noted that district offices do little monitoring and do not centrally report on the monitoring that is accomplished. Due to this lack of consistent monitoring, the report concludes by warning that problem allotments can be expected to remain in unsatisfactory condition or decline further (U.S. General Accounting Office 1991, 2–5).

Predator control in wilderness areas and WSAs is also regulated more stringently than on non-wilderness BLM lands. Predator control is allowed only when the activity is directed at a single offending animal, will not diminish the wilderness values of the WSA, and will not jeopardize the survival of other species in the area. The BLM allows for predator control in Wilderness Areas when threatened or endangered species are at risk, or on a case-by-case basis to prevent serious losses of domestic livestock. When predator control is necessary, the methods used must present the least possible hazard to other animals and wilderness visitors. For this reason, M-44 cyanide ejectors, poison collars, and poison-baited traps are not allowed. The state BLM Director must approve all other predator control actions by ADC, including aerial hunting, to ensure minimum disturbance to the wilderness and its visitors (BLM Utah 1990).

In 1986–87, the BLM documented predator control activities in grazing allotments that compromise sixteen of the eighty-three BLM WSAs. They estimated that 523 coyotes, eight foxes, and one bobcat were removed. However, only a portion of the predators were actually taken inside WSAs (BLM Utah 1990). The recent Animal Damage Control environmental assessment for the Southern Utah ADC district recognizes seven WSAs and one wilderness area that currently contain grazing allotments where predator control has taken place. The Northern Utah ADC environmental assessment recognizes no WSAs or wilderness areas that currently have wildlife damage management.

## IMPACTS ON THE GRAZING INDUSTRY

There is considerable resistance to wilderness designation within the Utah ranching community, demonstrated by the Utah Cattlemen's Association, which opposes "any further wilderness designation" because "the major use of western public lands is livestock grazing" (Esplin 1991). Both "neutral" observers and some wilderness activists agree that wilderness designation will affect existing operations. The debate centers on the degree of impact.[5]

The *BLM Statewide Wilderness Final Environmental Impact Statement* notes that approximately 339 livestock operators use an estimated 95,344 AUMs of forage in BLM WSAs. This represents just 3 percent of the total number of livestock operators in Utah utilizing 5 percent of the total AUMs allocated on Utah's public lands. Furthermore, the Final EIS also notes that the WSA portion of many grazing allotments is unsuitable or marginally suitable at best for livestock grazing due to rough terrain and a relative absence of vegetation and water. In total, WSAs contain approximately 1 percent of the estimated livestock forage utilized in the state.

Although WSAs account for a small percentage of total available livestock forage, there is no doubt wilderness designation would adversely affect some livestock operators. Booth Wallentine of the Utah Farm Bureau notes that "wilderness adversely impacts livestock producers, and whatever harms the livestock industry hurts rural economies" (Wallentine 1995). The number of operators affected seems relatively small. According to the BLM, most permittees do not depend on allotments within WSAs for the bulk of their AUMs (BLM Utah 1990, 142). At most, four hundred jobs could be affected by complete elimination of grazing privileges in WSAs. In a separate study, the Utah State Office of Planning and Budget, in its negative-impact scenario, suggests that a maximum of forty-two jobs would be lost assuming all 3.2 million acres of WSAs were designated and all grazing was eliminated on those lands (Utah Office of Planning and Budget 1991, 11). These seemingly insignificant numbers belie the fact that even in rural communities, the loss of even a few jobs could have significant impact.

As implied above, the extent to which wilderness designation affects livestock numbers is hotly debated. Many permittees believe that increasing regulations will make it economically impossible for them to continue profitable operations. Regulation of catchment basins has been a particularly sore issue among many permittees (Lane 1997). These basins are necessary to maintain stock, since the arid lands of the West necessitate supplemental watering. The basins are closely monitored by the federal agencies that manage the allotments on both WSAs and wilderness areas. The BLM maintains that the impact with regard to these basins has been minimal.

Motorized access is another source of considerable controversy. Many permittees are concerned that motorized access will be seriously curtailed by the more stringent access regulations on wilderness land (Thayn 1997). Individual instances of overzealous range managers have been recounted by grazing advocates. They include managers who would not allow trucks to transport salt, supplemental feed, equipment, or sick cattle to and from their allotment on wilderness land (Tanner 1997). Such instances only serve to create more suspicion on the part of ranchers, who fear that costs will increase to the point that they will be driven off their allotments, thus ending their way of life.

Many in the livestock industry also fear that wilderness designation will interfere with their ability to protect their stock from predation. According to ADC statistics for Utah in 1996, Utah wool growers lose about 10 percent of their animals each year to predators. Cattlemen suffer fewer, albeit still costly, losses to predators. Livestock losses to predators in Utah totaled approximately $2.3 million, even with a control program in place (State of Utah 1997). Livestock groups are fearful that further restrictions will increase losses and make ranching unprofitable. Environmental groups counter that it is the ADC itself that is unprofitable. According to Tom Skeele, director of the Montana-based Predator Project, ADC has

> yet to accomplish its goal of reducing livestock losses to a level where the
> rancher no longer complains. If it were an effective program, it would no

longer be needed. In 1994, the ADC spent over $19 million dollars in 17 west-ern states. Although federal appropriations accounted for 51% of this budget, the ADC received additional funding from state and county taxes as well as private donations. Ranchers do not have to pay directly for ADC service, nor are they required to change their management practices to try and minimize the need for ADC control work. For this reason, many fiscal conservatives, including Karl Hess with the Cato Institute, and Eric Stzepek with the Competitive Enterprise Institute, argue that the ADC amounts to a federal subsidy for ranchers that has outlived its usefulness. (Albert 1997)

Still, many ranchers feel that ADC control work is absolutely neces-sary, and would be hampered by wilderness designation.

Although both Section 4(d)(4)(2) of the 1964 Wilderness Act and Section 603(c) of FLPMA allow for continued livestock grazing where grazing is established prior to wilderness designation, some ranchers believe that a *de facto* elimination of grazing privileges is inevitable. Most rural county governments, whose economies may be heavily dependent on ranching federal land, were very clear in their opposition to the 1990 1.9-million-acre proposal, citing the potential loss of AUMs as a cause (Juab County 1990; Garfield County 1990).

The reality of wilderness impacts on individual permittees is difficult to quantify. Forest Service records reveal that there was no decrease in permit-ted livestock in Forest Service wilderness areas due to wilderness manage-ment practices (BLM Utah 1990). A study conducted by the New Mexico Department of Agriculture found similar results. This study surveyed the 170 permittees who graze existing wilderness allotments in New Mexico for their attitudes concerning wilderness. Of the 87 percent who responded, 46 percent said wilderness designation had not affected their ranch operations, 17 percent cited benefits to their operations, and 37 percent said wilderness designation had been detrimental. Most respondents indicated that wilder-ness designation had improved their quality of life, but even those who opposed designation indicated that wilderness would be acceptable if spe-cific problems were addressed, i.e., restrictions on improvements or range access (New Mexico Department of Agriculture 1990).

*CONCLUSION*

Although the intent of Section 4(d)(4)(2) is clear, implementation has been fraught with problems. Much of the difficulty stems from negotiat-ing the federal bureaucracy. The wilderness system is presently adminis-tered by four separate agencies in two different federal departments, making consistent application of congressional guidelines difficult at best. Consistent application of these guidelines would do much to allay the fears of the ranching community. However, vast discretionary powers can be exercised by individual range specialists, and this exacerbates the feeling of helplessness felt by some permittees.

Wilderness designation per se does not require curtailment of grazing operations. Protracted and acrimonious debate could be avoided if ranchers' concerns were included in the designation process. Unless the wilderness advocacy groups tone down their anti-livestock rhetoric, compromise seems unlikely. Perhaps wilderness advocacy groups within Utah could extend an olive branch to ranching interests to facilitate constructive discourse. Ranchers are not inherently anti-wilderness, they simply want their legitimate concerns recognized. The question remains, however, as to whether it is possible to manage grazing in wilderness areas so as to maintain essential wilderness values. The popular conception of wilderness-type lands is often incompatible with the statutory definition of wilderness.

In this chapter we have tried to demonstrate that, although they both have strong feelings for protecting the land, the permittees and wilderness advocacy groups have some distinctly different ideas about what wilderness means. This difference of opinion is exacerbated by the contradictory and ambiguous language of the Wilderness Act and its congressional interpretations. This is the dilemma the BLM has struggled with for twenty-three years.

This dilemma is at least partly responsible for the lack of constructive discourse concerning grazing privileges in potential wilderness lands. Equally culpable, however, is the lack of empathy shown toward the ranching community by wilderness advocates. This inability to breach traditional conceptions of rangeland and wilderness has hampered policy-makers and activists alike.

Change is inevitable, though, as the grazing tradition has run head-long into the newer conception of multiple use of public land. Ever greater numbers of recreationists encroach upon lands once utilized solely by livestock operators. This increased use has fostered concern about the health of public rangelands. Although active range management has greatly improved the once deplorable condition of the range, some argue that even tighter range restrictions are necessary. The growing clout of the recreationist and environmentalist lobbies will continue to encroach upon the economic power and political influence of the Utah rancher. Wilderness groups have a responsibility, nonetheless, to recognize the concerns of such permittees, as their decades-old way of life is perceived to be in jeopardy.

## ℂ  NOTES TO CHAPTER 9

1. Many in both the ranching and environmental communities continue to define rangeland solely as land where livestock graze. Interestingly enough, this relatively simplistic definition of rangeland is accepted by both ardent supporters and detractors of public-rangelands grazing (Heady and Child 1994).

2. Animal Damage Control recently changed its name to the more innocuous-sounding Wildlife Services.

3. For example, cutbacks occurred in the Woodenshoe Canyon, part of the USFS Dark Canyon Wilderness Area (Forrest 1997), and in the Bridger Wilderness Area in Wyoming (Hatch 1997).

4. Maintenance of such existing facilities is also regulated, and even where it is grandfathered, the BLM has been known to use such regulations to restrict motorized access to such basins.

5. Indeed, a few environmental groups see wilderness designation as a practical way to drive all the cattle off the land. They freely admit that increasing regulations on wilderness land will confirm ranchers' worst fears and "regulate them off the land." See, for instance, Forest Guardians, a New Mexico/Arizona group dedicated to removing livestock from public lands, at http://www.guardians.org/.

## ℂ  REFERENCES TO CHAPTER 9

Albert, Lisa. 1997. "Group calls for Retirement of Federal Predator Control Program" downloaded from www.wildrockies.org/Tango/PredProj.

*Animal Damage Control Act of March 2, 1931.* 46 Stat. 1468: 7 USC 426–426c, as amended.

Belnap, Jayne. 1995. Surface disturbances: their role in accelerating desertification. *Environmental Monitoring and Assessment,* 39–57.

BLM (Bureau of Land Management of the U.S. Department of the Interior). 1983. "Management of Designated Wilderness Lands." Document No. 8560, released August 22.

BLM Utah (Utah State Office, Bureau of Land Management of the U.S. Department of the Interior). 1990. *Utah BLM Statewide Wilderness Final Environmental Impact Statement.* Salt Lake City, UT: Utah State Office, BLM.

Chaney, E., W. Elmore, and W. S. Platts. 1993. "Livestock Grazing On Western Riparian Areas." Washington, DC: U.S. Environmental Protection Agency.

Clary, Warren P., and Bert F. Webster. 1989. *Managing Grazing of Riparian Areas in the Intermountain Region.* General Technical Report INT-263. USDA.

———. 1990. Riparian grazing guidelines for the intermountain region. *Rangelands* 12 (4): 209.

Esplin, Donald. 1991. Letter to Rep. James Hansen, May 24.

Forrest, Jimmy. 1997. Range Management Specialist, Monticello Ranger District UT, USFS. Telephone interview by authors, July 10.

Garfield County, Utah. 1990. Wilderness recommendations: A report issued to the governor's task force on wilderness designation.

Gerber, Grant. 1997. Chairman of the wilderness impact research center, Elko, NV. Telephone interview by authors, May 5.

Gregg, J., and Dale Bumpers. 1996. "Gravy Train for Corporate Cowboys," *Washington Times*, August 18, B3.

Hatch, Jeff. 1997. Range Management Specialist, Pinedale Ranger District, WY, USFS. Telephone interview by authors, May 7.

Haugrud, Jack K. 1985. *Wilderness Preservation: A Guide to Wilderness Selection on the BLM Lands*. Stanford: Stanford Environmental Law Society.

Heady, Harold F., and Dennis R. Child. 1994. *Rangeland Ecology and Management*. Boulder, CO: Westview Press.

Juab County, Utah. 1990. Wilderness recommendations: A report issued to the governor's task force on wilderness designation.

Kinsel, Sheldon. 1997. Consultant to the Utah Farm Bureau. Telephone interview by authors, April 4.

Lane, Doc. 1997. Chairman, Arizona Cattle Growers Association. Telephone interview by authors, May 1.

McClaran, M. P. 1990. Livestock in wilderness: A review and forecast. *Journal of Environmental Law* 20: 857–89.

———. 1991. Forest service and livestock permittee behavior in relation to wilderness designation. *Journal of Range Management* 44 (September).

Murray, Bruce. 1997. "Rangeland Changes in the Arid and Semi-Arid United States: The Need For Affordable Remote Monitoring." Downloaded from okin@arms.gps.caltech.edu.

New Mexico Department of Agriculture. 1990. The Wilderness Experience: New Mexico Ranchers on National Forest Wilderness. Special Report No. 7. Las Cruces, NM.

Rowley, William D. 1985. *United States Forest Service Grazing and Management Policies*. College Station, TX: Texas A&M University Press.

Snyder, Don, and B. E. Godfrey. 1991. "Draft economic analysis of wilderness designation." Unpublished draft report. Utah State University.

State of Utah. Department of Agriculture. 1991. Animal Damage Control. 1991 Environmental Assessment.

———. 1997. Animal Damage Control. 1996 Division Report. Downloaded from www.ag.state.ut.us/divisns/comisnr/97adc.htm.

Tanner, Brent. 1997. Vice-President, Utah Cattlemen's Association. Telephone interview by authors, April 22.

Thayn, Greg. 1997. 1990 EIS Coordinator, Bureau of Land Management, Utah State Office. Telephone interview by authors, April 5.

U.S. Congress. 1980. Conference Report 96-1126. *Grazing in National Forest Wilderness Areas*.

U.S. Congress, House. 1977. Report 620, 95th Cong., 1st sess.

———. 1978. Report 1321, 95th Cong., 2nd sess.

U.S. Department of Agriculture, Forest Service. 1981. *Forest Service Manual*. Title 2300, Sec. 2323.24.

U.S. District Court of Utah. 1993. Civil No. 92-C-0052A, *Southern Utah Wilderness Alliance, et al. v. H. Thompson, et al. Forest Supervisor*. January.

U.S. General Accounting Office. 1991. *Rangeland Management: Forest Service Not Performing Needed Monitoring of Grazing Allotments*. Washington, DC: GAO, GAO/RCED-91-148.

Utah Office of Planning and Budget. 1991. *Economic Analysis of Wilderness Designation in Utah*, Draft Report.

Utah Wilderness Education Project. 1995. Home page http://www.xmission.com/~uwep.html.

Wagner, Frederic H. 1988. *Predator Control and the Sheep Industry*, 70. Claremont, CA: Regina Books.

Wallentine, Booth. 1995. "USU Study Shows Ill Effects of Wilderness," *Deseret News*, April 20, A21.

Westbrooks, Randy G. 1993. *Biological Pollution: A Historical Perspective of Nonindigenous Invasive Plants of Grazing Lands in the United States*. North Carolina: USDA APHIS PPQ, Whiteville Noxious Weed Station. Downloaded from Grazing Lands Forum.

Wilkinson, Charles E. 1992. *Crossing the Next Meridian: Land, Water, and the Future of the West*. Washington, DC: Island Press.

CHAPTER 10

# Divided Highway
*The Politics of the Roadless Debate*

## Christa Powell

## Buck Swaney

*Searching for a definition of "road" is currently no different from uncovering a definition of beauty; both exist only in the eye of the beholder.*
—Representative James Hansen (R-Utah), 1997

## INTRODUCTION

Roadlessness is, and has been, a key criterion in the designation of wilderness on public lands. The roots of the idea that wilderness should be roadless can be traced to many early voices and leaders in the American wilderness debate. John Muir, Aldo Leopold, and Robert Marshall, to name a few of these early leaders, were all primarily concerned with saving wilderness from development, and nothing better exemplified development in their minds than roads. They assumed that designating land as wilderness and prohibiting road construction therein would in essence draw a line around it and prevent it from being changed. Wilderness to them would be a *roadless* area where the influence of modern man would remain absent.

Aldo Leopold envisioned wilderness as a "continuous stretch of country preserved in its natural state, open to lawful hunting and fishing, *devoid of roads* [emphasis added] . . . or other works of man" (Leopold 1921, 719). Robert Marshall wrote, "I shall use the word wilderness to denote a region that contains no permanent inhabitants, possesses no possibility of conveyance *by mechanical means* . . . this being that *all roads* [emphasis added], power transportation and settlements are barred" (Marshall 1930, 141). In Marshall's words we find much similarity to the federal agency definitions of wilderness in use today. Wilderness became in the modern American mind a natural environment that symbolized time away from social pressures, stimuli, and diversions, i.e., roads and the mechanized, technological era of modern man. It represents simplicity, and so it is that the primary criterion and seemingly simplest definition of wilderness has become land that remains *roadless*. Nevertheless, as we shall see in this chapter, *roadless* designation is anything but simple. Just as a definition of beauty, solitude, or untrammeled are elusive, so too is a definition of a *road*; it is around this elusive definition that the modern debate centers.

## THE HISTORY OF ROADLESS POLICY

The issue of roads on public lands can be traced to a one-sentence section of the 133-year-old mining statute, the 1866 Lode Mining Act. Section 8 of the Act, revised and renamed in 1873, became Revised Statute 2477 (R.S. 2477). This statute reads, "The right-of-way for the construction of highways over public lands, not reserved for public uses, is hereby granted." It was passed by Civil War–era lawmakers to give early prospectors easy access to their claims. However succinctly stated the law may seem, it has been an extremely contentious legal issue in recent years.

*Right-of-way* is the first term introduced in the law, and its implications in the wilderness debate are extremely important. Webster defines right-of-way as "a legal right of passage over another person's ground." In this case it is a legal right of passage over federal ground. R.S. 2477 rights-of-way first became an important issue in the 1860s when the federal government began its policy of land disposal. To reach a piece of remotely located homestead property, homesteaders had to cross many miles of federal land, and it became necessary to have some means by which the homesteaders could maintain access to their property. These rights of access through federal lands, usually along established trails to personal property or claims, are known as "rights-of-way." R.S. 2477 provided the legal go-ahead for construction of roads leading to those properties.

It wasn't until the early 1900s that Arthur Carhart and Aldo Leopold, working for the U.S. Forest Service, recognized the need for a land preservation policy. They asked the question: How much *roadless* land remained after nearly three centuries of development? This was the genesis of administrative regulation L-20 in 1929. The L-20 regulation was the first U.S. policy that focused on *roadless* areas and the need for their protection. In 1939, regulations U-1, U-2, and U-3 replaced the L-20 regulations. The U-regulations broadened the definition of wilderness to mean "Wilderness areas are the last frontier where the world of mechanization and of easy transportation has not yet penetrated . . ." (Hendee, Stankey, and Lucas 1990). The importance of these regulations is that, to this day, they have preserved much acreage in its original *roadless* state. The L-20 and U-regulations firmly laid the groundwork for what has become the primary criterion for wilderness designation, the absence of roads.

When the Wilderness Act of 1964 was passed there was no mention of *roads* or *roadlessness* anywhere in the definition of wilderness itself. In fact, the closest the Wilderness Act comes to defining *roadless* status in the definition of wilderness is "(1) [wilderness] generally appears to have been affected primarily by the forces of nature, with the imprint of man's work substantially unnoticeable." However, the act does specify in *Prohibition of Certain Uses, Section 4(c)* of the Wilderness Act:

> Except as specifically provided for in this Act, and subject to existing private rights, there shall be no commercial enterprise and no *permanent road* within any wilderness area designated by this Act and, except as necessary to meet minimum requirements for the administration of the area for the purpose of this Act (including measures required in emergencies involving the health and safety of persons within the area), there shall be no temporary road, no use of motor vehicles or motorboats, no landing of aircraft, no other form of mechanical transport, and no structure or installation within any such area. (Wilderness Act 1964, Sec. 4[c])

From the beginning[1] there was concern that the classification process used by the USFS to determine potential *roadless* areas would take too long, and in the meantime roads would be created in previously unmarked "potential" wilderness areas. The Roadless Area Review and Evaluation (RARE) was an attempt by the USFS to assemble an interdisciplinary team to complete the review and evaluation of the more than 1,449 potential wilderness areas. The first criterion was necessarily that the tracts are *roadless*, so, to begin, the total gross acres of *roadless* area were determined. Environmentalists criticized the process for failing, from its inception, to select areas located near population centers, such as Lone Peak near Salt Lake City, or areas that had within their boundaries "seeming" roads. (Hendee, Stankey, and Lucas 1990, 133). As dissatisfaction grew with the RARE I process, the team planned RARE II "to accelerate the planning process mandated by the Forest and Rangeland Renewable Resources Act of 1974 [P.L. 93-378] and the National Forest Management act of 1976" [NFMA, P.L. 94-588]. RARE II still used as its primary criterion *"roadless* tracts of land." Under RARE II the Wilderness Attribute Rating System (WARS) was created. This system allowed for a systematic rating system to identify wilderness areas. The lack of *roads* was essential to meet the criteria used by WARS, i.e., naturalness, opportunity for solitude, and primitive recreation.

With the passage of FLPMA (P.L. 94-579) in 1976, Congress mandated that previously uninventoried BLM lands be inventoried as well for potential wilderness designation. FLPMA Section 603 required the BLM to "review those *roadless* areas [emphasis added] of five thousand acres or more and *roadless* islands of public lands, identified during the inventory required in Section 201(a) of this Act as having wilderness characteristics described in the wilderness Act of September 3, 1964." For the purposes of this review and inventory BLM adopted a more precise definition of "roadless." It reads:

> The word roadless refers to the absence of roads that they have improved and maintained by mechanical means to ensure regular and continuous use. A trail maintained solely by the passage of vehicles does not constitute a road. (BLM Utah 1990, 393)

Further to clarify this definition the BLM applied the following sub-definitions:

> *"Improved and maintained"*: Actions taken physically by man to keep a road open to vehicular traffic.
> *"Improved"* does not necessarily mean formal construction.
> *"Maintained"* does not necessarily mean annual maintenance.
> *"Mechanical means"*: Use of hand or power machinery or tools.
> *"Relatively regular and continuous use"*: Vehicular use that has occurred and will continue to occur on a relatively regular basis. Examples are access roads for equipment to maintain a stock water tank or other established water sources, access roads to maintained recreation sites or facilities, or access roads to mining claims [emphasis in original]. (BLM Utah 1990, 394)

Keep in mind that this particular definition is very wilderness-friendly and that many definitions are much less so. There is hot debate regarding this attempt to clarify the "road" definitions. No better example of this can be found than within the internal debates of the Interior Department itself over the definition of a "highway" or *road*. In December 1988 then Secretary of the Interior, Donald Hodel, appointed under the Reagan administration, issued a statement in which he defined a "public highway":

> . . . a definitive route or way that is freely open for all to use. It need not necessarily be open to vehicular traffic for a pedestrian or pack animal trail may qualify. A toll road or trail is still a public highway if the only limitation is the payment of the toll by all users. Multiple ways through a general area may not qualify as a definitive route, however, evidence may show that one or another of the ways may qualify. (BLM 1988)

In 1994, under a new administration, Secretary of the Interior Bruce Babbitt proposed a new and different definition of *highway*.

> *Highway* means a thoroughfare that is currently and was prior to the latest available data used by the public, without discrimination against any individual or group, for the passage of vehicles carrying people or goods from place to place. Where State law, in effect on the latest available date, further limits the definition of highway, these limits also apply. (BLM 1994b, 43 CFR Part 39)

Babbitt developed these 1994 regulations in an attempt to "halt the abusive claims being made under the 1866 Mining Act" (SUWA 1997). These 1994 regulations were designed to eliminate questionable claims and alleged abusive practices. According to SUWA such regulations would clarify the requirement for all involved:

> Regulations would have required actual construction, not just the creation of a trail by the passage of horses or a vehicle. "Highway" would have been interpreted to mean a route between significant centers of public activity, and would rule out rights-of-way for dirt paths that fade out in the middle of the desert. Decisions concerning right-of-way claims would be made with fair and adequate opportunity for public participation and responsible, fact-based decisions. (SUWA 1997, 6)

It is interesting that, in these very different definitions, *road* came to be a *highway* because of the re-emergence of the R.S. 2477 debate; neither definition actually became accepted policy. The Hodel memo was not promulgated according to rulemaking procedures and therefore was never added to federal regulations. Babbitt's notice of the proposed rule published in 1994 was stopped by the Congress in 1996 when they attached a provision of appropriation and prohibited the regulations from taking effect without congressional approval (BLM 1997). The debates continue and attempts to clarify the issue of *roadless* designation are ongoing even within agencies.

## THE UTAH DEBATE

The issue of *roadlessness* has sparked hot debate and disagreement in the Utah wilderness battle for many reasons. The primary battle is over the *definition* of what constitutes a *road*. This definition, as we have seen, remains so elusive that most groups concerned with wilderness legislation in Utah have mapped and inventoried much of the state's remaining open spaces. These groups' zealous efforts to map all roads should not be construed, however, as anything resembling cooperation. Those who campaign for less

TABLE 10.1—Recognized and Pending Assertions of Right-of-Way Claims on Land Administered by the Federal Bureau of Land Management

| State | Recognized | Pending |
|---|---|---|
| Alaska | 2 | 10 |
| Arizona | 173 | 50 |
| California | 17 | 36 |
| Colorado | 53 | 8 |
| Eastern states | 1 | 10 |
| Idaho | 55 | 2 |
| Montana | 12 | 11 |
| Nebraska | 2 | 0 |
| Nevada | 137 | 4 |
| New Mexico | 171 | 0 |
| North Dakota | 0 | 0 |
| Oklahoma | 0 | 0 |
| Oregon | 450 | 1 |
| South Dakota | 0 | 0 |
| Utah | 10 | 5000+ |
| Washington | 17 | 0 |
| Wyoming | 353 | 0 |
| Total | 1,453 | 5,132+ |

Note: Numbers of potential claims are taken from BLM estimates in a preliminary draft of the Department of the Interior Report to Congress. They were not included in the final draft Report to Congress.

*Recognized Claims* are those claims that have been recognized by the BLM as R.S. 2477 rights-of-way.

*Pending Claims* are those submitted to but still waiting review by the BLM.

wilderness, such as county governments, map thousands of what they consider to be roads, some of them in very primitive areas. In Utah alone there have been more than five thousand R.S. 2477 claims filed by three counties, San Juan, Garfield, and Millard counties, far more than in any other state. Table 10.1 illustrates the disparity between Utah's claims and those of the other states.

The total number of formal pending claims in all the states equals 5,132, with five thousand of those in Utah. It becomes clear from this table that the R.S. 2477 debate is without doubt centered in Utah. San Juan County Commissioner Ty Lewis is proud that nearly two thousand of these claims are in San Juan County alone (Lewis 1997). The counties hope that establishing old R.S. 2477 claims on these roads will allow continued access to the land and keep its resources unregulated as wilderness. It is in the counties' interest, they believe, to map and record the location of every *road* that exists on 1976 topographic maps, especially if it runs through or near a proposed wilderness area. San Juan County is currently working with Utah State University on a project that uses satellite imaging to locate roads in proposed wilderness areas (*Salt Lake Tribune* 1998). In 1999 the Utah State Legislature provided funding for this survey.

Those who campaign for more wilderness, such as the Utah Wilderness Coalition's (UWC) Roadless Inventory Project, travel to these disputed areas with cameras, maps, survey equipment, and paper and pen, hoping to find fewer roads than the county claims to show. The Roadless Project members record what they see. Based on the current BLM definition of a road, they photograph every county claim. They believe these records prove that certain claims in given areas do not meet criteria established by the BLM to define a *road* and therefore such an area might remain *roadless*, and therefore remain eligible for wilderness designation (Catlin 1997). The UWC's maps, photographs, and surveys are shared with the BLM in the hope that they will influence the decision as to which R.S. 2477 claims are valid.

In 1998 the UWC's extensive two-year wilderness reinventory was completed, and the results unveiled at a series of open houses throughout the state. Nearly five thousand photographs were taken by hundreds of citizens reinventorying nearly twenty thousand acres of land. The results, according to UWC, showed that "about 1 percent of the old proposal has since been scarred by development; 99 percent remains in a relatively natural state. . . . Units were added in the Great Basin and Dinosaur areas in addition to biologically rich areas and connecting corridors" (SUWA 1998, 10). The reinventory concluded that nearly 9.1 million acres of land in Utah meet the criteria for wilderness designation. The UWC explained their approach to identifying roads and how it differed from their previous inventory:

> [We] use a slightly more conservative definition of "roadless." Even if a vehicle route fails to meet the BLM definition of "road" (usually because it is not maintained), we will sometimes exclude it from our wilderness proposal if we feel that it looks like a "road" to a hypothetical typical American, or if it serves some important purpose. (SUWA 1998, 14)

In these opposing inventories, one fact becomes clear: there is disparity between the assessments made by various groups of the locations and numbers of roads in these remote parts of Utah. The disparity probably exists for two main reasons: (1) competing groups seek to maximize their own interests, which naturally renders their judgment subjective, and (2) there is still considerable disagreement over the definition of *road*.

The controversy over the definition of *road* is currently marked "dead end." Neither the courts nor Congress have delineated a clear set of criteria that would define what constitutes a legal *road*. The number of definitions that can be given to the term *road*, then, are nearly infinite. The definitions differ dramatically because perceptions differ strongly. In Utah much of the issue is still to be decided in the courts where numerous issues are awaiting decisions. Furthermore, since Congress has failed to define what a road is, states must use their own definitions of what constitutes a road. This issue is discussed in more detail below.

## THE R.S. 2477 DEBATE

*The right-of-way for the construction of highways over public lands, not reserved for public uses, is hereby granted* (R.S. 2477, 1873).

*Until final rules are effective, the Bureau of Land Management will defer any processing of R.S. 2477 assertions except in cases where there is demonstrated, compelling, and immediate need to make such determinations* (BLM Report to Congress, 1993).

The R.S. 2477 statute has given rise to literally dozens of recent law review articles (Wolter 1996). In addition, there have been at least nineteen federal cases and thirty-seven Utah cases, thirty-five of which have taken place since the turn of the century (Hjelle 1997). R.S. 2477, although repealed in 1976 with the passage of FLPMA, has survived because Congress provided a clause in FLPMA that protects all R.S. 2477 claims existing prior to its passage (FLPMA 1976). No highway constructed after the passage of FLPMA can claim the same rights that an R.S. 2477 highway possesses. "The effect of recognition and use of R.S. 2477 right-of-way on manageability of wilderness areas and the WSAs is a special concern. It is this topic that elevated the R.S. 2477 issue to Congressional attention" (BLM 1993).

Environmentalists claim the counties have sought to "torpedo wilderness designation and National Lands protection by asserting approximately 5,000 dubious—and mostly unnecessary—road claims involving dirt trails, two-tracks, cow paths, sandy wash bottoms and even rivers. Most of these byways they assert are largely impassable by car" (SUWA 1997, 4). SUWA recently offered to donate $2,477 to charity if any county commissioner could drive a passenger car over certain road claims. On the other side, the counties making the claims maintain adamantly that all are valid, existing claims.

Within the wording of R.S. 2477 there are a few terms to be carefully considered if we are to understand the rights implicitly or explicitly created by this statute. Construction has been defined by many different federal entities, but the definition that pertains most directly to wilderness in Utah is in the BLM manual used during the second half of Utah's wilderness inventory:

> [A] physical act of readying the highway for use by the public according to the available or intended mode of transportation—foot, horse, vehicle, etc. Removing high vegetation, moving large rocks out of the way, or filling low spots, etc. may be sufficient as construction for a particular case. Road maintenance or the passage of vehicles by users over time may equal actual construction. (BLM 1979, 2801.48.B.1)

Construction then is interpreted by BLM land managers as a broad term with criteria that were fairly easy to meet but still open to considerable interpretation. Again, Congress has failed to set clear criteria by which an observer can determine whether construction has taken place on a disputed road.

The next term to be considered is probably the most widely debated, misunderstood, and misinterpreted. *Highway* was the word chosen by Congress in 1866 to define several different means of passage. In 1866, a "highway" would not have consisted of four lanes and asphalt. Highways were simply public roads or ways open to all passengers, and prior to the advent of the automobile, these highways could have been only wagon trails, equestrian trails, cowpaths, footpaths, or canals. A recent Utah law has used the original definition of highway to define highway today:

> Any road, street, trail, or other access or way that is open to the public to come and go or transport water at will, without regard to how or by whom the way was constructed or maintained; . . . and other areas that facilitate use of the highway by the public. "Highway" includes: pedestrian trails, horse paths, livestock trails, wagon roads, jeep trails, logging roads, homestead roads, mine-to-market roads, alleys, tunnels, bridges, and all other ways and their attendant access for maintenance; and irrigation canals, waterways, viaducts, ditches, pipelines, or other means of water transmission and their attendant access for maintenance. (UCA 27-16-101)

It is interesting to note here that claimants of R.S. 2477 rights-of-way point out that the legal list of necessary wilderness attributes does not equate the term "highway" with the term "road" or "roadless." Neither does this state law. The existence of a highway (i.e., an R.S. 2477 highway) across proposed wilderness, then, does not preclude the area from the possibility of designation as wilderness, so long as that highway is not a road, but is instead a footpath, a horse path, a ditch, etc. Most of the existing R.S. 2477 claims in Utah, however, are in fact road claims that often run across proposed or existing wilderness areas. Thus, R.S. 2477 highways can be divided into two groups of claims for convenience: (1) Those that necessarily take the form of a road, and thereby assume strategic importance in the wilderness issue, and (2) those that do not take the form of roads, so their existence does not affect the wilderness issue.

R.S. 2477 highways are an important legal issue for several reasons. The first is that they are almost completely immune from regulation. These rights-of-way often belong to individuals, which leads to the question of whether they constitute personal property rights. This is a point of confusion. One 1995 law review states: "R.S. 2477 has never been a grant of rights, but a statutory recognition of permissible encroachment upon public land" (Widmann 1995). Ten pages later the same review states: ". . . The fact that [R.S. 2477] roads are immune from regulation implies that they constitute vested property rights and any infringement of these rights may represent a taking under the Fifth Amendment." This, more than anything, illustrates the legal complexity of the entire issue. The majority of legislation and commentary consider these rights-of-way to be property rights as well. The extent of these rights is the issue under debate. At least one case, *Sierra Club v. Hodel*, clearly limited the extent of the rights issued under R.S. 2477: "The 'scope' of a right-of-way refers to the bundle of property rights possessed by the holder of the right-of-way. This bundle is defined by the physical boundaries of the right-of-way as well as the uses to which it has been put" (*Sierra Club v. Hodel* 1988). To whom the property right belongs is of minor importance, so long as the legal physical boundaries and uses to which it is limited are known and have been secured.

Ambiguity plagues the legal history of the establishment of R.S. 2477 claims. In an administrative memo we read: "The question of whether a particular highway has been legally established under R.S. 2477 remains a question of federal law." Later on in the same memo we read: "[This] would return us to the BLM's regulations: as a matter of federal law, state law has been designated as controlling [perfection of R.S. 2477 claims]" (Wolter 1996, 27).

The federal government has historically left the issue of identifying R.S. 2477 roads to the states, and this "tacit acquiescence" has led to 133 years of precedent in which the state has controlled its own R.S. 2477 issues and definitions. The situation is dichotomous, because federal law always takes precedence over state law (see chapter 2), and legal precedent is preferred over legal innovation. The Department of the Interior has met vehement opposition from many states in regard to its proposed R.S. 2477 regulations, which seek to change what counties and states perceive as established precedent. In fact, however, the states have control only insofar as the Congress does not take it away from them.

The political reality of R.S. 2477 is this: The law was open-ended and non-specific at the time of its inception, and since then it has been interpreted differently by successive presidential administrations, government agencies, and individual citizens. Yet when the various wilderness proposals are considered, we will gain a very critical understanding of the role roads play in the wilderness debate and of the effect that the mapping of "roads" may have on the final designation of wilderness lands in Utah.

## ROADS AND WILDERNESS DESIGNATION: A COMPARISON OF THE PROPOSALS

Investigating the number of legitimate R.S. 2477 claims in Utah is a daunting task. As yet, no final figures have been calculated; the counties and environmental interest groups are still mapping and/or filing their claims. However, some preliminary results of these surveys are available.

All sides, for various reasons, are hesitant to share their preliminary findings. While investigating the number of claims that have been filed, or are pending, we found that parties on both sides of the issue were exceedingly hesitant to share their information; they are concerned that it could somehow be used to advantage by the other side. For example, when we contacted state officials about sharing information on county claims they seemed more than willing, but when the Sierra Club requested the same information, the state offices declined to provide it.

Why are these claims held so secretively? The fact that these groups treat the issue as a covert operation suggests most certainly a lack of trust and perhaps a lack of survey integrity. As interested researchers, we found the groups' refusal to cooperate annoying and unproductive. In addition, the state's willingness to hide public-domain information is, at best, a breach of public trust. In the end we were able to find one reliable source of information regarding the number of county claims being filed with the BLM. This source asked to remain anonymous.

What we found was that most of the counties in Utah have only recently completed preliminary surveys of their R.S. 2477 claims, and a few counties are still incomplete. A preliminary survey is done by taking a topographic map of the county, highlighting the claimed existing roads, wagon trails, jeep trails, or other vehicle trails, numbering them, and sending the results to the state. The second phase, which will require a physical substantiation of the claims, has not yet been undertaken. The Utah Wilderness Coalition has completed their field surveying and documented

TABLE 10.2—Pending R.S. 2477 Road Claims in Some Southern Utah Counties

| County | Number of Claims |
|---|---|
| Emery County | 1,076 |
| Garfield County | 887 |
| Grand County | 1,166 |
| Kane County | 1,287 |
| Washington County | 857 |
| Millard County | >1,000 |
| Piute County | >1,000 |

Source: County officials

all the claims for which they have documentation. What they claimed to have found in their preliminary results is that many of the road claims cannot be substantiated according to the current BLM definition of road. This is probably the reason for the secretive nature of the county claims. They do not want their maps in the hands of the environmentalists until they have physically substantiated all their claims.

We were able to access exact preliminary totals for seven counties in southern Utah. It's important to note that these claims are only preliminary and the total number of actual claims will almost certainly change as the process of physical claim substantiation continues. Table 10.2 illustrates the preliminary results.

These numbers total 7,273 claims in just seven of Utah's twenty-nine counties. It is conceivable that the total number of claims in Utah could reach fifteen thousand or more by the time the entire survey is complete. This number far exceeds the next closest state, Alaska with an estimated 1,700 claims (Wolter 1996). These data also contradict the information on numbers of claims given by BLM in table 10.1. It appears that at this date the numbers continue to be fluid.

## CASE STUDY: THE BURR TRAIL CONTROVERSY

To date Utah has been the focal point for most of the current R.S. 2477 controversy. This is due in part to the case of the Burr Trail. The Burr Trail is a sixty-six-mile-long trail that winds through Capitol Reef National Park and Glen Canyon National Recreation Area, and borders a BLM Wilderness Study Area in southern Utah. It connects the town of Boulder, Utah, with Lake Powell's Bullfrog Basin Marina. Garfield County has maintained the Burr Trail as a one-lane dirt *road* since the early 1940s. In 1987, controversy erupted over the right to "improve and upgrade" this R.S. 2477 right-of-way. Plans by the county to "improve" the Burr Trail from a one-lane dirt road to a two-lane graveled or paved road caused the Sierra Club to file a suit against the Department of the Interior, BLM, and Garfield County (*Sierra Club vs. Hodel* 1988). The complaint alleged the following:

(1) The County's proposed improvements would extend the actual roadway beyond the right-of-way and encroach upon federal land;

(2) the County had not received authorization for this encroachment from the BLM, as required by the Federal Land Policy Management Act of 1976 (FLPMA);

(3) the improvements would unnecessarily and unduly degrade adjacent wilderness study areas and would impair the WSA's suitability for designation as wilderness; and

(4) the BLM had failed to study the environmental impact of the construction in violation of the National Environmental Policy Act of 1969. (*Sierra Club v. Hodel* 1988)

The complaint then requested an injunction against construction until Garfield County and BLM could comply with FLPMA and NEPA. This case led to extensive litigation in federal district court and ultimately in the Tenth Circuit Court of Appeals. The main issues of contention in this case were over "what rights, if any, the county had to improve the road and the federal government's ability to impose mitigation of impacts to WSAs, National Parks and Recreation Areas" (BLM 1993).

In 1993 the court ruled that the county did indeed have the right-of-way for portions of the Burr Trail that entitled it to provide "for reasonable and safe travel." The county then announced its intention to begin road construction. Once the Burr Trail was recognized in the courts as an existing R.S. 2477 highway, Garfield County claimed it had the right to improve the trail without permission or notice to any of the land management agencies responsible for the scenic lands surrounding the trail. But SUWA and other environmental groups disagreed and protested the development of the trail into a paved highway. Still the county laid an asphalt surface on the western portion of the Burr Trail. In 1996 the county bulldozed away a hillside in Capitol Reef National Park. The Park Service sued the county for trespass. The case at this date is still in litigation. Issues such as the width of the "improved" road and its impact on the surrounding environment are still being debated.

The case of the Burr Trail shows that, even if an existing R.S. 2477 claim is upheld in the courts, controversy continues. Questions continue to arise surrounding the Burr Trail case, such as these: To what extent can the trail be improved? Does the holder of the right-of-way need to inform the federal land managers of proposed improvements? Is the holder of the right-of-way responsible for the impact that use of the right-of-way will have on the surrounding environment? Can a one-lane dirt road be made into a well-traveled paved "highway"? If so, what will the impact of this be on the surrounding environment? The Burr Trail case study illustrates that, besides the multitude of questions that arise and must be answered, a "road" is not a simple definition that can, or cannot, define wilderness. Rather it presents a complex series of issues that must be mitigated, litigated, and resolved if we are to understand how it is to be defined in its relationship to wilderness.

## CONCLUSION: WILL EVER THE TWO PATHS MERGE?

> *Two roads diverged in a yellow wood,*
> *And sorry I could not travel both*
> *And be one traveler, long I stood*
> *And looked down one as far as I could*
> *To where it bent in the undergrowth;*
> *. . . and both that morning equally lay . . .*
> —Robert Frost

The *roadless* designation remains the primary criterion in the designation of land as wilderness. Because of this, as this chapter demonstrates, roads and roadlessness remain at the center of a spirited debate. If Congress could have seen into the future, perhaps legislators would have been more meticulous in their use of terms and meanings. They would have asked— and attempted to answer—many more questions. They would certainly have attempted to clarify a definition of what constitutes a *road.*

Furthermore, achieving a clear definition is only part of the solution; a related question concerns the relationship between the road and the surrounding federal land—an issue in the Burr Trail controversy. This is a critically important question with regard to wilderness designation due to the practice of "cherry-stemming." A cherry-stem is where wilderness boundaries are drawn tightly around a long segment of road that protrudes into a wilderness area. Does this practice violate the spirit of the Wilderness Act? Or is it a simple recognition that land adjacent to a jeep trail may be worth preserving? Even the cherry-stemming issue has vocal partisans, all with their own ideas about how close a wilderness area should be to a road.

Will the two paths of contention merge? Is it possible to reach agreement and pass legislation that will clarify the definitions and the issues?

How will this lack of clarity surrounding the *roads* and right-of-way issues impact future wilderness designation? One thing is clear as these issues proceed through litigation: legal definitions need to be developed to provide a solid base for determining future designation of rights-of-way. What remains unclear is whether the opposing sides in this debate will merge together with one understanding and agreement on definition and meaning.

## ℂ   NOTES TO CHAPTER 10

1. When the Wilderness Act was passed in 1964 it applied only to the U.S. Forest Service, national parks, and wildlife refuges. The BLM was exempt until 1976, with the passage of FLPMA.

## ℂ   REFERENCES TO CHAPTER 10

BLM (Bureau of Land Management of the U.S. Department of the Interior). 1979. *Interim management policy and guidelines for lands under wilderness review.* December 12, 1979.
——. 1982. Wilderness study policy: policies, criteria and guidelines for conducting wilderness studies on public lands. Federal Register 47 (23): 5098–5122.
——. 1984. *Scoping the Utah Statewide Wilderness Environmental Impact Statement Public Scoping Issues and Alternatives.* July 20, 1984. Denver, Colorado: U.S. GPO.
——. 1985. CFR 8560. Federal Register, February 21, 1985.
——. 1988. Secretary Hodel Letter on "Policy regarding rights-of-way on public lands under the 1866 Act of Congress."
——. 1993. Report to Congress on R.S. 2477, "The History and management of R.S. 2477 rights-of-way claims on federal and other lands," June.
——. 1994a. Federal Register 59:146. Revised Statute 2477 Right-of-Way. 43 CFR Part 2820.
——. 1994b. 43 CFR Part 39.
——. 1997. Memorandum, January 22, "Interim Departmental Policy on Revised Statute 2477 Grant of Right-of-Way for Public Highways; Revocation of December 7, 1988 Policy."
BLM Utah (Utah State Office, Bureau of Land Management of the U.S. Department of the Interior). 1990. *Utah BLM Statewide Wilderness Final Environmental Impact Statement.* Salt Lake City, UT.
Catlin, Jim. 1997. Utah Wildlands. Telephone interview by authors, May 25.
*Endangered American Wilderness Act.* 1978. Act of February 24, 1978. P.L. 95-237. 92 Stat. 40.
*Federal Land Policy and Management Act of 1976.* Act of October 21, 1976. P.L. 94-579. 90 Stat. 2743.
Frost, Robert. 1971. "The road not taken," in *The Road Not Taken.* New York: Holt, Rinehart, Winston, 1971.
Hansen, James. 1997. U.S. Congressman from Utah. Personal interview by authors, May 17, University of Utah.

Hendee, J., G. Stankey, and R. Lucas. 1990. *Wilderness Management.* Golden, CO: North American Press.

Hjelle, Barbara, attorney. 1997. Telephone interview by authors.

H.R. 1500. 1989. Utah Wilderness Coalition bill before the House of Representatives.

H.R. 1501. 1989. Rep. Hansen's bill before the House of Representatives. BLM Final Environmental Impact Statement, vol. 1, Overview, Appendix 2 (reaction to H.R. 1500).

Leopold, Aldo. 1921. The wilderness and its place in forest recreation policy. *Journal of Forestry* 19(7): 7.

Lewis, Ty. 1997. San Juan County Commissioner. Personal interview, April 19, San Juan County.

Marshall, Robert. 1930. The problem of wilderness. *Scientific Monthly* 30.

*Mining Act of 1866.* R.S. 2477.

*National Environmental Policy Act* (NEPA). 1974.

*National Forest Management Act.* 1976. P.L. 94-588.

Register of Public Access, P.L. 93-378.

*Rights-of-way Across Federal Lands Act.* 1993. Utah State Law, Public Access Across Federal Lands, 27-16-101.

*Salt Lake Tribune.* 1998. December 6, C7.

*Sierra Club v. Hodel.* 1988. Case Study. P.L. 87-2832, 88-1130, and 88-1161. U.S. Court of Appeals Tenth Circuit.

Six County Commissioners Organization. 1983. "Wilderness Recommendation of 241,480 Acres of Public Land" (personal communication). June 12, 1983. Richfield, Utah.

SUWA (Southern Utah Wilderness Alliance). 1997. The 1866 Mining Act: Imminent Threat to Protection of America's National Lands. SUWA Publications.

————. 1998. "Wild Utah Unveiled." SUWA Newsletter 15 (No. 2, Summer).

U.S. Congress, House. 1973. Ninth Annual Wilderness Report. House Document No. 93-194.

U.S. Congress, Senate. 1933. National Plan for American Forestry. S. Doc. 12, 73rd Cong., 1st Sess.

U.S. Department of Agriculture, Forest Service. 1973. *Final Environmental Statement: Roadless and Undeveloped Areas,* 690.

————. 1978a. *Roadless area review and evaluation (RARE II).* Draft environmental impact statement 78-04.

————. 1978b. *RARE II, Supplement to Draft Environmental Statement Roadless Area Review and Evaluation.* Denver, CO: GPO.

————. 1979. *Final RARE II environmental impact statement.*

————. 1985. Wilderness, primitive areas, and wilderness study areas. In *Forest Service Manual,* chapter 2320.

Utah Wilderness Coalition. 1997. Citizen Reinventory of R.S. 2477 Claims in Utah Wilderness Study Areas. SUWA (unpublished).

Widmann, Brian. 1995. Tenth Circuit survey: land and natural resources survey. *Denver University Law Review* 72: 763.

*Wilderness Act.* 1964. Act of September 3, 1964. P.L. 88-577, 78 Stat. 890.

Wilderness Society. 1984. *The Wilderness Act Handbook,* 64. Washington, DC: The Wilderness Society.

Wolter, Michael. 1996. *Dickson School of Law Journal of Environmental Law and Policy* 5 (Summer): 315–73.

# CHAPTER 11

# Pottery and Pithouses

## Archaeological Resources in Wilderness

### R. Kelly Beck

Eleven thousand years ago the North American continent was changing. The Ice Age was drawing to a close, several species of animals that had flourished during the Ice Age were becoming extinct, and humans, living in temporary camps, were following large prey across the continent into South America. These ancient Native Americans had begun forming this continent's archaeological record, consisting of sites and artifacts, in their respective contexts including their surrounding environment. It is this archaeological record that we call archaeological or cultural resources, a resource that, like fossil fuel, is not renewable. Archaeological artifacts, such as stone tools, bones, pottery, and basketry, can be recovered and are often sent to museums for safe keeping. However, the association between these artifacts and other features of a site, such as fire pits, trash piles, and walls or other physical structures, cannot be picked up and sent to a museum. These aspects of an archaeological site are perhaps the most important, as it is this information that needs to be linked to the movable artifacts in order to effectively and accurately interpret the archaeological site. Once the context and associations between artifacts and features at an archaeological site have been destroyed, they are gone forever.

Archaeological resources have been suffering the ravages of destruction since the beginning of the archaeological record itself. People seem to have an insatiable interest in ancient items. Federal protection of archaeological resources began in this country in the late nineteenth century with an effort to protect archaeological resources that were already on federal lands. Protection of cultural resources was, in fact, one of the many reasons cited in support of the formation of this nation's first national park, Yellowstone.

It was, however, not until 1889 that the government acted to preserve an area primarily for its archaeological resources. This was at Casa Grande, Arizona, in an effort to stabilize and protect that area's rapidly crumbling ruins. During the 1890s public interest in Civil War battlefields began to increase. People were visiting battlefields in greater numbers, and many were collecting Civil War artifacts. This prompted the federal government to acquire and protect, through condemnation, several privately owned battlefield areas. This was the first time the government acted to protect cultural resources found on private lands (Fowler 1974).

The 1890 census found no western frontier, due in a large part to five-fold growth of the nation's railroad system. The railroad had two major impacts on the archaeological resources of the West. It dramatically increased access to the West, and it provided a means for easily transporting artifacts to eastern markets. A rapid increase in the destruction of archaeological resources during this time alarmed archaeological resource preservationists.

Advocates of preservation formally petitioned Congress in 1882 to formulate legislation to protect archaeological resources, but to no avail (Hutt, Jones, and McAllister 1992). Then, in 1888, Richard Wetherill discovered Mesa Verde. Intense publicity about Wetherill's spectacular discovery led to explosive public interest in the prehistoric past. Congress finally took action in 1906 with the passage of the Antiquities Act. This act was essentially the beginning of the nation's commitment to protecting its cultural heritage, and as such was the first in a long series of laws, directives, and executive orders aimed at protecting and preserving archaeological resources. Despite these protective efforts, many archaeological resources have been lost forever; much of the remaining resource is found on undeveloped federal lands. In other words, wilderness—both *de facto* and *de jure*—is where America's remaining archaeological resources are concentrated.

This chapter is an evaluation of the impact of wilderness designation on the preservation and protection of prehistoric archaeological resources on federal lands administered by the Bureau of Land Management (BLM). After first examining factors that affect archaeological resources on federal lands in general, it will then discuss how these factors are likely to change with the designation of wilderness.

## DESTRUCTION OF ARCHAEOLOGICAL SITES

The archaeology of Utah's potential wilderness is significant. It is also largely unknown. Garth Portillo, the BLM State Office archaeologist, commented that we know very little about the archaeology in most potential wilderness areas (Portillo 1997). What we do know is due, in large part, to luck. Each year the BLM State Office receives reports of forty-five to fifty thousand acres of land surveyed. With each new acre surveyed a little more information about the prehistory of Utah is learned. The nature of this dynamic research environment suggests that any list of numbers of located sites will be obsolete in a very short period of time. However, the most up-to-date estimates are found in table 11.1. Site density estimates from the 1990 *BLM Environmental Impact Statement* were used to calculate an estimated number of archaeological sites found within potential wilderness.

Density estimates within the BLM EIS were given for individual WSAs. To calculate regional site density estimates I used the lowest density estimate given for an individual WSA within each region for the density of that region. In Table 11.2, estimates were calculated for the UWC's 5.7-million-acre proposal, the 3.2 million acres of WSAs, and the 1.9-million-acre BLM proposal.

### TABLE 11.1—Regional Density Estimates

| Region | Density Estimate |
|---|---|
| West Desert | 6/ 640 acres |
| Zion | 4/ 640 acres |
| Escalante | 11/ 23,000 acres |
| Henry Mountains | 864/ 23,000 acres |
| Canyonlands–La Sal | 411/ 23,000 acres |
| San Rafael | 115/ 23,000 acres |
| Book Cliff–Uintah | 39/ 23,000 acres |

### TABLE 11.2—Estimated Archaeological Sites Comparison

This shows the density estimates that were used to calculate regional site estimates. Densities were taken from the BLM Final EIS, and the lowest number of sites per acre were used.

| Region | Proposal | | |
|---|---|---|---|
| | UWC | WSA | BLM |
| West Desert | 6,429 | 4,349 | 2,010 |
| Zion | 1,866 | 908 | 464 |
| Escalante | 609 | 415 | 168 |
| Henry Mountains | 23,019 | 16,009 | 11,237 |
| Canyonlands–La Sal | 23,870 | 8,342 | 7,863 |
| Ran Rafael | 3,764 | 1,310 | 1,211 |
| Book Cliffs–Uintah | 1,269 | 985 | 506 |

Utah is an environmentally diverse state, from high mountain alpine areas in the Uintahs, to the redrock desert of southern Utah, to the sparse and hostile Great Basin desert in the west. This variation in environment requires some regional distinction in establishing site density estimates because a single statewide density would mask some significant spatial variability. The seven geographical regions chosen for this study follow the regional boundaries found on Pocket Map 4 in the *BLM Statewide Wilderness Final EIS* (1990). From these data it is easy to see that there are literally thousands of archaeological sites within potential wilderness areas. Therefore it is important to evaluate how these sites will be affected by wilderness designation.

The major issues concerning the protection and preservation of archaeological resources have been categorized by Nickens, Larralde, and Tucker (1981). These issues are broadly divided into two major categories: natural agents and human agents. Natural agents are those forces that, while in some instances they are precipitated by humans, are typically conducted without the direct action of humans.

The second category, human agents, can be subdivided into two sections: incidental actions, and intentional actions. Incidental actions are those that are not directly involved in archaeological resource destruction. These incidental actions include development (roads, pipelines, etc.), natural resource exploration, and recreation. Intentional actions are those that are directly involved in resource destruction. Examples of intentional actions are archaeological research and looting or vandalism of a site. It can be argued that these forces that destroy archaeological resources are harmful, but a great number of sites have been exposed and discovered due to these very actions. This chapter will focus on the destructive impacts of these factors.

### Natural agents

Natural agents, primarily erosion, are often the factors that lead to the discovery of a previously unknown archaeological site. However, these same natural agents are more often the factors that lead to the destruction and eventual loss of a site and the information contained within that site (Gaede and Gaede 1977).

An example of the destructive force of erosion on an archaeological site will help to demonstrate this point. In 1875, William H. Jackson accompanied the Hayden Survey on an expedition to the Southwest. Jackson was the first photographer to be taken on a survey expedition. His assignment was to document the cliff dwellings of the Southwest and the Pueblo villages located south of the San Juan River. It was on this 1875 expedition that Jackson took the first pictures of Poncho House, a cliff dwelling found on the Navajo reservation of southeastern Utah. Jackson took three photographs of Poncho House, and also took detailed notes and made scale drawings of the site. While at Poncho House, Jackson found seven large ceramic vessels at the base of one of the towers. These vessels were left in place at that time. Forty-eight years later, archaeologist Samuel Guernsey excavated Poncho House and took a photograph of the central portion of the site at the same angle as Jackson. Comparison of these two photographs did not show any noticeable change in the ruin. However, all seven ceramic vessels were gone. The Monument Valley–Rainbow Bridge Expedition of 1933 also photographed Poncho House and few major changes were noted in relation to those taken ten years before. In 1962 the Museum of Northern Arizona conducted the Monument Valley Survey for the Navajo tribe. This survey of the Poncho House area documented substantial change to the ruin. An entire portion of a three-story wall had collapsed. Many interior walls had fallen, and a roof that had been previously intact had caved in. At the time of the museum report in 1965, natural erosion, primarily arroyo cutting in the canyon below the site, was putting the site at considerable danger of increased destruction. Due to the imminent loss of a potentially valuable resource by erosion, a project to stabilize Poncho House ruin was suggested in the 1965 report of the Museum of Northern Arizona (Gaede and Gaede 1977).

Clearly, the forces of nature cannot be controlled. This is as true in wilderness as in any other place on earth. The BLM has developed a plan for dealing with potential loss of archaeological resources within wilderness due to natural causes. In chapter 3, section B, of the BLM Wilderness Management Policy (BLM 1990, 213–30), it is stated that cultural resources will be subject to the forces of nature as will all other wilderness resources. The BLM policy then states that

> Management direction for cultural resources that qualify for nomination to the National Register of Historic Places is subject to section 106 of the National Historic Preservation Act and 36 CFR 800. A decision to remove, maintain, or allow historic or prehistoric structures to deteriorate naturally is a Federal undertaking which will affect the resources. In working through the compliance processes, a determination will be made as to what feasible and prudent alternatives exist to satisfactorily mitigate adverse effects of the proposed decision on the cultural resources. (1990, 216)

Under Section 106 of the National Historic Preservation Act (P.L. 89-665), any action that the federal government takes, approves, or permits must account for any effect on a site that has been included in the National

Register of Historic Places that may be affected by any given action. If a negative effect is likely, then the site must be mitigated in some manner. Mitigation typically involves rerouting the proposed action, capping the site with topsoil, or complete excavation and data recovery. In the case of erosion in wilderness the option to stabilize the site is also considered.

### Human Actions

Human actions have been a source of destruction of archaeological resources since the beginning of the formation of the archaeological record itself. Currently, archaeological resources are facing a full spectrum of destructive human forces, ranging from incidental destruction such as development, natural resource exploration, and recreation, to intentional looting and vandalism, and archaeological research itself. These issues will be discussed more completely below and evaluated for their impact on archaeological resources within wilderness.

The impacts of development, in the form of roads, pipelines, and structures, on archaeology have not been systematically studied. This is due in large part to the difficulty in quantifying these impacts and the resulting change of the archaeological record. However, it does not take any stretch of the imagination to see the potential impacts that these actions could have on archaeological resources. One of the most important pieces of information to come from a site is the relationship between artifacts and features, or, in other words, the context in which the artifact is found. The action of blading a road, providing access to a pipeline, or digging a foundation can be destructive to any archaeological resource that is encountered. Development changes the surrounding environment, and in doing so also changes the environment, or context, of an archaeological site.

Development of a road, pipeline, or structure on BLM land in general requires, at a minimum, approval of the BLM. This approval process by the BLM constitutes a federal undertaking and is thus subject to Section 106 approval under the National Historic Preservation Act (NHPA). Wilderness, however, by its very definition, does not have noticeable signs of humankind and will be managed to preserve this quality. Therefore, the threat of development as a destructive force for archaeological resources is negligible within wilderness, with, of course, a few exceptions. These exceptions consist primarily of the requirement that access to inholdings or valid existing rights be maintained.

Natural resource exploration, like development, has not been the focus of much research as far as archaeological resource destruction is concerned. However, a look at the process of natural resource exploration will show that, like development, it too is a source of inadvertent archaeological resource destruction. Mineral extraction and drilling for oil both have similar destructive mechanisms. Both penetrate the ground surface in search of subsurface materials. In the process of preparing to penetrate the surface, each operation will clear an area on the surface for equipment and other operation requirements. The action of clearing an area will obliterate any surface evidence of an archaeological site. Often it is these surface observations that are the only clue that a buried site might be found. After the surface area is cleared, the subsurface exploration begins. This process in and of itself is detrimental to any archaeological site that it might encounter. The subsurface exploration will completely remove archaeological materials from their contexts or mix the sediments in which the archaeological materials are found so as to render any sort of contextual interpretation meaningless.

Two other problems for archaeological resource protection arise from natural resource exploration. The first concerns the requisite access roads that all mining or drilling operations require, and the second is vandalism at sites by natural resource workers due to the proximity of workers to archaeological sites. The access road issue has been previously discussed in this chapter as well as in chapter 10 (vandalism will be discussed in greater detail below). The problem of natural resource workers participating in destructive activities is demonstrated in the Poncho House report (Gaede and Gaede 1977). Gaede and Gaede cite the 1965 Northern Arizona University report stating that oil exploration crews that had been working in the area of Poncho House were responsible for toppling parts of the front walls in the western half of the ruin. The report also states that there were stories of uranium miners in the 1950s setting off dynamite charges inside one of the towers that had been a part of Poncho House.

Exploration of natural resources on BLM land requires that a permit be granted by the BLM. This permit constitutes a federal undertaking and is subject to Section 106 review under NHPA. Any adverse effect on archaeological sites that are a part of the National Register of Historic Places must undergo some sort of mitigation to eliminate or minimize the effect on the site. Wilderness designation will affect natural resource exploration in that it will limit new mining or drilling projects.

Recreationists are another source of impacts on archaeological resources. Wilderness and recreation go hand in hand. Part of the definition of wilderness in the Wilderness Act is the opportunity for primitive recreation. This opportunity for recreation, for some people, is the opportunity to visit archaeological sites in an area that has not been developed, to experience the area around the site in much the same way that we envision the native occupants of the site did. This desire to experience archaeology in its natural setting, however, also leads to the destruction and eventual loss of the archaeology that brought people to the area in the first place. This is an example of a classic tragedy of the commons. Everybody wants to visit a site in its natural setting, yet in the process of visitation, the site and its natural setting are destroyed so that the site can no longer be seen within its natural setting. An example of destruction of archaeological sites due to recreation and increased visitation can be found at Poncho House. During the 1962 Monument Valley Survey by the Museum of Northern Arizona, Poncho House was observed to have undergone substantial damage due in part to an increase in visitation. Gaede and Gaede state that the effects of erosion at sites such as Poncho House increase in proportion to human activity; as more people visit a site, the site is increasingly destroyed (1977).

Recreation in wilderness, as stated by the Wilderness Act, is an important and accepted use of wilderness. Recreational use of archaeological sites, however, is only marginally manageable; it is not possible to control the recreational use of every single archaeological site. The *Utah BLM Statewide Wilderness Final Environmental Impact Statement* provides a brief analysis of recreational use of Wilderness Study Areas. It assumes recreational use of WSAs will increase from 264,898 visitor days per year to between 497,868 and 1,725,861 visitor days per year by the year 2020 (BLM 1990, 125). However, the EIS also cites a study done by McCool (1985) stating that, in the long term, wilderness designation does not substantially increase recreational use compared to use that would occur without designation.

Intentional agents of archaeological resource destruction include the seemingly obvious and occasionally well publicized actions of site vandalism and looting, but they also include the act of archaeological research. This may seem counterintuitive, but when one considers the finality of site excavation and the constraints put upon research, this seemingly incongruous relationship becomes more obvious. The process of archaeological research, as in all scientific research, is constrained by limited funding and deadlines. All too often the needs of a research project exceed the time and money allocated to it, forcing the archaeologist to either limit the scope of the project or to hurry an excavation process that should be done with great care and meticulous attention to detail. On occasion, researchers take on too many projects and are unable to follow a project through to publication, thus not making data available for other archaeologists to test and verify. This problem is being solved through pressure from other professional archaeologists, and is becoming less common. Today a permit is required to conduct legitimate archaeological field research. The permit process was begun with the passage of the 1906

Antiquities Act and then made more comprehensive under the Archaeological Resources Protection Act (ARPA) of 1979 (P.L. 96-95).

## WILDERNESS AND ARCHAEOLOGY

Research within wilderness is viewed as a valid and important use of wilderness, as stated by the BLM Wilderness Management Policy (BLM 1990, 230). As with all archaeological research on federal lands, a permit is required to fulfill the requirements of ARPA; however, research within wilderness must be conducted in a manner that does not degrade the characteristics that made an area wilderness. This would exclude the use of any permanent facilities or motorized equipment unless approved by the State Director. This approval would likely come only in situations where research was needed to protect wilderness values.

Looting and vandalism of archaeological sites is often seen as the most difficult problem to control. Looting and vandalism of archaeological sites has received much attention from Congress, the courts, and archaeologists (U.S. General Accounting Office 1987; Nickens, Larralde, and Tucker 1981; Green and Davis 1981; Ahlstrom et al. 1992). The result of this extensive body of research is the establishment of several factors that affect looting and vandalism of archaeological resources. Common to all studies of looting factors is the effect of site type/visibility and access. Nickens, Larralde, and Tucker (1981) studied the extent of vandalism in southwestern Colorado and noted that site types with the highest visibility were the most heavily vandalized. These high-visibility sites include surface pueblos, towers, granaries, storage cysts, rock shelters, and cliff dwellings. Wilderness designation will not change a site type or visibility, and by definition wilderness is free of access roads. Roads, however, are often used as boundary lines for wilderness, and some dead-end roads are included in wilderness through the "cherry-stemming" process.

Nickens, Larralde, and Tucker (1981) examined the relationship between site vandalism and distance to the nearest road and found a statistically significant relationship (1981, 70). Archaeological sites closer to roads were more likely to have been vandalized than sites located away from roads. In interviews with residents of southwestern Colorado who admitted to participation in looting, 85 percent expressed a willingness to walk half a mile or less to a site from the nearest road (Nickens, Larralde, and Tucker 1981, 108). Nickens also examined the relationship between the type of nearest road and the presence of site vandalism. Roads were given a rank of type 2 (a gravel road) through type 5 (a track or jeep trail). There was not a statistically significant relationship between road type and vandalism (1981, 60). This study suggests that better protection of archaeological resources from vandals would occur in wilderness areas with two characteristics. First, the wilderness area should encompass a large, uninterrupted area. Second, the wilderness area should be bounded by geographic features rather than roads and should not contain "cherry-stemmed" roads.

## SOLUTIONS

With so many factors contributing to the destruction of archaeological resources within wilderness, protection of these resources will be an important task. Three protective actions can be readily found. Periodic re-evaluation of protective legislation can be used to find any shortcomings present in current laws. The Archaeological Resources Protection Act of 1979 demonstrates the utility of evaluating law for flaws.

The following cases illustrate how the law has to evolve in order to maintain protection. They are taken largely from accounts in Hutt, Jones, and McAllister (1992). In 1972, Ben Diaz located what he thought to be the cave of an Apache medicine man. From the cave, Diaz removed twenty-two face masks, headdresses, and other religious items. Diaz placed these items on sale at a consignment shop in Scottsdale, Arizona, where a collector offered $1,200 for the collection. Diaz refused, thinking that he could get more. The next people who contacted Diaz were the FBI. Diaz was charged under the Antiquities Act, even though the masks were less than five years old. During the trial, an anthropology professor testified that an item could be considered an antiquity the day it was made as long as it was used in an ancient ceremony. Diaz was convicted and appealed to U.S. District Court, where the conviction was upheld. Diaz then appealed to the Ninth Circuit Court of Appeals and argued that the ruling should be overturned because the term "antiquity" was unconstitutionally vague. The judge agreed with Diaz, and ruled that the criminal provisions of the Antiquities Act could no longer be used.

Five years later three people, Jones, Jones, and Gevara, were caught digging in an archaeological site in Tonto National Forest, Arizona. The three had excavated pottery, grave goods, and human skeletons. They had even taken photographs of themselves holding human skulls from the site. Since the Antiquities Act could no longer be used in Arizona to prosecute archaeological vandals, the three were charged under the general crimes of theft and destruction of government property. Prior to trial, the defense made a motion to dismiss the case, arguing that charges should be made under the most specific law, which was the invalid Antiquities Act, and thus the case should be dropped. The court held that prosecutors could use specific or general laws unless the congressional history of a specific law held that it was to be the only law used. There was no such history in the Antiquities Act, so the charges held. These two cases became an incentive to re-evaluate the Antiquities Act and subsequently formulate and pass the Archaeological Resources Protection Act to compensate for the flaws of the former.

Enforcement of current protective laws within wilderness will be problematic. Backcountry access will be limited not only for visitors but for law enforcement personnel as well. Nobody can use mechanized modes of travel within wilderness. Law enforcement agencies require adequate staff as well as adequate funding, both of which are currently lacking. For example, there are only two rangers for all 100,000-plus acres of Grand Gulch and only one law enforcement person for all of the Moab resource area (Portillo 1997).

Educating the public on the importance of archaeological resource preservation is perhaps the most effective means of protecting cultural resources. A visitor aware of the significance of the whole archaeological context will be less likely to destroy a site and will be more likely to report such actions if they are seen. A curriculum for wilderness education, to be used in both primary and secondary schools, has been developed by the Forest Service, the BLM, the National Park Service, and the U.S. Fish and Wildlife Service. This curriculum includes sections on prehistoric land use and wilderness archaeology (Moe 1997). The importance of education in protecting archaeological resources has been recognized at the highest levels. On March 20, 1990, Secretary of the Interior Manuel Lujan issued a directive that had four parts. At the very top of this four-part directive were the words "Emphasize public education" (Preface C of Smith and Ehrenhard 1991).

The evaluation of archaeological resource protection in wilderness is much more complex than a simple "it is good/it is bad" statement. Clearly there are several issues at hand that all need to be considered before any final decision is made. It is my hope that this chapter will help inform the decision in relation to the preservation of our nation's finite cultural heritage.

## ℚ REFERENCES TO CHAPTER 11

Ahlstrom, Richard V. N., Malcom Adair, R. Thomas Euler, and Robert C. Euler. 1992. *Pothunting in Central Arizona: The Perry Mesa Archaeological Site Vandalism Study.* Cultural Resources Management Report No. 13. USDA Forest Service, Southwestern Region. USDI Bureau of Land Management, Arizona.

BLM Utah (Utah State Office, Bureau of Land Management of the U.S. Department of the Interior). 1990. *Utah BLM Statewide Wilderness Final Environmental Impact Statement.* Salt Lake City, UT.

———. 1991. *Utah Statewide Wilderness Study Report.* Salt Lake City, UT.

Fowler, John M. 1974. "Protection of the Cultural Environment in Federal Law." In *Federal Environmental Law*, edited by Erica L Dolgin and Thomas G. P. Guilbert. St. Paul, MN: West Publishing Co., 1466–1517.

Gaede, Marc, and Marnie Gaede. 1977. 100 years of erosion at Poncho House. *The Kiva* 43:37–48.

Green, Dee F., and Polly Davis. 1981. *Cultural Resources Law Enforcement: An Emerging Science*, 2d ed. USDA Forest Service, Southwestern Region. Albuquerque, NM.

Hutt, Sherry, Elwood W. Jones, and Martin E. McAllister. 1992. *Archaeological Resource Protection.* Washington, DC: The Preservation Press.

McCool, Stephen F. 1985. "Does wilderness designation lead to increased recreational use?" *Journal of Forestry.* January 1985.

Moe, Jeannie M. 1997. Utah State BLM Education Coordinator. Personal communication, May 28.

Nickens, Paul R., Signa L. Larralde, and Gordon C. Tucker, Jr. 1981. *A Survey of Vandalism to Archaeological Resources in Southwestern Colorado.* Cultural Resources Series No. 11. USDI Bureau of Land Management, Colorado State Office. Denver, CO.

Portillo, Garth. 1997. Utah State BLM Archaeologist. Personal communication, May 28.

Smith, George S., and John E. Ehrenhard, eds. 1991. *Protecting the Past.* Boca Raton, FL: CRC Press.

U.S. General Accounting Office. 1987. *Cultural Resources: Problems Protecting and Preserving Federal Archaeological Resources.* Washington, DC: GAO, GAO/RCED-88-3.

# CHAPTER 12

# The Cost of Solitude

## Chris Perri

### INTO THE DEN OF WOLVES

Wilderness in Utah is a very delicate topic. There are many pros and cons to the Utah wilderness issue from an economic perspective. Economic arguments are often used by both sides of the wilderness debate, each emphasizing only those statistics that buttress their own claims. A basic problem with the use of economic arguments is the difficulty in measuring wilderness in dollars and cents. How is it possible to put a value on an item that has no marketable value? This point was made in a study on wilderness by Utah State University researchers:

> The conceptual methodology suggests that one must determine the benefits and costs *with* versus *without* the action proposed. Unfortunately, the analytical methodology needed to fully implement the conceptual analysis is less well-developed. Measuring the costs and benefits of goods not typically traded in the market is particularly difficult, and wilderness has typically been described as having several non-use values including those associated with preservation, option, bequest, existence, and non-uses. (Snyder 1995)

This chapter will explore the main economic areas surrounding wilderness proposals in Utah. The fundamental uses and non-uses of wilderness will be discussed, including the income derived from those uses. Also included is a discussion of the potential benefits and costs if wilderness does become a reality. A discussion of whether wilderness *should* be debated along economic lines is omitted; that is best left to the philosophers.

### USES OF WILDERNESS

Wilderness has many varying uses, and trying to name them all is nearly as problematic as counting grains of sand on a beach. The main uses of wilderness are recreation, habitat, and grazing. From a recreation perspective, studies at Utah State University show that the numbers of people entering and staying in wilderness areas are declining (Snyder 1995). Professor Thomas Power (1991) believes this is primarily due to the aging baby boom generation, who are becoming less physically active. Conversely, Utah's younger age group is expected to increase at a growth rate of twice the national average (State of Utah 1997). With 40 percent of wilderness users between sixteen and twenty-five years of age, Power is certain that usage will rise sharply as that age group grows rapidly in the near future (1991). A common belief concerning the number of wilderness users is that usage will skyrocket after designation, mainly because of the publicity surrounding designation. Nevertheless, a study by Stephen F. McCool in 1985 found that not only is this "designation effect" difficult to report, it is also based on many variable characteristics of each area, and is not as pronounced as once thought. His study of the Rattlesnake National Recreation and Wilderness Area found that usage actually dropped after designation (McCool 1985).

## The Economy of Utah

To get an accurate understanding of the economic aspects of wilderness, it is important to understand the economy of the state of Utah. The most stable economy is one that is very diversified. According to Natalie Gochnaur at the Governor's Office of Planning and Budget, a diversified economy is superior in two ways. First, diversification reduces the risk of potential failing industries. Boom-bust cycles, common in southern Utah in the past, could be mitigated by diversification. Second, diversification means self-reliance and less dependence on others. The state of Utah is now seventh in the nation in measures of economic diversity, far above the national average. This growth is primarily due to (1) the decline of the mining industry and downsizing of federal government employment, and (2) the growth of service industries, tourism, and manufacturing (State of Utah 1997). A good example of the benefits of diversification is Grand County. In 1981, 25 percent of Grand County's employment was mining related. By 1993, 80 percent of these jobs had been lost, yet the county's economy did not collapse, due to rapid growth in other stable areas, such as services (Power 1995).

A reliance on recreation and tourism creates economic dilemmas for rural counties in Utah. Tourism-related jobs are usually low paying, low skill, and seasonal. Also, tourism in Utah faces some unique challenges. First, tourism's infrastructure is weak. Roads, lack of facilities (including campgrounds, motel/hotels, restaurants), lack of air transportation, and lack of access to scenic sites are just a few. Second, Utah's available tourism promotion budget is minuscule compared to our neighbor Colorado.

Utah's potential to benefit from tourism is equal to Colorado's, but the financial backing does not exist in this state (Warner 1989).

Demographics is another important factor in understanding how Utah is most likely to grow. Although the state's population as a whole increased at 2.2 percent in 1996, which is over two times the national average of .9 percent, 87 percent of this growth occurred in the urban areas. Besides the Wasatch Front counties (comprising 82.6 percent statewide growth) the state is also populous in two other areas: (1) counties adjacent to the Wasatch Front, such as Cache, Wasatch, Tooele, Summit, Juab, Morgan, and Sanpete; and (2) southwest Utah, composed of Iron and Washington Counties. Washington County (St. George area) is growing at an amazing annual rate of 6.6 percent, ahead of all the other counties in the state. Through the year 2020, population growth is expected to continue in southwest Utah, the Wasatch Front, the Wasatch Back (Summit and Wasatch Counties), and Grand County (State of Utah 1997).

What is the relationship between the phenomenal growth in Washington County and wilderness in Utah? Is wilderness responsible for its numbers? According to Natalie Gochnaur, Washington County is popular for several reasons. Climate and scenic amenities play a role. Another reason is the number of young people living there. Dixie College brings many students into the county. It also attracts urban professionals and many retirees. Many of the immigrants to the county are from within the state.

How much of this is due to the nearby national parks and wilderness areas? Undoubtedly, they play an important part. However, wilderness and national parks are almost opposites on the developmental scale. Attributing wilderness to growth such as that in Washington County is not a fair comparison, even though most of the land within Zion National Park is *de facto* wilderness. It is also important to understand the amount of publicity that national parks receive compared to wilderness areas.

What are possible future trends? First, diversity in rural economic growth will probably continue. Reliance on one large industry will not support these struggling counties. Second, state population growth will continue to outpace the nation, but most of this growth will occur in metropolitan areas. Third, population gain is more common where retailing is a major activity (Johnson 1985).

## What Makes Rural Utah Tick

Several enormous money-makers for the state, and particularly the rural counties of the state, are located in or near proposed wilderness areas in southern Utah. The first of these is recreation and tourism. In 1996, tourism in Utah generated $3.8 billion dollars in revenue for the state and employed 91,000 workers, making it one of the top five industries in the state. The single largest recreation-related money-maker that takes place inside of or adjacent to proposed wilderness areas is river outfitting and guiding (State of Utah 1997).

The second source of revenue, mining, will be the most impacted by wilderness designation, as nearly all mining will cease in areas that are designated as wilderness. This basically means the loss of a modest number of jobs and approximately $4.4 million in lost income for the government in the form of lease payments (BLM Utah 1990). As the number of proposed wilderness acres increases, the dollar value of forgone oil, gas, and mineral leases increases (see chapter 7).

Grazing is the third source of wilderness revenue. As pointed out in chapter 9, it is permitted, but there is concern that AUMs will eventually be reduced. These three activities—recreation, mining, and grazing—are the largest potential money-makers from undeveloped public lands. Many other indirect benefits of wilderness exist, such as the amenity value and non-use value of wilderness, which will be discussed later.

## RECREATION AND ECONOMICS

### Recreation and Tourism's Financial Impact

Utah has some of the most outstanding recreational resources in the country. Because of this, Utah tourism is a $3.8 billion industry. The Economic Report to the Governor estimates that tourism, travel, and recreation employ about 9.5 percent of the population (91,000 people) (State of Utah 1997). Tourism is one of the top five industries in the state and continues to grow rapidly, slowed only by the state's infrastructure. Garfield County's largest industry is commercial recreation, a $3.7 million industry (Snyder 1995). However, due to the enormous number of people who invade Garfield County each year, it also has a large infrastructure problem, including lack of facilities, maintenance problems, and trash (Kinsel 1997). This problem is not confined to Utah; others have found this to apply generally to rural and recreation-based counties nationwide (Johnson et al. 1995).

### Potential Impact of Wilderness Designation

How will wilderness designation affect the counties' income derived from recreation and tourism? This is a difficult question to answer because the research done to date is incomplete and inconsistent. Utah State University researchers conducted a survey of wilderness users in four wilderness areas in southern Utah. An average daily expenditure of $33.42 was spent per group.[1] This is less than the average daily expenditure for motorized recreation. A recent study of power boaters suggests average expenditures of $50 to $75 a day (Snyder 1995). Along similar lines, it is easy to see how off-road vehicle (ORV) users spend more per day than wilderness users.

Currently, 80 percent of the WSAs in Utah have vehicle routes within them. This percentage translates to 679.3 miles of vehicle routes, roughly 2 percent of the state's total number of ORV routes. Currently, 601.8 of these miles of vehicle routes are open in the WSAs. ORV users constitute 9 percent of all public recreation use on BLM land (BLM Utah 1990). In addition, many other activities often involve driving off-road, such as camping, hunting, etc. When this is taken into account the number of ORV users is higher. With wilderness designation, much of this ORV use will be transferred to nearby surrounding areas or elsewhere. However, some of the 601.8 miles of vehicle routes located within WSAs are considered "destination" areas for some, and their closure represents a significant loss of recreation potential. Regarding the economic loss associated with primitive versus developed (motorized) recreation, Power states:

> This has led some to postulate a significant recreational opportunity cost associated with wilderness classification. In evaluating this tradeoff between different types of recreational use, the relative supply of one type of recreational land base has to be taken into account. If, for instance, there is an excess supply of one type of recreational land, adding to that supply may add little of economic value. Usage of that land will simply be offset by declining usage elsewhere. (Power 1995)

*Wilderness Value as a Recreational Resource*

It is obvious that wilderness is a precious and valuable resource for recreation, even though it is difficult to assign a value to it. Pope and Jones state:

> Many goods and services, including environmental amenities, are not traded in the marketplace. Non-market goods, such as air quality, wilderness preservation, unique scenic vistas, dispersed recreational opportunities and wildlife have value. Quantifying their value is a growing area of interest by scientists. (1990, 160)

A common way to determine the value of a non-marketable object is willingness to pay, or contingent valuation. Respondents are asked how much they would be willing to pay to preserve an area of land in one of several scenarios, such as land in a state of wilderness, multiple use, etc. The Pope and Jones study found that 86 percent of respondents rate wilderness preservation as either "very important" or "important." The average willingness-to-pay values for 5, 10, 15, and 30 percent of Utah's land area to be preserved as wilderness are, respectively, $53, $64, $75, and $92 (Pope and Jones 1990). To understand how much land is represented by these numbers, the BLM proposal of 1.9 million acres is 3.8 percent of the state, and all of the land currently in WSA status (3.2 million acres) is only 6.2 percent. UWC's new 9.1-million-acre reinventory is approximately 17 percent of the land area in Utah. One problem in doing a contingent valuation survey, such as the one used by Pope and Jones, is the use of percentages to represent the amount of land protected; it is difficult to grasp how much land is represented by a percentage. Also, these numbers do not necessarily correspond to political reality; no one expects 30 percent of the state to become wilderness, regardless of willingness to pay.

Utah State University researchers also conducted a willingness-to-pay survey that included more information, such as surveying urban versus rural opinion, and asking which wilderness proposals respondents support. This survey found that people who oppose wilderness in general are willing to spend a maximum of $540.44 a year to preserve multiple use of the land, compared to only $75.22 for those who support wilderness in general (Snyder 1995).

Another problem with the data concerns people's misunderstanding of the wilderness concept. In the USU survey many people stated that they had used recreational vehicles inside of a wilderness area or WSA (where they are not allowed and usually posted as such). Are these people confused about the purpose of wilderness or are they purposely violating the law?

## EXTRACTION AND WILDERNESS

Chapter 7 describes the long conflict between mining and wilderness. According to some, the closure of public lands to future mining represents an irreplaceable loss. To many others, the designation of wilderness will permanently protect these lands from future damage at the hands of the mining industry, if it in fact makes a comeback.

### Future Expectations

What future potential for mineral development is there in the deserts of southern Utah? And if there is significant potential, should we become reliant on this type of industry? Historically, extractive industries have brought much economic disruption to local communities. Thomas Power suggests protecting local economies by making the transition away from the historical extractive base that has disrupted local economies in the past (Power 1995). Power argues that it is inaccurate to figure out the forgone value of minerals by multiplying the amount of mineral by its estimated market value. The problems with this system of valuation are (1) the amount of minerals is uncertain—many of the estimates are simply best guesses; (2) the costs of access, extraction, and transportation must be taken into account (when transportation costs alone are taken into account, many of the potential mineral sites become economically unfeasible to mine); and (3) many alternate sources of supply are more readily available than the mineral deposits in Utah (Power 1991). One thing is certain; once wilderness designation is made, the mineral potential will never be known because all surveying will cease.

### Known Possibilities and Reliance on Minerals

The contribution of mining to the state's economy has been declining since the 1960s, and is expected to continue to decline (Power 1991). According to one estimate, eight-tenths of one percent of all jobs in Utah are in the mining industry (Spomer 1996). By the year 2010, it is projected that that number will fall to six-tenths of one percent (Power 1995).[2] Of course, few if any people currently employed in mining work in WSAs; much of the current mining employment occurs in underground coal mining that is not threatened by wilderness consideration. However, wilderness also employs few if any people.

Despite the declining employment in the mining sector, tax revenues from mining contribute significantly to some county budgets. According to the Snyder study,

> Even though gross sales from the mining and minerals industries may be relatively small in some of these counties, the proportion of property taxes paid by these extractive industries often comprised a significant share of the total property taxes collected by the county, a major source of revenue for local governments for school, streets, etc. (Snyder 1995, 257)

Duchesne County received 43–65 percent of its property taxes from the mining sector from 1989 to 1992. Similarly, Grand County's property tax receipts from mining-related industry ranged between 17 percent and 24 percent (Snyder 1995). Again, wilderness designation in the short run is not expected to significantly impact this number, but it could affect future mining in areas that become wilderness.

### WILDERNESS VALUATION: AN ECONOMIC APPROACH

### Ways to Value Wilderness

The most difficult question is how to place an economic value on wilderness. It is as subjective as it is scientific. For example, compare the following studies: The Leaming study estimated a $91 million loss due to the loss of uranium mining in wilderness, while a study by Thomas Power arrived at a different answer: zero loss. Several comprehensive studies have been done on the wilderness issue. The main studies were done by Power at the University of Montana, Snyder at Utah State University, Leaming, and Pope and Jones. The Power study and the Pope and Jones study are usually regarded as pro-wilderness studies, whereas the other two are viewed as supporting multiple-use designation regardless of the effect it has on potential wilderness areas.

In respect to wilderness, there are several types of values. The first two are use versus non-use values. Use value is economic well-being derived directly from the use of a wilderness area. Non-use value can be obtained without actually visiting wilderness. Even though a person may never set foot in a wilderness area, that person may still be willing to make economic sacrifices to protect and preserve it. Many studies suggest that these non-use values actually exceed the use values. A recent study by Pope and Jones suggests a value of $10 to $40 million per year due to non-use values, depending on the amount of land that is designated (1990). Wilderness also has "existence value," which is the value of its resource potential even if it is not actively used. Finally, bequest value is the value derived in preserving a unique landscape for the benefit of future generations.

Closely related to use and non-use values is opportunity cost. When opportunity cost is used in the context of wilderness, it is often defined as forgone uses that are lost in the stead of another choice. There are many forgone losses if wilderness designation occurs. Some are associated with developed recreation, which includes lost development opportunity, the value derived from developed recreational activities, future jobs related to developed recreation, and income to surrounding communities that support these recreational activities. Another forgone loss is the activity associated with the extraction of oil, gas, tar sands, coal, and other precious minerals, and the employment tangentially related to mining.

If wilderness lands are opened to development, several forgone losses occur due to loss of protection. These include protection of watershed, protection of airshed (and the chance to prevent pollution as a by-product of development), wildlife protection, and protection from formal development of vast stretches of untrammeled and pristine land. Remember, however, that wilderness does not equal total protection; primitive recreation can also damage the land, especially if it occurs in large numbers.

*Why Wilderness Is So Popular*

There are many aspects of wilderness that make it attractive to people and communities. First, it has amenity value; people like to live near wilderness and are willing to make sacrifices to ensure their surroundings are natural and pleasant. Many reports support this. In the 1980s, the only group of non-metro counties that had above-average growth rates were "amenity" counties where natural and social environments supported both recreation and retirement benefits (Deavers 1989). Also, a review of counties adjacent to classified wilderness reveals that population growth rates are two to three times that of other non-metropolitan counties. Furthermore, a survey of recent immigrants to wilderness counties shows that the presence of wilderness was a major factor in the location decisions of 60 percent of newcomers (Rudzitis and Johansen 1989).

Another group that is attracted by wilderness characteristics is that of retirees. Often referred to as "footloose" income because it is not associated with the current work force, the income of this group makes a significant impact in the growth of local communities. For instance, in Grand County, estimated retirement income is three times as large as extractive income, and it continues to grow as extractive income declines (Power 1995). Determining where to retire is largely dependent on environment and climate. This is obvious when all of the amenities around St. George are taken into account. Another point to make concerning retirees is the relative non-use of wilderness by this group; retirees value wilderness as protected landscapes more than as a natural playground.

## State Impact from Wilderness
In 1991 the Utah Office of Planning and Budget conducted a study to determine potential impacts of wilderness designation. Three scenarios were proposed: negative, neutral, and positive. The negative scenario assumed 3.2 million acres of wilderness and estimated $67 million in personal income losses and 1,700 job losses. The neutral scenario assumed two million acres (the BLM proposal), and estimated personal income losses at $360,000 and fourteen lost jobs. Finally, the positive scenario assumed two million acres and estimated gains in personal income of $15 million and six hundred new jobs (State of Utah 1991). These scenarios demonstrate how difficult it is to evaluate the future economic impact of wilderness designation.

## Wilderness and Employment
One of the largest concerns of rural Utahns with regard to wilderness is the loss or gain of jobs that will accompany designation. Over the last four years, Utah's job-growth rate has exceeded 5 percent, and every major industry has grown except mining, which has decreased 3.7 percent. The top two industries are construction and services.

According to the BLM EIS, local employment (under the 3.2-million-acre proposal) is expected to generate only a very small number of new jobs (primarily seasonal recreation guides), and potential employment from mineral activity will be forgone. The EIS concludes that employment gain or loss from wilderness designation will be inconsequential on a statewide basis but will significantly affect some counties.

Aside from total employment estimates, there is also a difference in the kind of jobs created. Wilderness tends to create service employment, in contrast with the higher-paying jobs in extractive industries. Generally it takes three service jobs to equal one mining job (Snyder 1995). Service jobs (more specifically recreation/tourism–related jobs) are usually seasonal and lower paying. However, there are other factors to be considered. First, even though mining jobs pay more, they can interrupt local economies because of their dependence on the mineral market, which often ends abruptly in boom/bust cycles. Second, when new mining begins in an area, not all of the resulting jobs are filled by local people. Mining companies often bring outside workers with them (Garrity 1997). According to Glenn Eurick of the Barrick Gold Corporation, dependency on local employees for mining operations depends greatly on the type of technology used to remove the ore. The higher the technology, the slimmer the chance of finding local people with those skills. However, in many of Barrick's Nevada mines, 85 percent of employees were locals (Eurick 1997). Third, many of the local people who go to work for a mining company were previously employed somewhere else and have to quit a current job to begin working for the mining company. When a mining company announces X number of new jobs, these jobs are not really new, the company is simply rearranging the job situation (Power 1997). Nevertheless, it adds to the local economy.

In order to keep up with its population growth, Utah needs to create twenty thousand to thirty thousand new jobs each year. Most of these jobs come from land in private ownership (Utah Public Lands Multiple Use Coalition 1997). Neither mining jobs nor recreation jobs can approach this number. On the one hand, wilderness designation could restrict economic possibilities, but on the other hand, designation may provide such an outstanding environment that it will attract thousands of people to nearby communities, boosting local economies.

*CONCLUSION*

So, in which direction should we proceed? This is a question with many answers, none of which is necessarily "right." One of the main questions that needs more research is the actual benefit of wilderness as a preserve. Will wilderness really become such an attraction as to become a self-producing fully independent source of local income? Will wilderness attract droves of people into the counties of southern Utah (above and beyond their current growth rates) that will diversify and expand their economies to an extent that is unattainable without wilderness? Will Utah ever see the $10 to $40 million dollars in non-use value that is predicted? If wilderness is not designated, are we not only seriously jeopardizing the future protection of that land, but also missing a greater economic benefit that could be gained with wilderness protection?

There are many variables that make the whole economic question very unpredictable: *if* mineral reserves are mined, *if* the mining companies employ many locals, *if* a number of touring businesses spring up to take advantage of the wilderness recreation, *if* there is a way to capitalize on non-use value, and *if* wilderness really is a people magnet. And none of these variables helps us answer the larger question: Do we really want hordes of people coming to the remote, beautiful places of southern Utah, whether they be miners, backpackers, or retirees?

Is it possible to have the best of both worlds? A possible solution may be to determine which of the many variables has the greatest potential of becoming a significant future economic event; gauge that variable in terms of percentage of change against the growth of the county it would occur in and the state as a whole. Use 5 percent or 10 percent change as a measure of acceptance. Next, take the largest possibilities on each side (variables resulting from wilderness designation, and variables resulting from no designation) and work out a way to keep the largest possibilities on each side. This will mean reducing the acres of potential wilderness on the one side and reducing the number of development sites on the other. The only way for this type of approach to work is to eliminate all non-compromising attitudes of the various parties, which is desperately needed. Without an acknowledgment by all of their willingness to work together, the wilderness debate in Utah will never be settled.

## ₵ NOTES TO CHAPTER 12

1. Expenditures were collected on a per household, per trip basis. The average expenditure was divided by the average number of days spent, and the four averages for the four wilderness areas surveyed were then averaged to come up with the $33.42 figure.

2. It should be noted that mining accounts for 23 percent of the job force in some rural counties such as Emery County (State of Utah 1997).

## ℭ *REFERENCES TO CHAPTER 12*

BLM Utah (Utah State Office, Bureau of Land Management of the U.S. Department of the Interior). 1990. *Utah BLM Statewide Environmental Impact Statement, Final.* Salt Lake City, UT.

Deavers, Ken. 1989. The reversal of the rural renaissance. *Entrepreneurial Economy Review* (September/October): 3–5.

Eurick, Glenn. 1997. Barrick Gold Corp. Personal interview by author, May 28.

Garrity, Michael T. 1997. University of Utah Economics Dept. Personal interview by author, April 15.

Johnson, Kenneth M. 1985. *The Impact of Population Change on Business Activity in Rural America.* Boulder, CO: Westview Press.

Johnson, Kenneth, John P. Pelissero, David B. Holian, and Michael T. Maly. 1995. Local government fiscal burden in nonmetropolitan America. *Rural Sociology* 60 (Fall): 381–98.

Kinsel, Sheldon. 1997. Utah Farm Bureau. Personal interview by author, May 21.

McCool, Stephen F. 1985. "Does wilderness designation lead to increased recreational use?" *Journal of Forestry* (January): 39–41.

Pope, C. Arden, III, and Jeffery W. Jones. 1990. Value of wilderness designation in Utah. *Journal of Environmental Management* 30 (August): 157–74.

Power, Thomas M. 1991. *Wilderness Preservation and the Economy of Utah.* Missoula: University of Montana.

———. 1995. The economics of wilderness preservation in Utah: testimony for the U.S. House of Representatives. *Southern Utah Wilderness Alliance* (Winter): 1–8.

———. 1997. University of Montana Economics Department. Telephone interview by author, May 22.

Rudzitis, Gundars, and Harley E. Johansen. 1989. *Amenities, Migration, and Nonmetropolitan Regional Development, Report to the National Science Foundation,* Department of Geography. Moscow: University of Idaho.

Snyder, Donald L. 1995. *Potential Economic Impacts of Wilderness Designation.* Logan: Utah State University.

Spomer, Dan. 1996. The economics of wilderness. *Canyon Echo* (September).

State of Utah. 1991. Office of Planning and Budget, *Economic Analysis of Wilderness Designation in Utah,* Draft Report.

———. 1997. *Economic Report to the Governor.* Salt Lake City: Governor's Office of Planning and Budget.

Utah Public Lands Multiple Use Coalition. 1997. "Ten Wilderness Issues."

Warner, Fara. 1989. Utah's $2.2 billion tourism industry. *Utah Business* (March): 19–22.

# Lessons from the Past, Proposals for the Future

In an informal get-together between the authors of this book and several residents of southern Utah, everyone discovered they had something in common: no one wanted Utah's last best places to be overrun with "outsiders." The local residents had been visiting the area's canyons and mesas for many years, and harbored a sense of ownership and responsibility for them. They viewed southern Utah's spectacular redrock country as part of their heritage, and they did not want to see it engulfed by people who might interfere with their long-time usage. As one elderly local put it, "I don't want to take my family down one of these canyons and run into a bunch of skinny-dipping hippies."

The wilderness advocates at the meeting also expressed a fear that the most scenic and secluded backcountry locations would be overrun by visitors who would appear in such large numbers that all opportunity for solitude would be lost. As one wilderness supporter said, "I don't want to backpack into my favorite spot and find a crowd of tourists there." Finally, after some good-natured debate, everyone at the get-together came up with a solution: SWAs, or Secret Wilderness Areas. It was agreed that these areas would be managed with sufficient latitude to encompass the needs and activities of both rural and urban Utahns, which would not be difficult if the needs of "outsiders" could be ignored. The SWA idea generated lots of laughs and a sense of camaraderie.

But of course, in the hard-bitten world of wilderness politics, such a "solution" is not feasible. The

215

reality is that federal public lands in Utah belong to all the people of the nation, and everyone in the country has a potential interest in the Utah wilderness debate. No matter how much Utahns care for the land, we cannot make BLM land in southern Utah a private enclave. Thus, it is within the national political context that we must find a solution to this conflict.

This final section of the book focuses on two approaches that might hopefully yield some solutions. First, we need to examine past successes. To many people, the wilderness issue seems intractable and never-ending. After twenty years of conflict, we appear to be no closer to resolution. According to this view, it just is not possible to make a decision. History gives us a different message, however: it *is* possible to pass a wilderness bill for Utah. In 1984, after years of debate, twelve new wilderness areas were designated in Utah. In chapter 13, Richard Warnick describes the process that led to the designation of those wilderness areas. Perhaps we can learn important lessons from this past success.

A second approach is to do the unconventional. The status quo is not working. Perhaps it is time to consider some new ideas about how to resolve the problem—and do so without imposing a burden on certain groups of people or the land. In the final chapter we propose a "community context approach" that we hope will open some doors, and allow the debate to move to the next level.

—The Editors

# CHAPTER 13

# The Year of Utah Wilderness
## Lessons from 1984

### Richard Warnick

President Ronald Reagan signed the Utah Wilderness Act, Public Law 98-428, on September 28, 1984. The following August, a Utah wilderness dedication at Mirror Lake in the High Uintas marked both the culmination of years of negotiations and the beginning of a long period of polarized debate over the future of Utah wildlands. Under a brilliant midday sun, the U.S. Forest Service set up wooden wilderness trail signs, one for each national forest wilderness in Utah. At the start of the ceremony, only the sign with the name of Utah's first designated wilderness area—Lone Peak—faced the crowd. Then the rest, each representing one of the twelve new areas, were turned around one by one.

Applause marked the debut of the Mount Naomi, Wellsville Mountain, Mount Olympus, Twin Peaks, Deseret Peak, Mount Timpanogos, Mount Nebo, Box–Death Hollow, Ashdown Gorge, Dark Canyon, Pine Valley Mountain, and the High Uintas wilderness areas. Each of these simple signs represented a hard-fought compromise. In the case of the High Uintas, the deliberations took twenty years. The total acreage for these wilderness areas is shown in table 13.1.

The Utah Wilderness Act was part of an unprecedented package of twenty-one statewide wilderness bills enacted in the 98th Congress. This act proved that Utahns could, literally, find common ground and work out compromises on wilderness issues. In addition, the Arizona Wilderness Act of 1984 (P.L. 98-406) established two Bureau of Land Management (BLM) wilderness areas—Beaver Dam Mountain and Paria Canyon–Vermilion Cliffs—that extend into southern Utah. Including

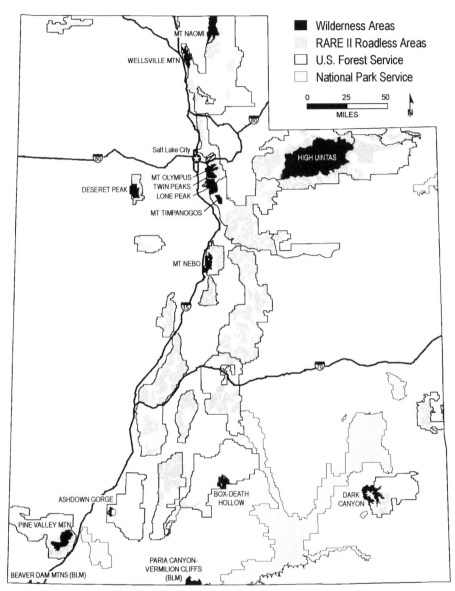

Map 13.1—Utah's National Forest Wilderness in 1984
(Sources: Utah Automated Geographic Reference Center, USFS 1979)

TABLE 13.1—Utah National Forest Wilderness Acreages, 1979–1984

| | USFS RARE II[1] | Conservationist Proposal[2] | Delegation July 1983 Proposal | H.R. 4516 S. 2155 | Utah Wilderness Act |
|---|---|---|---|---|---|
| Ashdown Gorge | 7,024 | 7,024 | 7,000 | 7,024 | 7,000 |
| Box–Death Hollow | FP 31,600 | 31,600 | 31,600 | 31,600 | 26,000 |
| Dark Canyon | 48,000 | 48,000 | 30,000 | 45,000 | 45,000 |
| Deseret Peak | 43,824 | 55,000 | 15,000 | 0 | 25,500 |
| Fishlake Mountain | 24,280 | 24,280 | 18,000 | 0 | 0 |
| High Uintas | 512,000 | 659,000 | 415,000 | 448,000 | 460,000 |
| Mount Naomi | FP 66,320 | 66,320 | 0 | 41,500 | 44,350 |
| Mount Nebo | FP 36,860 | 36,800 | 0 | 23,500 | 28,000 |
| Mount Olympus | 15,985 | 24,800 | 15,985 | 15,985 | 16,000 |
| Mount Timpanogos[3] | Not studied | 14,500 | 0 | 10,750 | 10,750 |
| Mount Watson | 0 | 80,000 | 0 | 0 | 0 |
| Pine Valley Mountain | 83,500 | 83,500 | 45,000 | 48,500 | 50,000 |
| Red Canyon | 13,655 | 14,555 | 0 | 0 | 0 |
| Thousand Lake Mountain | 0 | 43,000 | 0 | 0 | 0 |
| Twin Peaks | 12,364 | 12,364 | 12,264 | 12,364 | 13,100 |
| Tushar Mountains | 0 | 36,000 | 0 | 0 | 0 |
| Wellsville Mountain | 22,513 | 22,513 | 22,500 | 22,513 | 23,850 |
| Totals | 917,925 | 1,259,256 | 612,349 | 706,736 | 749,550 |

Notes: All acreage figures are approximations

[1] "FP" indicates the area was recommended for "further planning" instead of wilderness.

[2] The "critical areas" proposal supported by the Utah Wilderness Association and nine other conservation groups.

[3] Mount Timpanogos, as an administratively designated scenic area, was not studied in RARE II.

Lone Peak, designated by the omnibus Endangered American Wilderness Act of 1978, Utah now had fifteen wilderness areas.

Comments made at the dedication reflected sharp philosophical differences. Representative Jim Hansen (R-Utah) stated his belief that only the most rugged and remote areas ought to be set aside. Looking toward Hayden Peak, he said, "I don't see we've protected this by a wilderness designation. The Lord's protection is more than a wilderness designation will ever do." Max Peterson, Chief of the Forest Service, summed up that agency's skeptical view of preservation by emphasizing the concept of "wise use of natural resources," with wilderness playing a relatively small role (Wharton 1985). Utah Wilderness Association coordinator Dick Carter also qualified his acceptance of the compromise. "We . . . aspired to an exceptional bill and it didn't happen. It stopped short," he said. "I emphasize it is not even close to over yet. The battle's going to go forward" (Carter 1985).

Some conservationists, particularly the newly organized Southern Utah Wilderness Alliance, took an even more critical view. Politicians "browbeat conservationists into accepting terrible legislation," according to one complaint (Weed 1985). Others characterized it as a "Wasatch Front pocket wilderness bill" and a "paper success" (SUWA 1984). Wilderness advocates wanted far more than they got in 1984, but they were forced to weigh the pain of compromise against the chance of finally obtaining a High Uintas wilderness and other critical core areas on national forest and BLM land. "A wilderness today is worth more than a wilderness ten years from now," said Carter in an interview during the bill negotiations. "Wilderness is static in time . . . resource conflicts go on and on. Had we designated the High Uintas last year, we wouldn't be talking about oil and gas conflicts on the High Uintas" (Wheeler 1984, 76).

## FINDING A WAY TO THE WILDERNESS

One lesson that can be learned from looking back is that the Utah political hierarchy has always been slow to respond to calls for wilderness preservation. Years of seemingly fruitless discussion preceded the decisions of 1984, although it can be said that this gradual process served to familiarize decision-makers with the issues. Much debate focused on the High Uintas, at that time the largest undesignated roadless area in the national forest system.

The interior of the High Uintas wildlands, first set aside in 1931, was one of thirty-four national forest primitive areas subject to wilderness studies mandated by the 1964 Wilderness Act. In 1966 the Forest Service recommended enlarging the 247,000-acre primitive area into a 322,998-acre wilderness. Action on this proposal was deferred indefinitely because the Uintas are the main source of water for the Central Utah Project, and politicians were concerned that some of this land would be needed for dams and reservoirs (Fradkin 1989). In the early 1970s the Forest Service expanded its Wilderness Act mandate with the Roadless Area Review and Evaluation (RARE). RARE was criticized in Congress, which essentially repudiated the first RARE study (Roggenbuck, Stankey, and Roth 1990). One result of the RARE I controversy was the omnibus Endangered American Wilderness Act, which designated the Lone Peak Wilderness (U.S. Congress 1978).

RARE II was initiated by the Carter administration in 1977 in an attempt to correct the earlier flaws. But RARE II ran into dissension from conservationists who believed they had a right to expect more generous wilderness recommendations from a president who seemed personally to favor land preservation. Timber and oil company representatives, on the other hand, expressed relief at the extent of areas recommended for non-wilderness uses (Nice 1978).

In Utah, RARE II studied 3,045,081 acres of national forest roadless areas and recommended 783,145 acres of wilderness in ten areas;[1] three more areas totaling 134,780 acres were proposed for "further planning." As it did in other states, RARE II helped set the agenda for Utah's national forest wilderness debate. The list of roadless areas recommended for wilderness and "further planning" by the Forest Service included nearly all of the areas that later received legislative attention (U.S. Department of Agriculture 1979). By contrast, the 80,000-acre Mount Watson proposed wilderness, just west of the High Uintas, received a "nonwilderness" recommendation. Despite the verdict of RARE II, conservationists still give the area a high priority (Smart 1997). The Tushar Mountains and Thousand Lake Mountain are two more examples of areas that received negative Forest Service recommendations. Other Utah roadless areas were simply ignored during RARE II.

In 1977 Governor Scott Matheson assembled a State Wilderness Committee (SWC), composed of state and local government officials and staff members of the Utah congressional delegation. Governor Matheson felt the state needed an overall wilderness plan because RARE II, national park wilderness studies, and the early stages of the BLM wilderness inventory were all under way at the same time. The SWC discussed a response to RARE II from July through September, 1978. The local officials on the committee, led by San Juan County Commissioner Calvin Black, one of the leaders of the "Sagebrush Rebellion" movement, refused to accept any more than 300,000 acres of national forest wilderness. The committee's majority called for the designation of approximately 684,000 acres, plus four areas for further study including another 123,400 acres.

Governor Matheson had hoped to bring some of the state's rural opinion leaders to a better understanding of wilderness issues, but also deliberately stacked the SWC against them. The five local officials "voted against the proposed recommendations and immediately swarmed to my office to protest," Matheson later recalled (Matheson and Kee 1986, 140). Cal Black's revolt persuaded the governor to refrain from issuing a formal state position on the RARE II study. The "north versus south" conflict between state government officials and southern Utah county commissioners became a recurring theme in the wilderness debate.

Although a final, comprehensive wilderness plan was never produced, the SWC continued in existence through the rest of the Matheson administration and was revived for a time by his successor, Governor Norm Bangerter. The committee focused public attention on the wilderness issue, provided the governor with some control over the discussion, and generated media attention. At its peak, the SWC was meeting regularly with members of interest groups and the public.

Congressional interest in Utah's forest wilderness began to coalesce in 1981. The Reagan administration took office, and the GOP won control of the Senate in the 1980 elections. The chairman of the House public lands subcommittee, Representative John Seiberling (D-Ohio), and Representative Beverly Byron (D-Maryland), came to Utah in August and took a helicopter tour of Mount Naomi and the High Uintas with Representatives Jim Hansen and Dan Marriott.[2] Seiberling talked about the possibility of a RARE II bill, but the Utah Republicans cautioned against any action that might hamper the oil exploration boom the state was then enjoying (Bauman 1981).

Following the tour, Seiberling asked his aide Andy Weissner to gather more information. Weissner, who was in close contact with Utah conservationists, wrote a detailed memo with specifics on a number of areas proposed for wilderness designation (Weissner 1981). A month later, Dick Carter wrote a letter to the Utah congressional delegation urging them to introduce a bill (Carter 1981). Governor Matheson offered encouragement. In a speech at the March 1982 annual meeting of the Utah Wilderness Association, he declared, "I'd really like to cut a ribbon for a High Uintas Wilderness . . . while I'm still governor. . . . If we work together to reach agreement on areas, boundaries and management that represents the broad balance of Utah interests, Utah wilderness is not that far away" (Perry 1982).

The discussions about a forest wilderness bill soon took on a new urgency. In *California v. Block*, the Ninth Circuit Court of Appeals upheld an earlier federal court ruling that the RARE II EIS was inadequate (1982). The court required the Forest Service to go back and study roadless areas yet again. Utah was not among the seven states immediately affected by the Ninth Circuit Court decision, but in February 1983 Assistant Secretary of Agriculture John Crowell announced a "RARE II re-evaluation" (immediately dubbed "RARE III" by the media) that would include every state that was not covered by RARE II "release" and "sufficiency" legislation (USDA 1983).

Suddenly, not only the conservationists but also other interest groups, such as the timber and petroleum industries, could see a need for legislation. Wilderness advocates knew they could expect no improvements from a Reagan administration roadless area study, which Crowell wanted to incorporate in forest plans scheduled for completion in 1985. The multiple-use side was impatient with the lengthy RARE process, and sought relief from Congress. A proposed nationwide release bill did not get far. Individual state bills would be needed.

*California v. Block* was a catalyst, but only where the political ground-work had been laid. Utah was ready, but other western states that were even more bitterly divided on the wilderness issue, notably Idaho and Montana, never reached a compromise on RARE II.

## A UTAH WILDERNESS BILL TAKES SHAPE

Jake Garn, Utah's senior senator, had strong views about doing a "Utah wilderness bill instead of a Seiberling wilderness bill" (Husselbee 1983). Garn also favored a three-agency approach, which would resolve the questions of national forest, national park, and BLM wilderness all at once (Wharton 1983). Dick Carter thought that a three-agency bill would be too controversial. He warned Ted Stewart, chief aide to Representative Hansen, that it could lead to a failure to reach a consensus locally and might provoke a national debate over Utah wilderness reminiscent of the bitter Alaska lands dispute (Ford 1983). Hansen, in turn, helped persuade Senator Garn to agree to a separate Forest Service bill because the BLM was still too far from a final wilderness recommendation (Hansen 1997a).

In the wake of RARE II, Carter's Utah Wilderness Association (UWA) had produced a 1.6-million-acre citizens' forest wilderness proposal also supported by the Utah Chapter of the Sierra Club, the Utah Audubon Society, the Wasatch Mountain Club, and other local conservation organizations. It included a 659,000-acre proposal for a High Uintas Wilderness. UWA then began drawing up a "critical areas" list to highlight areas in the proposal that had the most support and the fewest resource conflicts.

The feeling that the High Uintas ought to be included in a statewide bill was nearly unanimous. Governor Matheson and the congressional delegation were also interested in releasing the bulk of RARE II roadless areas to non-wilderness uses. The other elements of a bill remained undecided until after a series of informal staff-level discussions around the state. Congressional aides met behind closed doors with Governor Matheson, county commissioners, and various interest groups to find out what wilderness area designations they could accept (Thalman 1983).[3] In a May 16th meeting with conservationists, Ted Stewart and the other delegation staffers made it clear that they intended to assiduously avoid resource conflicts between wilderness and non-wilderness land uses by erring on the side of less wilderness acreage (Bauman 1983a).

Tension began to arise between UWA and the local Sierra Club leadership over the "critical areas" list. UWA sought to emphasize about 1.2 million of the 1.6 million acres, but the Sierra Club saw this as a pullback from the joint proposal. The difference in positions became public in

June, when Alan Miller, chairman of the Sierra Club's Utah chapter, wrote a letter to the *Deseret News* (Miller 1983). The Sierra Club began work on a separate proposal, formally announced eight months later, which called for 2.6 million acres of national forest wilderness in Utah.

On July 1, the governor and the delegation made public a draft Utah wilderness bill for a little more than 612,000 acres. This "discussion proposal" was greeted with tacit approval from multiple-use groups; wilderness advocates expressed dismay. This starting bid on wilderness acreage was well below the Forest Service RARE II recommendations and a million acres short of what conservationists had proposed. The proposal included only a 415,000-acre High Uintas Wilderness, and no designations at all for the Mount Naomi and Mount Nebo areas. Mount Naomi was the third-largest RARE II area in Utah; Nebo is the highest peak in the Wasatch Range.

Release language specified that roadless areas not designated wilderness would be "managed for multiple uses other than wilderness" and excluded from further wilderness study indefinitely (Utah Congressional Delegation 1983). This went a step beyond the concept of "hard release" as it was then understood. It was the "permanent release" desired by the oil and gas industry (Cash 1983).

Broad, unprecedented exceptions to standard wilderness management appeared in the discussion proposal. For example, there was special language permitting the routine use of motor vehicles for a wide variety of purposes, including recreational access for handicapped and elderly visitors. There was a provision that would have allowed continued mineral leasing.[4] Another section required the Forest Service to increase the authorized grazing within Utah wilderness areas "as range conditions permit." Additional construction of water development facilities was authorized inside wilderness areas (Utah Congressional Delegation 1983). The information presented earlier, in chapter 6, makes it obvious that the Utah delegation's proposal was quite extreme in this regard.

The delegation appeared to envision a separate category of "Utah wilderness" within the National Wilderness Preservation System, managed according to different policies. Representative Dan Marriott described the discussion proposal as "really a quasi-wilderness bill" (Fitzpatrick 1983). Nothing like it had ever been introduced in Congress; it seemed inconceivable that Seiberling's subcommittee would seriously consider such unprecedented management language.

Crowded public hearings held in Roosevelt, Salt Lake City, Cedar City, and Logan, and hundreds of written comments sent to Governor Matheson and Utah's senators and congressmen, were dominated by criticism of the proposal. The Salt Lake hearing on July 11 was the most contentious. Angry wilderness supporters filled the State Office Building auditorium, ready to confront all five members of the congressional delegation. Senator Garn, who chaired the meeting, threatened to walk out unless everyone came to order. Three-quarters of the speakers wanted more wilderness areas, and denounced the release and exception language. Under the delegation's proposed management rules, said one, nearly all of Utah could be designated wilderness without curtailing anyone's normal activities (Bauman 1983b).

Representatives of multiple-use interest groups largely agreed with the discussion proposal, but they still weighed in with now-familiar rhetoric. To the Utah Wool Growers, wilderness would "allow for a breeding ground for predators" (Acord 1983). Kaibab Industries lamented that "future generations will be deprived of needed wood for shelter" (Fordyce 1983). The Utah Petroleum Association said the proposal was "clearly excessive and ignores the multiple use concepts" on federal lands (Peacock 1983).

A few comments came from Utahns who viewed wilderness as an exclusive preserve for backpackers. One letter said, "I attend church on Sundays, leaving time to enjoy these great outdoors we speak of, very limited. On a Friday after work and a Saturday, there just isn't enough time to walk in very far!" (Brewer 1983). Commenting on the High Uintas, another writer asked, "What good is a wilderness if only a select few can ever see it? What good are natural resources if no one can use them?" (Wilcken 1983).

The Utah delegation made some improvements to the wilderness bill by the time they introduced it in November 1983, just before the end of the congressional session.[5] Mount Naomi, a big issue at the Logan hearing in July, was added, along with Mount Nebo and Mount Timpanogos. Deseret Peak and Fishlake Mountain were now gone from the bill. Most of the other areas, especially the High Uintas, had larger boundaries. More than 94,000 additional acres were in the bill, which then received a cautious endorsement from Governor Matheson.

The permanent release language had been replaced with "Wyoming" hard release that postponed further wilderness studies until the third round of forest planning—around the year 2010. And the management language no longer contradicted the 1964 Wilderness Act (U.S. Congress 1983).

Rob Smith, the Utah representative for the Sierra Club and the Wilderness Society, wondered at the changes: "There is an immense philosophical barrier to overcome with our delegation. It is difficult for them to acknowledge there is a wilderness constituency at all. So in Utah, it represents a truly major step to even come up with a wilderness bill that doesn't have a lot of funny items in it" (Marston 1983).

What was now before Congress was the result of extensive public comment as well as private discussions. A critical mass of public concern about wilderness in Utah coincided with a national window of opportunity for RARE II wilderness legislation. A conservationist agenda to set aside a core of national forest wilderness areas came together, for a brief time, with the agenda of industry and multiple-use groups that wanted roadless areas released from wilderness study.

### "There Were No Easy Areas"

In 1984, the fact of an imminent decision on Utah wilderness led to sharpened debate on specific areas. A February 9th Senate hearing presided over by Senator Malcolm Wallop (R-Wyoming) provided a forum for the oil and gas industry to call for eliminating several areas from the bill. The region of complex faulting along the Utah-Wyoming border that geologists call the "Overthrust Belt" had been known for its oil seeps as early as 1847, when pioneers used them to lubricate the axles of their wagons. Large-scale commercial oil exploration began in the late 1970s, and required lots of exploratory drilling because it is difficult to predict where the oil accumulates underground (Alt and Hyndman 1995).

Atlantic Richfield, Conoco, and other oil industry representatives wanted to take Mount Naomi and the north slope of the High Uintas out of the bill for the sake of pending lease applications. Conservationists pointed out that the U.S. Geological Survey rated petroleum potential in the wilderness as "low." On the Uintas, the North Flank Fault divided the high and low potential areas; UWA's proposed boundary ran south of the fault, minimizing the conflict. Even if oil exploration uncovered new reserves, these would amount to no more than a few days of national consumption, they argued (U.S. Senate 1984).

Box–Death Hollow, near Escalante, became the most controversial area in Utah when Mid-Continent Oil found large quantities of carbon dioxide ($CO_2$) in an anticline 3,000 feet below the proposed wilderness. The $CO_2$ could be used to enhance oil recovery in old Texas oilfields; if a pipeline could be built into the area, the Box–Death Hollow deposit was said to be worth between $2 billion and $8 billion. A geologic map showed potential drilling locations on Antone Bench, the high ground between The Box and Death Hollow (U.S. Senate 1984). The $CO_2$ issue was a major topic of the House hearings, held March 26–27 before Representative Seiberling's Subcommittee on Public Lands and National Parks. Oil and gas spokesmen wanted Box–Death Hollow eliminated from consideration (U.S. House of Representatives 1984). $CO_2$ is abundant elsewhere in Utah, but that was not a winning argument for wilderness advocates. There were three options: ask Seiberling to kill the entire bill, add precedent-setting language to allow drilling rigs to enter a wilderness area, or redraw the boundaries of Box–Death Hollow so as to exclude Antone Ridge.

During "mark-up" of the bill, Seiberling finally negotiated an altered boundary for Box–Death Hollow, excluding a six-mile corridor on Antone Ridge and making three smaller boundary indentations. As part of the compromise, Section 306 of the Utah Wilderness Act of 1984 allowed leasing in the excluded areas only for $CO_2$ and only for a single term of ten years. Restrictions on lease development were also written into the act to minimize impact on the adjacent wilderness (U.S. Congress 1984b). The Southern Utah Wilderness Alliance (SUWA) decried the "sacrificing" of Box–Death Hollow and took a position against passage of the bill. "We cannot support legislation that barters the gems of Utah's wild lands to satisfy the unproved promotional schemes of special interests," read a statement from SUWA (Bauman 1984a). Even before the Utah Wilderness Act had been signed into law, Mid-Continent Oil had government approval to drill a well on Antone Bench. Wilderness visitors were greeted by signs that said, "Keep Out. Authorized Personnel Only." After several years, the hoped-for $CO_2$ development never proved profitable (Bauman 1987). Representative Seiberling could and did barter Utah wilderness. In exchange for the Box–Death Hollow concessions, he demanded more land for the High Uintas, Mount Naomi, and Mount Nebo and the addition of Deseret Peak—a total of about 35,000 new acres.

The most crucial decisions about the High Uintas were made on April 13. The delegation staff and Dick Carter made a helicopter trip to the north slope oil fields, and spent four hours in the Kamas Ranger District office drawing lines on the map. Carter eventually acceded to the demands of the oil companies while obtaining wilderness status for Bull Park and several other north slope wildlife habitat areas threatened by timber sales. The UWA strategy was to protect the most vulnerable wildlands first (Carter 1984a).

Negotiations between the delegation and conservationists continued through a good part of the summer. The Senate committee mark-up brought another compromise, this time over helicopter skiing. Wasatch Powderbird Guides had a permit from the Forest Service to operate in what was about to become the Mount Olympus Wilderness. Bill language approved on the House side would have allowed the helicopter flights to continue, while giving the Forest Service the power to restrict this use and eventually cancel the permit. The Sierra Club's Washington representative, Tim Mahoney, argued that allowing helicopter skiing to continue in a wilderness area, even on a limited basis, would set a bad precedent. So the Sierra Club and the Wilderness Society negotiated with Jake Garn to remove Alexander Basin and Gobblers Knob from the Mount Olympus Wilderness, adding a smaller area on Butler Fork as compensation (Mahoney and Kish 1984). From the perspective of Utah conservationists, including UWA and the Wasatch Mountain Club, this deal made no sense at all (Bauman 1984b). Why formally concede 1,500 acres in the middle of the Mount Olympus area to helicopter skiing, a use that could have been phased out? But ultimately the deal stuck and the boundary of the Mount Olympus Wilderness ended up looking like a puzzle with a missing piece.

While the final details of the Utah bill were being debated, the question of release language was settled in May when Senator James McClure (R-Idaho) agreed to a "soft release" provision, allowing national forest roadless areas to be studied again for wilderness in the second round of forest plans.

"It was clear that there were no easy areas," Dick Carter wrote when the negotiating came to an end. "We simply could not accept nor afford another year of acquiescing to no wilderness" in Utah. Conservationists met every instance of an alleged resource conflict with a suggested compromise, because they believed that the only way to win was by getting a bill enacted (Carter 1984b).

For UWA, the satisfaction of designating a dozen new wilderness areas was soon tinged with frustration. The first winter after the Utah Wilderness Act took effect, the Forest Service moved to permit the helicopter gunning of coyotes in the Mount Naomi Wilderness as part of a predator control program, something that the agency had never before allowed in a wilderness area. Other wildlife controversies came later, such as stocking non-indigenous species of fish in High Uintas lakes by the Utah Division of Wildlife Resources, and transplanting mountain goats, which biologists say are not native to Utah, into wilderness areas.

The preparation of wilderness management plans for the High Uintas, Mount Naomi, and other areas took many years. Because of the intense public interest in the Uintas, the Forest Service sponsored a citizen task force. The inconclusive talks dragged on for two years, and UWA representatives found themselves sitting across the table from some of the same people who had fought against wilderness designation in the first place (Nickas 1997). The High Uintas management plan was not completed until October 1997; in it, the Forest Service opted for the status quo, postponing some hard decisions on grazing, recreation, and wildlife management (U.S. Department of Agriculture 1997).

*LESSONS*

Conservationists learned from the RARE II negotiations that if all politics is local, wilderness politics may be even more so. Most of the areas included in the 1984 act came with a substantial local constituency. Congress did not take the Sierra Club's 2.6-million-acre proposal seriously because obscure areas such as the Raft River Mountains and Impossible Peak did not have enough advocates (Sierra Club 1984). Suitable wilderness acreage is not hard to find in Utah, but political support proved to be a limiting factor.

Another lesson was that negotiations over a statewide wilderness package tend to pit disparate areas and constituencies against one other. Seiberling's decision to take acreage away from Box–Death Hollow in southern Utah and expand the High Uintas and other northern areas caused misunderstanding and hard feelings among conservationists.

With the Utah BLM wilderness issue coming on the heels of RARE II, the Utah Wilderness Association sought a legislative strategy that would avoid the disadvantages of a statewide bill. They didn't have to look far, because the Arizona Wilderness Act of 1984 provided a model for a regional approach to wilderness (U.S. Congress 1984a).

The Arizona Strip is the sparsely populated area of northwestern Arizona separated from the rest of that state by the Grand Canyon. Geographically, it is really a part of Utah. The region has some of the world's richest uranium deposits, which could be refined profitably even as prices declined. In 1982, top officials of Denver-based Energy Fuels Nuclear, a mining firm, met with Russell D. Butcher of the National Parks and Conservation Association (NPCA) to discuss wilderness. Energy Fuels wanted access to BLM wilderness study areas and national forest roadless areas for mineral exploration, but those areas would be off-limits until a wilderness bill was passed (National Parks and Conservation Association 1984).

A unique dialogue emerged, in which Butcher and company officials toured the Arizona Strip wildlands together by helicopter and found that the conflicts between proposed wilderness and uranium resources could be resolved. Negotiations in Phoenix later included BLM officials, the Wilderness Society, and the Sierra Club. A meeting with ranchers in St. George garnered additional support for the NPCA's proposal.

In the end, participants in the Arizona Strip negotiations agreed to add nine areas totaling 394,900 acres of BLM and Forest Service land to the National Wilderness Preservation System and to release some 672,270 acres from study.[6] The conservation groups even agreed to "hard release" language because they felt satisfied with the lands to be designated wilderness (Bauman 1983c). The Arizona Strip bill found essentially unanimous support. Arizona Senator Barry Goldwater and Utah Senators Jake Garn and Orrin Hatch cosponsored it, and the House version had the full backing of the Arizona delegation. An elated Goldwater called it "conservation by consensus," something that was possible because of the regional focus and the relatively small number of stakeholders (Goldwater 1984). Even Cal Black, the sagebrush rebel, testified in favor, saying "this novel approach to solving the wilderness dilemma . . . has greatly lessened many of the concerns and much of the distrust felt by many of the residents of southern Utah." NPCA's Butcher said it was "an exciting adventure in the democratic process" (U.S. Senate 1984).

The Utah Wilderness Association formed a task force to explore a "regional approach" based on the Arizona Strip example. The BLM was preparing a huge, unwieldy environmental impact statement for its Utah wilderness study.[7] Would it not be good strategy if conservationists made an effort to narrow the focus? On the statewide level, the wilderness issue had always been an ideological stalemate in Utah—a shouting match. But Arizona had shown how limiting the debate to one region of the state, and dealing with a more manageable set of issues and people, could lead to agreement on wilderness boundaries without the need for a broader philosophical consensus.

UWA proposed grouping individual BLM wilderness study areas into nine regions: the West Desert, Desolation Canyon/Book Cliffs, Escalante, Canyonlands/Dirty Devil, Henry Mountains, Grand Gulch Plateau, Kaiparowits Plateau, Zion/Canaan Mountain, and the San Rafael. "The tradeoffs have to be within each region," Dick Carter explained. "We don't want the delegation to pit the Escalante against the Book Cliffs. . . . They're not as pretty. But they're more important biologically" (Bauman 1985). A decade later, even in the context of a deeply polarized political situation, the regional approach had a successful trial in the San Rafael region under the auspices of the Coalition for Utah's Future. Emery County agreed with conservationists on a joint wilderness proposal, but it was rejected for inclusion in the Utah delegation's 1995 BLM wilderness bill (Callister 1995). The delegation eventually included a scaled-back San Rafael proposal in a huge omnibus bill, which was soundly defeated in the House of Representatives in October 1998. This was the first Utah wilderness bill to come to a vote in the Congress since 1984.

In October 1996, Governor Mike Leavitt suggested an "incremental wilderness strategy" based on the regional approach. The governor wanted to try a series of BLM bills as an alternative to the statewide bill that had failed in Congress earlier that year (Woolf 1996). Leavitt's incremental strategy attracted little enthusiasm from interest groups on both sides of the wilderness issue, even when he suggested a process reminiscent of Governor Matheson's State Wilderness Committee.

The resistance of national environmental groups to the regional approach dated back to a January 1985 meeting with Utah conservationists. Debbie Sease, the Sierra Club BLM Coordinator, and Terry Sopher, Public Lands Specialist for the Wilderness Society, came to Salt Lake City to urge local activists not to adopt the UWA regional plan. The outlines of a BLM wilderness proposal were taking shape at around 3.8 million acres—twice the agency recommendations. Sease insisted on a much larger acreage, saying, "Whatever we propose now will become the upper limit from this point forward" in the debate. "Now is not the time to be pragmatic," she said (Sease 1985).

Jim Catlin, then Conservation Chair of the Sierra Club's Utah chapter, agreed. So did Clive Kincaid of SUWA. Frustrated by their lack of clout during the 1984 bill negotiations, both favored a "national approach" that would attempt to bypass the Utah congressional delegation in the halls of Congress. Even though they themselves had decided to break ranks with other groups on national forest wilderness just a year earlier, Catlin and Kincaid argued that UWA ought to embrace their ideas for the sake of unity among conservationists. In contrast, Dick Carter and the UWA contingent believed the regional approach was right for Utah wilderness, and predicted that a Washington-based strategy would not be as effective. An inflated proposal might do more to energize the opposition than to move the designation process along. Following a series of BLM wilderness strategy meetings, it was clear that there would be no consensus among the Utah wilderness advocates. On March 9, 1985, UWA made a final offer to join with the other groups in a common BLM wilderness proposal, which was rejected. The split among Utah conservationists became permanent, and continues to affect the Utah wilderness debate.

At first, the differences were more over strategy than proposals. In 1989, when Representative Wayne Owens first introduced H.R. 1500 as a way to spur debate of the merits of BLM wilderness, his goal was to reach a compromise of at least four million acres (Owens 1992). This was essentially the same goal UWA advocated. Later, after Owens gave up his House seat[8] and the national environmental groups turned to Rep. Maurice Hinchey (D-New York) to keep H.R. 1500 in play on Capitol Hill, positions hardened.

The names of the two rival BLM wilderness bills introduced in 1995 revealed how polarized the issue had become. "America's Redrock

Wilderness Act" (H.R. 1500) significantly omitted the name of the state, and the Utah delegation's "Utah Public Lands Management Act" (H.R. 1745 / S.884) omitted the word "wilderness" from its title. The Sierra Club and other groups of the Utah Wilderness Coalition proclaimed a "no compromise" stance (Wright 1997). Representative Jim Hansen has said he is open to working out a compromise (Hansen 1997b). In October 1997, Hansen proposed the designation of 2.7 million acres of BLM wilderness, 50 percent more acreage than the delegation's 1995 bill (Fantin and Woolf 1997).

In sum, a number of elements contributed to the passage of a Utah wilderness bill in 1984: the threat of another national forest roadless area study, political momentum at the national level, active support from the governor, frustration with the status quo on both sides of the issue, and a general willingness to negotiate. All of these factors helped stakeholders reach a compromise. If the environmental groups can find a way once again to work with the Utah congressional delegation, perhaps there can be another year of Utah wilderness.

### ⊊ NOTES TO CHAPTER 13

1. For simplicity, some adjacent areas are counted here as one (for example, RARE II studied Mount Nebo as two roadless areas).

2. At the time, Utah had only two congressional districts. Redistricting created a third in 1982.

3. Delegation staff met separately with representatives of the Utah Cattlemen's Association, Utah Farm Bureau Federation, Utah Wool Growers' Association, Utah Petroleum Association, and conservationist groups.

4. Under the terms of the 1964 Wilderness Act, all designated wilderness areas were to be withdrawn from mineral leasing effective January 1, 1984 (U.S. Congress 1964).

5. Representative Hansen and Senator Garn introduced two identical bills, H.R. 4516 in the House and S. 2155 in the Senate.

6. Approximately 67 percent of the RARE II roadless areas and 21 percent of the BLM wilderness study areas received wilderness designation.

7. In Colorado and other states, the BLM conducted wilderness studies for individual resource areas rather than on a statewide basis.

8. He ran unsuccessfully for the U.S. Senate.

### ⊊ REFERENCES TO CHAPTER 13

Acord, Clair. 1983. Letter to the Utah Congressional Delegation and Governor Scott Matheson, July 7. MS 85.*

Alt, David, and Donald W. Hyndman. 1995. *Northwest Exposure: A Geologic Story of the Northwest.* Missoula, MT: Mountain Press Publishing Co.

Bauman, Joseph. 1981. "Visiting Officials Look at Utah's Wilderness," *Deseret News,* August 11, B1.

———. 1983a. "Utah Needs More Wilderness," *Deseret News,* June 10, A5.

———. 1983b. "S.L. Speakers Want More Wilds Protected," *Deseret News,* July 12, B1.

———. 1983c. "Utah Can Learn From Arizona," *Deseret News,* July 20, A5.

———. 1984a. "Wilderness Compromise Divides Environmentalists," *Deseret News,* June 29, B8.

———. 1984b. "Garn Might Drop Acres From Study Area," *Deseret News,* July 27, B1.

———. 1985. "Carter Urges Environmentalists to Change Tactics," *Deseret News,* May 10, A9.

———. 1987. "Where's Utah's Huge Gas Strike?" *Deseret News,* April 3, B2.

Brewer, Doug. 1983. Letter to Utah Congressional Delegation, August 19. MS 85.*

Callister, Deborah Cox. 1995. *Community & Wild Lands Futures: A Pilot Project in Emery County, Utah.* Salt Lake City, UT: Coalition for Utah's Future.

Carter, Dick. 1981. UWA letter to Senators Garn and Hatch, Representatives Hansen and Marriott, October 14. MSS 200.**

———. 1984a. Letter to wilderness activists, May 31. MSS 200.**

———. 1984b. *At Last . . . Wilderness.* Salt Lake City, UT: Utah Wilderness Association.

———. 1985. No title. Speech given at the Utah Wilderness Dedication Ceremony, Wasatch-Cache National Forest, Utah, August 28. MSS 200.**

Cash, R. D. 1983. Letter from the Rocky Mountain Oil & Gas Association to Utah congressional delegation, June 24. MS 85.*

Fantin, Linda, and Jim Woolf. 1997, "More Wilderness in New Hansen Bill," *Salt Lake Tribune,* September 27, A1.

Fitzpatrick, Tim. 1983. "Congressmen Told Wilderness Bill Is Full of Holes," *Salt Lake Tribune,* July 17, B1.

Ford, Jerry. 1983. "No Consensus Means No Utah Wilderness Bill," *Logan Herald-Journal,* April 29.

Fordyce, Dave. 1983. *Statement by Kaibab Industries on the Utah Wilderness Proposal.* July 21. MS 85.*

Fradkin, Philip. 1989. *Sagebrush Country: Land and the American West.* New York: Alfred A. Knopf.

Goldwater, Barry. 1984. "Conservation Through Consensus." *National Parks,* July/August, 14–15.

Hansen, James. 1997a. Personal communication, April 21.

———. 1997b. "It Is Time for the Environmentalists to Compromise," *Salt Lake Tribune,* October 12, AA6.

Husselbee, Paul. 1983. "Garn Tells Five County Group: Utah Needs Own Wilderness Bill," *Cedar City Spectrum,* February 11, 14.

Mahoney, Tim, and Carla Kish. 1984. Letter to Senator Jake Garn, August 2. MS 85.*

Marston, Ed. 1983. "1984 May Be a Wilderness Year," *High Country News,* December 12, vol. 15, no. 22, p. 1.

Matheson, Scott, and James Edwin Kee. 1986. "Wilderness: Who Is To Say." In *Out of Balance.* Salt Lake City, UT: Peregrine Smith Books.

Miller, Alan. 1983. "Utah Wilderness Association Is Not an 'Umbrella Group,'" (letter to the editor), *Deseret News,* June 13, A4.

National Parks and Conservation Association. 1984. "Arizona Strip Bill a Model for the Future." *National Parks*, May/June, 35–36.

Nice, Joan. 1978. "RARE II Tables Turn; Conservationists Enraged," *High Country News*, June 30, 1.

Nickas, George. 1997. Personal communication, February 13.

Ninth Circuit Court of Appeals. 1982. *California v. Block*. 690 F.2d 753. October 22.

Owens, Wayne. 1992. "Is Preservation of Utah's Remaining Wilderness in Utah's Best Interest?" In *Wilderness Issues in the Arid Lands of the Western United States*, edited by Samuel I. Zeveloff and Cyrus M. McKell, 13–34. Albuquerque: University of New Mexico Press.

Peacock, Jim. 1983. Statement by Jim Peacock, Executive Director, Utah Petroleum Association on the Utah Wilderness Proposal, July 11. MS 85.*

Perry, Janice. 1982. No title. United Press International wire story, March 27. NEXIS.

Roggenbuck, Joseph W., George H. Stankey, and Dennis M. Roth. 1990. The wilderness classification process. In *Wilderness Management*, edited by John C. Hendee, George H. Stankey, and Robert C. Lucas, 2d ed., revised, 123–56. Golden, CO: North American Press.

Sease, Debbie. 1985. Remarks to Utah Statewide BLM Information and Strategy Meeting, University of Utah Law School, January 12 (author's notes).

Sierra Club. 1984. *Sierra Club Proposal for Forest Service Wilderness in Utah*. Salt Lake City: Utah Chapter Sierra Club, February 9.

Smart, Christopher. 1997. "High Uintas preservation: don't say 'wilderness.'" *Mountain Times*, August.

SUWA (Southern Utah Wilderness Alliance). 1984. We Lost . . . Box–Death Hollow and the 1984 Utah Wilderness Act. *Southern Utah Wilderness Alliance* newsletter, August 15, 5.

Thalman, James. 1983. "Wilderness Meetings Exclude Public," *The Herald Journal*, May 19, 1.

U.S. Congress. 1964. *Wilderness Act*. P.L. 88-577. 78 Stat. 890.

———. 1978. *Endangered American Wilderness Act of 1978*. P.L. 95-92 Stat. 40.

———. 1983. H.R. 4516. *To designate certain national forest system lands in the State of Utah for inclusion in the National Wilderness Preservation System, to release other forest lands for multiple use management, and for other purposes.*

———. 1984a. *Arizona Wilderness Act of 1984*. P.L. 98-406. 98 Stat. 1485.

———. 1984b. *Utah Wilderness Act of 1984*. P.L. 98-428. 98 Stat. 1657.

U.S. Department of Agriculture, Forest Service. 1979. *RARE II Final Environmental Statement*. Department of Agriculture.

———. 1997. *Final Environmental Impact Statement for Management of the High Uintas Wilderness*. Salt Lake City, UT: Ashley and Wasatch-Cache National Forests.

U.S. Department of Agriculture, Office of Governmental and Public Affairs. 1983. *National Forest Areas Subject to Re-evaluation*. Washington, D.C.: U.S. Department of Agriculture news release. MS 85.*

U.S. House of Representatives, Committee on Interior and Insular Affairs. 1984. *Additions to the National Wilderness Preservation System*. Serial No. 98-3, Part X. Hearings before the Subcommittee on Public Lands and National Parks.

U.S. Senate, Committee on Energy and Natural Resources. 1984. *Designating Certain National Forest System Lands and Public Lands in Utah and Arizona as Wilderness*. S. Hearing. 98-779. Hearing before the Subcommittee on Public Lands and Reserved Water.

Utah Congressional Delegation. 1983. *Utah Wilderness Discussion Proposal,* July 1. MS 85.*

Weed, Robert. 1985. "Wilderness Politics" (letter to the editor). *Outside,* March, 8.

Weissner, Andy. 1981. Memo to Rep. Seiberling re Utah RARE II, September 11. MSS 200.**

Wharton, Tom. 1983. "Utah Wilderness Bill Slated," *Salt Lake Tribune,* March 16, C1.

———. 1985. "Utah's Officials Dedicate New Wilderness Areas," *Salt Lake Tribune,* August 29, B1.

Wheeler, Raymond. 1984. Gunfight in God's Country. *Utah Holiday,* May, 44–76.

Wilcken, G. Paul. 1983. July 21. *The Wilderness; By a Man Who Has Been There.* MS 85.*

Woolf, Jim. 1996. "Leavitt Backs Series of Wilderness Bills," *Salt Lake Tribune,* October 12, B1.

Wright, Jim. 1997. "What's True in Debate on Wilderness?" *Standard-Examiner,* September 11, D1.


* In Jake Garn Papers, MS 85, Manuscripts Division, University of Utah Marriott Library, Salt Lake City, Utah.

** In Utah Wilderness Association Papers, MSS 200, Special Collections, Utah State University Merrill Library, Logan, Utah

# CHAPTER 14

# The Community Context Approach

## Doug Goodman

## Daniel McCool

### INTRODUCTION

A lot has been written lately about a new epoch—a whole new era for humankind—corresponding to the new millennium. The industrial age has been replaced by the information age, causing dramatic changes in government, the economy, and society. Yet at the same time there is a greater consciousness of our past, a need to maintain cherished traditions and remember how it used to be. Perhaps this nostalgia provides us with a certain measure of security—a cultural reassurance of who we are—as we enter a period of rapid change with unforeseen consequences.

As the American West goes through convulsive change, many people realize that it will take a concerted effort to preserve our past, our culture, our land. Of course, land and culture have a profound impact on each other, and any effort to preserve one should be tied to an effort to preserve the other. In the American West, what is truly distinctive in the culture is not derived from the burgeoning cities, which tend to be quite similar to other cities in the nation and are often populated with people from other regions. Rather, the heart of western culture is found in the rural West, where the land has had its greatest impact on the population. In the rural West, the nature of the land determines population patterns, economic activity, and social and recreational activity. Thus it makes sense that any effort to preserve the land must be tied to an effort to preserve the rural West. Without a doubt wilderness is a precious resource, the value of which will only increase as it becomes more scarce relative to population. But the cultural traditions of the rural West also constitute a national treasure. The real challenge is to tie the two together as part of an effort to preserve both.

236

## THE PUBLIC INTEREST

There is a voluminous literature in political science regarding the nature of government and how it can best serve the public. Much of the discussion concerns the relationship between individual costs and benefits, and efforts to serve the larger public interest. Deborah Stone succinctly explains this trade-off:

> Situations where self-interest and public interest work against each other are known as commons problems. . . . There are two types of commons problems. In one, actions with private benefits entail social costs; for example, discharging industrial wastes into a lake is a cheap method of disposal for a factory owner but ruins the water for everyone else. In the other, social benefits necessitate private sacrifices; for example, maintaining a school system requires individual tax payments. (1997, 22)

These kinds of trade-offs are found in nearly every activity that involves government. After all, we do not give the easy problems to government; if there are only benefits to be had, people simply do it themselves. Government intervenes when there is conflict between who benefits and who pays. Thus, the basic question in formulating government policy is to decide the allocation of costs and benefits. This much is obvious, but it leads to a more difficult question: if a certain policy benefits the public at large, yet also imposes a cost on certain individuals or subgroups, does the public have an obligation to mitigate the negative impact on those individuals?

To a great extent, the answer to this question depends on how readily the winners and losers can be identified, and if there is any significant overlap between them. For example, in regard to paying for public schools, there is a tremendous overlap in the population that pays and the population that benefits; both groups are nearly universal. The clearest opportunities for mitigating losses occur when there is a clear demarcation between those in society who benefit, and the subpopulation that bears much of the cost.

At its core, this is a moral question; if society, via its government, imposes a cost upon some of its members in order to create a benefit for the greater society, is there a moral obligation to attempt to compensate those who, in effect, bear a disproportionate share of the costs of serving the community as a whole? The answer would have to be yes if we believe that government should be responsive to all its citizens, especially those whose misfortune was visited upon them by government. To do less would seem to be a let-them-eat-cake attitude toward some of the members of our national community.

But there is also a practical side to this question. If significant costs are imposed on a subgroup in the name of a larger public interest, then the subgroup has a powerful incentive to oppose all public-interest policies. This makes the political process exceedingly conflictual, with high costs imposed on everyone when policies serving the larger public interest are held up by a concerted minority that is willing to expend considerable resources to avoid bearing a disproportionate part of the burden. To avoid this, public policy should meet two goals: serve the larger public interest, and compensate those who bear a disproportionate burden of the costs of that policy. This dilemma, presented in the abstract, is exactly what has happened in the wilderness debate.

## THE COMMUNITY CONTEXT APPROACH

We regard wilderness as a highly valued resource. Contrary to opponents' statements, it does not "lock up" any land. Just the contrary, wilderness on public land is open to anyone who wishes to use it without destroying it. There is no exclusive access; rather, each interested person makes an individual decision about whether to access this public asset. In other words, it is a common good that is available to society as a whole. But the costs of wilderness are not borne equally by all citizens. Wilderness areas are not carved out of people's backyards in the city; they typically surround small rural communities and rural parcels of private land. Thus rural people disproportionately bear the burdens of wilderness designation.

These burdens consist of three types. First, wilderness designation may terminate certain ongoing activities that are valued by people living adjacent to the areas, and may include profit-making activities as well as social or recreational activities. A second cost involves the imposition of additional public services and duties that result from wilderness designation. An influx of wilderness users places a considerable burden on local infrastructure, including roads, parking, law enforcement, search and rescue, restrooms, fire, emergency medical services, and other public amenities. The third type of cost is of much greater long-term importance: rural people are subjected to what economists call opportunity costs. These are activities that are precluded because some other activity has been given precedence. Opportunity costs are by nature hypothetical; they concern potential assets that may or may not have future economic value. This does not make them any less real, only more difficult to identify and quantify. These difficulties are quite evident in the chapters of this book in section III; lost opportunities for mining, grazing, school trust lands, and developed recreational activities are clearly important in the wilderness debate.

Of course, the allocation of wilderness costs and benefits is not totally separated into two distinct groups of beneficiaries and burden-bearers. Local economies gain from increased tourism and visitation to wilderness areas, especially in the provision of services and the sale of outdoor equipment. And local people are entitled to the same wilderness benefits as everyone else; indeed, due to proximity their opportunity to enjoy wilderness is greater than that of individuals who must travel long distances. In terms of bearing costs, local people do not shoulder this entire burden. The cost of maintaining a federal land management capability is borne by all taxpayers. And opportunity costs affect everyone; forgone economic activity impacts more than just the local economy.

Still, there is a clear demarcation between those who will benefit the most from wilderness and those who will bear a disproportionate cost of wilderness. It is no accident that most wilderness proponents are urban people whose livelihood is not affected by wilderness designation, and most opponents are rural people whose livelihood may be directly and perversely affected by wilderness. Designing a just and fair wilderness policy entails an attempt to establish wilderness to serve the larger public interest, and at the same time ameliorate the impact it has on local communities. Thus the larger the wilderness acreage, the larger society's obligation to compensate the bearers of disproportionate costs.

In an effort to solve this dilemma, we have developed what we call the community context approach to wilderness policy. This approach is based on two basic assumptions. First, wilderness cannot be considered in isolation; rather, we should make policy in light of the impact it has on the larger human and biological context. Among public land management agencies, ecosystem management is now in vogue; it assumes that land management is best when an entire ecosystem is managed as a unit, rather than being broken up into arbitrary jurisdictional components with no coordinated management goals. We think this concept needs to be expanded to include the people who live in the ecosystems. The community context approach looks at wilderness as part of a larger biological, economic, and political community. We can best preserve any one of these elements if we pay attention to the others.

Second, wilderness, and the larger society it serves, are better off if we preserve the vitality of local communities. One of the greatest threats to wilderness is the activity that occurs outside wilderness boundaries. This has become a major problem for many of our national parks (Freemuth 1991; Clarke and McCool 1996, 90). We cannot create an isolated island of wilderness; every wilderness area is surrounded by other land that may or may not be used in a manner that is compatible with wilderness. A wilderness area surrounded by a cattle ranch is quite different from one surrounded by a rash of new condominiums. If local communities are economically harmed by wilderness designation, how will they compensate for the loss? Sell land to developers? Subdivide ranches into second homes? Replace modest homes with large hotels? If you are camped on the edge of a wilderness, which would you prefer to encounter: a local rancher, or a real estate developer from L.A. with "plans" for the area? In short, we can protect the integrity of wilderness by minimizing the impact it has on local communities.

Wilderness is part of a larger rural community; this community context must be taken into consideration when designating wilderness. We propose that this can done by adopting four related policies: compensating for losses; charging a user fee for wilderness use; providing for local participation; and creating a Wilderness Management Commission.

## COMPENSATION

In the United States, as of 1996, there were 622 BLM wilderness study areas, totaling more than 17.4 million acres; all of them have yet to be acted upon by Congress (BLM 1997a, 140). For some groups this is too much wilderness, and for others it is not enough. Compensation for economic losses (perceived and real) associated with wilderness is an issue that needs to be addressed. If the compensation could be addressed, then perhaps various interest groups and Congress can come together to protect some of the nation's scenic and "untouched" lands.

This volume discusses many uses of public lands, ranging from economic uses to recreational uses. One of the fears of designating public lands as wilderness concerns its economic impact. As discussed in chapter 9, grazing is the only extractive industry allowed in wilderness areas. Designating wilderness precludes mining and other substantial developments. It also reduces the potential for local tax revenue.

In a 1995 study of fiscal burdens in nonmetropolitan counties, the authors found that the tax burdens in rural America are comparable to those of inner-city ghettos (Johnson et al. 1995). Rural western economies are limited, and extractive industries have traditionally played a major role. By necessity some rural communities have relied on public lands for economic viability. Ranching, timber, and mining are three industries that are prevalent in the rural American West. Tourism can be lucrative, but it has its own drawbacks. Furthermore, wilderness areas attract visitors, but not to the same extent as national parks or monuments (McCool 1985). In other words, wilderness imposes significant opportunity costs on some rural western communities. Although the role of extractive industries has declined dramatically in the last two decades, they are still an important economic activity in some western communities.[1]

In many parts of the West, tourism is seen as the wave of the future. Indeed, tourism is already the dominant economic activity in Utah. In 1997, seventeen million out-of-state visitors came to Utah for leisure or business (State of Utah 1998, 187). Local communities that rely on tourism or recreation bear a heavy burden of added infrastructure costs (Johnson and Beale 1995; Johnson et al. 1995). As mentioned earlier, wilderness is generally found in rural areas. In Utah, many of the counties outside of the Wasatch Front are large in area with little population; table 14.1 illustrates the number of acres owned by federal and state governments in Utah.[2] Many of these counties, such as Garfield County and Kane County, have little private property: only 4.7 percent and 1.5 percent respectively is privately held (State of Utah 1992). This leaves very little taxable land, thus the tax burdens for these rural communities are large.

The federal government tries to offset some of this burden by providing payments in lieu of taxes (PILT) to counties with substantial nontaxable federal land (see GAO 1998a). Table 14.2 provides the total PILT payments to counties in Utah under the current law. We propose to increase PILT on wilderness acreage to offset the losses to rural communities due to wilderness designation.[3] Increasing PILT accomplishes three important goals in preserving America's wilderness. First, it would help compensate communities for perceived and actual losses. Second, the increased tax base would ease tax burdens on rural communities. Third, it would also help build infrastructure associated with increased tourism on federal lands.

PILT payments are based on two criteria: population and acreage. We propose to quadruple this payment for every acre that is declared wilderness.[4] The current level of payment, set by Congress, is $0.93 per acre (P.L. 103-397), which, if quadrupled, would total $3.72 per acre, per annum. Table 14.2 illustrates the PILT payment counties would receive under three different wilderness proposals: current BLM WSAs (3.2 million acres), BLM's proposed wilderness (1.97 million acres), and UWC's original proposal (5.7 million acres). The additional PILT funding for wilderness acreage would be substantial for counties that encompass large wilderness areas. For example, Kane County would net $887,662 of additional PILT if 1.9 million acres were declared wilderness. If the UWC 5.7-million-acre proposal becomes law, that total would jump to $3.5 million. For a county with roughly 6,000 residents, that is a substantial amount of assistance to the county. This additional PILT would help offset potential

TABLE 14.1—Estimated Land Ownership in Utah

| | | | | | Federal | | | | | | American Indian | | State | | | | | |
|---|---|---|---|---|---|---|---|---|---|---|---|---|---|---|---|---|---|---|
| County | July 1, 1996 Pop. | Total Acres | BLM Acres | FS Acres | NP Acres | BOR Acres | DOD Acres | F&W Acres | Total Federal Acres | Federal as a % of Total | Indian Reservation Acres | Indian as a % of Total | State Park Acres | School Trust Acres | State Sovereign Acres | Wildlife Resources Acres | Total State Acres | State as a % of Total |
| Beaver | 5,607 | 1,660,137 | 1,249,120 | 138,469 | 0 | 0 | 0 | 0 | 1,387,589 | 83.6% | 0 | 0.0% | 207 | 145,606 | County | 11,974 | 157,787 | 9.5% |
| Box Elder | 39,484 | 4,303,250 | 808,255 | 100,674 | 2,203 | 12,760 | 797,221 | 65,029 | 1,786,142 | 41.5% | 0 | 0.0% | 0 | 188,924 | Distribution | 25,670 | 214,594 | 5.0% |
| Cache | 82,097 | 749,325 | 0 | 269,389 | 0 | 1,368 | 0 | 0 | 270,757 | 36.1% | 0 | 0.0% | 10 | 33,492 | unavailable | 19,523 | 53,025 | 7.1% |
| Carbon | 21,420 | 952,990 | 430,190 | 30,199 | 0 | 2,542 | 0 | 0 | 462,931 | 48.6% | 0 | 0.0% | 30 | 94,637 | | 7,449 | 102,116 | 10.7% |
| Daggett | 803 | 459,553 | 76,505 | 260,256 | 0 | 33,744 | 0 | 0 | 370,505 | 80.6% | 0 | 0.0% | 0 | 31,193 | | 6,570 | 37,763 | 8.2% |
| Davis | 219,644 | 406,834 | 0 | 37,525 | 0 | 2,711 | 8,466 | 0 | 48,702 | 12.0% | 0 | 0.0% | 25,790 | 267 | | 1,434 | 27,491 | 6.8% |
| Duchesne | 14,032 | 2,078,400 | 201,200 | 727,635 | 0 | 40,563 | 0 | 0 | 969,398 | 46.6% | 390,892 | 18.8% | 85 | 49,610 | | 86,023 | 135,718 | 6.5% |
| Emery | 10,810 | 2,860,019 | 2,083,363 | 212,888 | 1,734 | 2,817 | 0 | 0 | 2,300,802 | 80.4% | 0 | 0.0% | 2,293 | 299,015 | | 1,255 | 302,563 | 10.6% |
| Garfield | 4,386 | 3,337,814 | 1,423,433 | 1,045,677 | 433,588 | 39,007 | 0 | 0 | 2,941,705 | 88.1% | 0 | 0.0% | 3,597 | 237,456 | | 74 | 241,127 | 7.2% |
| Grand | 8,797 | 2,363,192 | 1,530,942 | 57,527 | 66,602 | 0 | 2,746 | 0 | 1,657,817 | 70.2% | 0 | 0.0% | 4,988 | 374,791 | | 4,903 | 384,682 | 16.3% |
| Iron | 28,031 | 2,117,153 | 909,780 | 243,464 | 9,006 | 0 | 0 | 0 | 1,162,250 | 54.9% | 2,506 | 0.1% | 11 | 136,754 | | 8,060 | 144,825 | 6.8% |
| Juab | 7,444 | 2,175,867 | 1,486,302 | 118,418 | 0 | 679 | 200 | 17,992 | 1,623,591 | 74.6% | 37,525 | 1.7% | 184 | 178,322 | | 14,718 | 193,223 | 8.9% |
| Kane | 5,956 | 2,629,767 | 1,647,964 | 124,283 | 465,606 | 141,172 | 0 | 0 | 2,379,025 | 90.5% | 0 | 0.0% | 3,730 | 207,249 | | 0 | 210,979 | 8.0% |
| Millard | 11,958 | 4,376,977 | 3,028,011 | 362,134 | 0 | 0 | 0 | 0 | 3,390,145 | 77.5% | 1,156 | 0.0% | 4 | 401,999 | | 35,422 | 437,425 | 10.0% |
| Morgan | 6,693 | 390,408 | 3,749 | 13,996 | 0 | 2,696 | 0 | 0 | 20,441 | 5.2% | 0 | 0.0% | 0 | 5,728 | | 7,039 | 12,767 | 3.3% |
| Piute | 1,508 | 489,777 | 158,112 | 190,466 | 0 | 0 | 0 | 0 | 348,578 | 71.2% | 0 | 0.0% | 120 | 64,208 | | 4,600 | 68,927 | 14.1% |
| Rich | 1,822 | 694,370 | 170,059 | 49,398 | 0 | 0 | 0 | 0 | 219,457 | 31.6% | 0 | 0.0% | 906 | 44,554 | | 1,992 | 47,453 | 6.8% |
| Salt Lake | 818,860 | 516,169 | 2,872 | 95,497 | 0 | 77 | 9,798 | 0 | 108,244 | 21.0% | 0 | 0.0% | 2,200 | 160 | | 2,376 | 4,735 | 0.9% |
| San Juan | 13,188 | 5,071,757 | 1,760,403 | 450,707 | 578,612 | 110,641 | 0 | 0 | 2,900,363 | 57.2% | 1,209,026 | 23.8% | 92 | 295,752 | | 0 | 295,844 | 5.8% |

TABLE 14.1 (Continued)

| County | July 1, 1996 Pop. | Total Acres | Federal | | | | | | | | | American Indian | | State | | | | | |
|---|---|---|---|---|---|---|---|---|---|---|---|---|---|---|---|---|---|---|---|
| | | | BLM Acres | FS Acres | NP Acres | BOR Acres | DOD Acres | F&W Acres | Total Federal Acres | Federal as a % of Total | Indian Reservation Acres | Indian as a % of Total | State Park Acres | School Trust Acres | State Sovereign Acres | Wildlife Resources Acres | Total State Acres | State as a % of Total |
| Sanpete | 19,999 | 1,025,500 | 201,248 | 389,152 | 0 | 6,728 | 0 | 0 | 597,128 | 58.2% | 0 | 0.0% | 61 | 36,736 | | 28,564 | 65,362 | 6.4% |
| Sevier | 17,682 | 1,230,612 | 263,363 | 711,552 | 4,488 | 0 | 0 | 0 | 979,403 | 79.6% | 1,283 | 0.1% | 889 | 56,463 | | 0 | 57,352 | 4.7% |
| Summit | 23,562 | 1,199,872 | 954 | 514,522 | 0 | 4,335 | 0 | 0 | 519,811 | 43.3% | 0 | 0.0% | 0 | 11,665 | | 19,794 | 31,459 | 2.6% |
| Tooele | 30,492 | 4,669,616 | 1,443,283 | 150,234 | 0 | 0 | 1,026,184 | 0 | 2,619,701 | 56.1% | 18,723 | 0.4% | 1,199 | 259,066 | | 1,650 | 261,915 | 5.6% |
| Uintah | 24,275 | 2,882,017 | 1,329,960 | 268,864 | 51,379 | 11,008 | 0 | 8,754 | 1,669,965 | 57.9% | 426,304 | 14.8% | 2 | 237,884 | | 11,647 | 249,533 | 8.7% |
| Utah | 317,879 | 1,370,386 | 71,494 | 486,414 | 250 | 126,364 | 16,648 | 0 | 701,170 | 51.2% | 0 | 0.0% | 416 | 50,158 | | 42,948 | 93,522 | 6.8% |
| Wasatch | 12,585 | 772,736 | 4,270 | 426,554 | 0 | 106,144 | 0 | 0 | 536,968 | 69.5% | 3,200 | 0.4% | 21,279 | 7,368 | | 36,105 | 64,753 | 8.4% |
| Washington | 72,888 | 1,557,657 | 585,279 | 394,556 | 130,798 | 0 | 0 | 0 | 1,110,633 | 71.3% | 27,524 | 1.8% | 6,287 | 98,581 | | 0 | 104,869 | 6.7% |
| Wayne | 2,389 | 1,579,287 | 849,931 | 160,349 | 278,216 | 0 | 0 | 0 | 1,288,496 | 81.6% | 0 | 0.0% | 0 | 189,808 | | 1,129 | 190,937 | 12.1% |
| Weber | 178,068 | 422,982 | 80 | 67,790 | 0 | 5,955 | 3,006 | 0 | 76,831 | 18.2% | 0 | 0.0% | 88 | 1,455 | | 16,331 | 17,874 | 4.2% |
| Total | 2,002,359 | 54,344,423 | 21,720,122 | 8,098,589 | 2,022,482 | 651,311 | 1,864,269 | 91,775 | 34,448,548 | 63.4% | 2,319,301 | 4.3% | 74,468 | 3,738,901 | 1,500,000 | 397,250 | 4,210,620 | 10.5% |

Source: State of Utah, Governor's Office of Planning and Budget, Demographic and Economic Analysis Section, "Estimated Land Ownership in Utah: 1992," and State of Utah, Governor's Office of Planning and Budget, *Economic Report to the Governor*, 1997.

TABLE 14.2—Various BLM Wilderness Proposals and PILT by County

| County | BLM Wilderness | BLM WSAs Acres | BLM Proposed | UWC** Proposed | PILT | Additional PILT* | | UWC Proposal |
|---|---|---|---|---|---|---|---|---|
| | | | | | | WSAs | BLM Proposal | |
| Beaver | 0 | 7,140 | 7,140 | 76,915 | 236,159 | 26,561 | 26,561 | 286,124 |
| Box Elder | 0 | 0 | 0 | 23,469 | 866,661 | 0 | 0 | 87,305 |
| Cache | 0 | 0 | 0 | 0 | 172,006 | 0 | 0 | 0 |
| Carbon | 0 | 87,020 | 68,000 | 113,125 | 338,202 | 323,714 | 252,960 | 420,825 |
| Daggett | 0 | 0 | 0 | 11,472 | 36,345 | 0 | 0 | 42,676 |
| Davis | 0 | 0 | 0 | 0 | 16,016 | 0 | 0 | 0 |
| Duchesne | 0 | 0 | 0 | 7,357 | 482,168 | 0 | 0 | 27,348 |
| Emery | 0 | 428,030 | 385,109 | 844,364 | 340,898 | 1,592,272 | 1,432,605 | 3,141,034 |
| Garfield | 0 | 528,958 | 298,411 | 888,598 | 202,600 | 1,967,724 | 1,110,089 | 3,305,585 |
| Grand | 0 | 347,495 | 190,245 | 559,607 | 250,000 | 1,292,681 | 707,711 | 2,081738 |
| Iron | 0 | 4,433 | 1,607 | 4,273 | 571,653 | 16,491 | 5,978 | 15,896 |
| Juab | 0 | 92,390 | 62,340 | 124,986 | 277,379 | 343,691 | 231,905 | 464,948 |
| Kane | 20,000 | 639,958 | 218,608 | 939,163 | 239,688 | 2,455,044 | 887,622 | 3,568,086 |
| Millard | 0 | 265,600 | 106,418 | 298,587 | 404,587 | 988,032 | 395,875 | 1,110,744 |
| Morgan | 0 | 0 | 0 | 0 | 0 | 0 | 0 | 0 |
| Piute | 0 | 0 | 0 | 0 | 52,433 | 0 | 0 | 0 |
| Rich | 0 | 0 | 0 | 0 | 78,495 | 0 | 0 | 0 |
| Salt Lake | 0 | 0 | 0 | 0 | 38,640 | 0 | 0 | 0 |
| San Juan | 0 | 387,595 | 365,905 | 912,953 | 396,726 | 1,441,853 | 1,361,167 | 3,396,185 |
| Sanpete | 0 | 0 | 0 | 0 | 0 | 0 | 0 | 0 |
| Sevier | 0 | 0 | 0 | 24,325 | 431,806 | 0 | 0 | 90,589 |

TABLE 14.2 (Continued)

| County | BLM Wilderness | BLM WSAs Acres | BLM Proposed | UWC** Proposed | PILT | WSAs | Additional PILT* | |
|---|---|---|---|---|---|---|---|---|
| | | | | | | | BLM Proposal | UWC Proposal |
| Summit | 0 | 0 | 0 | 0 | 0 | 0 | 0 | 0 |
| Tooele | 0 | 99,150 | 39,364 | 190,914 | 671,818 | 368,835 | 146,434 | 710,200 |
| Uintah | 0 | 44,958 | 0 | 86,701 | 604,871 | 167,244 | 0 | 322,528 |
| Utah | 0 | 0 | 0 | 0 | 462,945 | 0 | 0 | 0 |
| Wasatch | 0 | 0 | 0 | 0 | 285,080 | 0 | 0 | 0 |
| Washington | 2,600 | 88,501 | 65,858 | 167,529 | 827,367 | 338,896 | 254,664 | 632,880 |
| Wayne | 0 | 188,706 | 164,034 | 453,044 | 200,000 | 701,986 | 610,207 | 1,685,324 |
| Weber | 0 | 0 | 0 | 0 | 68,078 | 0 | 0 | 0 |
| Total | 22,600 | 3,209,934 | 1,973,039 | 5,727,382 | | | | |

Source: State of Utah, 1992, Utah Wilderness Acres by County—Draft; BLM *EIS*; State of Utah, 1995, Utah BLM Wilderness Proposals by County; CPPA *Survey of Local Government Finances.*

PILTs for Wayne and Grand Counties are estimated.

*These columnse 26,000 acres in BLM wilderness for Washington and Kane Counties.

*Includes school trust lands.

**Includes school trust lands.

losses to tax revenue because of potential property devaluation and potential loss of extractive industries.[5]

As illustrated in table 14.2, the more wilderness that is designated, the larger the PILT payment to affected counties. The extra money would help counties cover extra infrastructure costs associated with wilderness recreation. Moreover, this source of perpetual revenue would be an incentive for rural counties to accept wilderness designation. We note that our proposal relies on federal funds to assist impacted local governments; it is not a transfer of the taxpayer's money to a private corporation or individuals. We are *not* suggesting another costly subsidy for special private interests (we already have too much of that). Rather, we are proposing that the national community provide assistance to impacted local communities; this means spending public money for public purposes. Wilderness is indeed a national treasure; it is surely worth a modest investment in local communities.

Counties should be free to use their additional PILT money in any manner that serves a public purpose; they may build infrastructure, or choose to support their school systems, or decide to fund job-retraining and college scholarships. The only prohibitions should be that counties may not directly allocate this money to private interests, and it should not be used for lobbying. The objective is to compensate communities in order to keep them viable and well maintained.

### User Fees for Wilderness

BLM estimates the number of visitors to wilderness areas will increase from about 250,000 visitors a year to more than 1.7 million visitors per year by 2020 (BLM Utah 1990, 125).[6] A second component of the community context approach is to charge user fees for access to wilderness. In this way wilderness users will help maintain the public lands they enjoy, and help mitigate the impact their usage has on surrounding communities. User fees have gained popularity since the early 1980s. A fee permit system would allow the BLM to track the number of visitors and raise funds to properly manage wilderness areas. Money would be used for on-site improvements, wilderness education, and hiring more people to help monitor wilderness areas.[7] Permit fees collected by BLM would stay in the district, and thus would be similar to the National Park Service demonstration fee program, which permits parks to collect gate fees and use the revenue in-park (see GAO 1998b). The BLM fee we are proposing would range from $5.00 a day to $15.00 a week for access to wilderness areas, depending on popularity and hence the potential for damage to the resource.[8]

User fees are not new, even to BLM. Fees are paid for river rafting on some rivers, camping, and access to some popular wilderness and primitive areas. BLM has over two hundred recreation fee sites that generated nearly $2 million in 1996 (BLM 1997a, 127–29). Furthermore, BLM charges $5.00 a day for overnight camping permits at Grand Gulch Primitive Area (also a WSA) in southeastern Utah.[9] User fees will be used to hire additional BLM staff, and help ameliorate the impact of increased visitation on area infrastructure. We suggest that permit fees could also be used to help fund local search and rescue and law enforcement. Additionally, BLM could give hiring preference for some of these jobs to local citizens, thereby providing local stable jobs.

*Local Participation*

A third aspect of the community context approach is to incorporate local participation in the administration of wilderness areas after they have been designated. When wilderness areas are created, the way they are managed has a direct impact on local and regional citizens. Local participation in wilderness management would help mitigate the feeling that public lands are managed by faceless Washington bureaucrats with little understanding of how their decisions affect the people of Utah.

Local citizen participation has been utilized successfully in other administrative processes. Interior Secretary Bruce Babbitt initiated such a process for designing a management plan for the Grand Staircase–Escalante National Monument. Babbitt allowed Utah's Governor Michael Leavitt to appoint five members to the management board for the new monument in southern Utah (BLM 1997b). This board is somewhat similar to Governor Matheson's State Wilderness Committee, which provided local feedback during the Forest Service wilderness process (see chapter 13).

A second example of local participation can be found in the Department of Defense's base closing process (Goodman 1997). Local governments and citizens determine uses for former military facilities, and they are given considerable control over redevelopment of military facilities (U.S. Department of Defense 1995). This has reduced the negative impact that base closings have on local economies, and helped local communities exploit the benefits of base closing.

A similar process for BLM wilderness use would assure that all voices are heard. A local board, consisting of representatives from economic interests, wilderness user-groups, and area and regional officials, could determine permit fees and management plans for wilderness areas. In addition, the board should have input on various impact determinations. For example, if BLM determines that grazing AUMs should be reduced or increased in a wilderness area, then the local board could review the data and make a recommendation.

As with the new Grand Staircase–Escalante National Monument's planning strategy, these local boards would focus on the values of the wilderness areas and their community context. These values would include, but are not limited to, historic use, geological resources, recreational and aesthetic resources, impact on private land, water use, paleontological resources, and current and future land uses (BLM 1997b). This would help BLM consider the impact that wilderness use has on local communities.

Local participation, where all stakeholders have a voice, would reduce the misunderstanding and miscommunication that have characterized the wilderness debate. For many years both sides have talked past one another. This might be avoided if all interested parties were part of a regular administrative process, sitting face to face, discussing wilderness management and developing mutually agreeable recommendations.

### Wilderness Management Commission

A fourth component of the community context approach is applicable to all future wilderness controversies. We propose a special commission to make formal proposals for wilderness designation using a multi-agency, multi-state approach. As illustrated throughout this volume, there are many conflicts over wilderness designation. In Utah the process has become mired in disagreement. Special interest groups on both sides of the issue have vowed not to budge from their positions. Neither side can see the other side's concerns. The rationale for a commission is to take some of the politics out of the decision-making process, and attempt to develop more definitive designation criteria that would guide the designation process.

A lesson can be learned from the base closing controversy. From the mid-1970s through much of the 1980s, the Defense Department was unable to close or realign military bases. The parochial demands of members of Congress had allowed unnecessary bases to stay open because individual members of Congress would stall closures in their districts (Twight 1990; Twight 1989; Armey 1988). Closing bases became more feasible politically after the Grace Commission recommended closing such bases (Grace 1984). But only after the base closing process was reformed did military bases actually begin to close.

A similar process could be used for wilderness designation.[10] A bipartisan commission would reduce conflict and allow for a less politicized decision-making process. Patterned after the Base Closure and Realignment Commission, the Wilderness Management Commission (WMC) would function in a similar manner. Commission members would be appointed by the president with advice from both political parties, Congress, and governors. The appointment procedure would include an allocation formula that guaranteed a balance of party and regional interests. The Secretary of the Interior and the Secretary of Agriculture (for the Forest Service), would make wilderness recommendations to the WMC for the BLM, National Park Service, U.S. Fish and Wildlife Service, and U.S. Forest Service. The proposed wilderness areas would become wilderness study areas while the WMC considers them on their merits. The commission would then review the secretaries' proposals, relying upon specific written criteria and procedures developed by the Commission. Commission members would visit potential sites and hold public hearings, and would have the authority to add or subtract wilderness acreage from the list of proposed areas.

The Commission would also devise exemptions, if any, for the various wilderness areas. At the completion of their review they would present the list to the president, who would have to accept or reject the list as a whole; the president could not add to or take away any areas on the list. After the list is accepted by the president, Congress would have sixty days to accept or reject the list as a whole. Again, they could not adjust the recommendations. After Congress accepts the list, the Secretaries of the Interior or of Agriculture would develop management plans for each region/ecosystem, and the Secretary would have five years to trade out or buy inholdings such as school trust lands. All areas not designated by the commission and accepted by Congress would revert back to multiple-use designation, but could be reconsidered for wilderness in subsequent Commission recommendations.

Utilizing such a commission would allow for wilderness designations to cross agency boundaries and state boundaries and focus on ecosystems or regions; this makes more sense than limiting wilderness areas to arbitrary political boundaries between agencies or states. There is precedent for this: the Arizona Wilderness Act of 1984, described in chapter 13, established the Paria Canyon Wilderness Area, which traverses the Utah state line. Also, a number of wilderness areas have been established because they are coterminous with similar units managed by other federal agencies. Thus wilderness designation and management would follow the precepts of ecosystem management.

The proposed Wilderness Management Commission is also congruent with a significant innovative trend in the management of environmentally sensitive areas. A number of volatile resource conflicts have been resolved or mitigated by a new conflict resolution process, called "new governance," or the network approach, that focuses on common goals, cross-jurisdictional partnerships, and "information-based, learning-oriented action"

(Reid and Lovan 1993: 2–3). This approach has been especially useful in managing conflict over rural development. Radin et al. describe the success of these "multiple partnership configuration" networks:

> They [networks] were able to provide brokering and mediation functions; they were able to defuse past antagonisms, unfreeze some policy logjams, and smooth out conflicts as they created opportunities for participants to deal with one another in face-to-face, personal terms. They were also able to broaden the issue beyond traditional actors . . . and sensitize some participants to the potential breadth of expertise that might be utilized to solve rural development problems. (Radin et al. 1996, 312)

Regarding innovative management of natural resource issues, there are a number of models from which to choose. For example, the Sierra Nevada Ecosystem Project was established with five objectives:

(1) improve return from beneficiaries of the Sierra to those who will maintain and enhance the ecosystem qualities from which benefits flow,

(2) strengthen cooperation among federal, state, and local governments and agencies whose authorities and resources overlap in the ecosystem and strengthen cooperation between the public and private sectors,

(3) increase community involvement,

(4) provide legal, regulatory, and financial support to advance such reforms beyond current levels of ad hoc spontaneity,

(5) take advantage of characteristic aspects of Sierra Nevada regions to leverage progress on issues of regional and rangewide scale (Sierra Nevada Ecosystem Project 1996).

Another example is the Northwest Power Planning Council, which is a "planning and policy-making body" in the Columbia River Basin that is responsible for inter-agency electric power planning, a program to protect and rebuild fisheries, and public involvement "in the Council's decision-making process" (Northwest Power Planning Council n.d.). In Utah, important resource conflicts in the St. George area have been addressed by the Southwest Utah Planning Authorities Council. Its mission is to "create a structure and develop a process for coordination of the planning processes for all levels of government in southwestern Utah with representatives from every level of government participating in a collaborative and interactive partnership" (Barber 1994).[11] It is clear that the wilderness controversy would benefit from a new approach that emphasizes collaborative problem-solving rather than conflict and posturing.

## CONCLUSION

We agree that Utah's wilderness is a critically important national asset that should be preserved. Given its importance, surely the nation is prepared to pay a modest amount for its preservation. The amount of federal funding that would be required to fund the community context approach would be a tiny percentage of the federal budget. Is America's Red Rock wilderness worth that much to us as a society? If wilderness is truly a national treasure, the nation should be willing to make a contribution to its protection.

We also agree with rural people who fear that additional wilderness will have a negative impact on their economic viability. It undoubtedly will. Although mining is now only 1 percent of the state's economy, and ranching is less than 1 percent, in some rural communities these traditional extractive activities are essential to their continued viability. For example, mining accounts for 24 percent of Emery County's workforce, and it accounts for 11 percent of southeastern Utah's jobs (State of Utah 1998, 86). Are we so callous as a society that we would destroy rural communities in order to serve a larger public interest? Or have we progressed to the point where we are willing to ameliorate the impact society has on small groups of rural Westerners? We cannot replace the lost opportunity for a mine any more than we can replace a lost wilderness. But we can adopt an approach to wilderness designation that focuses on the entire community of rural Utah and the West. If we save wilderness but in the process destroy livelihoods without any effort to compensate for it, then we have not achieved a just settlement of the issue.

In the meantime, the conflict continues. A recent newsletter of the Wilderness Society noted that "Sometimes it seems there's a new wilderness story every day in Utah" (*Wilderness Society News* 1998, 3). That organization recently devoted a feature story in its national magazine to the latest Utah wilderness conflicts (Aplet 1998). A recent article in a local newspaper covered the new SUWA proposal under a headline that read: "New Battle Plan: SUWA ups the ante—calling for even more wilderness in the war over Utah's public lands" (Smart 1998).

In the meantime, Congressman Chris Cannon introduced a bill to create a San Rafael Swell National Heritage and Conservation Area (H.R. 3625). Local officials were quite supportive of the bill (*Emery County Progress* 1998), but wilderness advocates called it "another rotten anti-wilderness bill" (SUWA 1998, 28). Congressman Hansen continues to introduce wilderness bills, the latest being titled the "Utah Wilderness and School Trust Lands Protection Act of 1997." Meanwhile the UWC is sponsoring meetings across the United States in an effort to generate support for its latest 9.1-million-acre proposal.

The community context approach is designed to move the wilderness debate beyond this stalemate. All parties have adopted rigid positions that are devoid of an awareness of the other side's needs. The wilderness debate is not about right or wrong; it's about needs and values. When we begin to consider all of these needs and values, then we will find a solution. In the long run that is best for both wilderness and the people who live nearby.

## ₵ NOTES TO CHAPTER 14

1. Thomas Michael Power makes a convincing argument that, on a region-wide basis, traditional extractive industry is no longer critically important to the economy as a whole. However, it is still very important in some communities. See Thomas Michael Power, *Lost Landscapes and Failed Economies* (Washington, DC: Island Press, 1996).

2. It is important to note that, while rural Utah counties have a high percentage of federal land, the amount of private land per capita in rural Utah is very high.

3. The BLM recently gave Garfield County a $100,000 grant to assist with law enforcement and search and rescue for the new monument. The grant is for only the current year. It helps offset some initial start-up costs, but does not continually provide funds to the county (Madsen 1997).

4. We chose this multiplier because it requires at least a fourfold increase in payments to generate sufficient revenue to significantly impact local public budgets.

5. There is substantial disagreement over the impact that wilderness designation has on private property values. Many rural Utahns believe property values and tax revenues have decreased since the designation of wilderness study areas. Although there could be other reasons for the decline, they associate the drop in valuation with the loss of land "locked up" in wilderness. In terms of local property taxes, both private and centrally assessed, wilderness designation reduces potential income from mining and forestry, but increases potential income from property values that have increased due to tourist and recreational potential.

6. Some areas receive more visitors than others. An assessment of visitor estimates from the *EIS* illustrates that some areas like French Springs WSA receive fewer than fifty visitors a year while others like Desolation Canyon or Phipps–Death Hollow WSAs receive thousands of visitors each year (BLM Utah 1990).

7. As noted in chapter 11, there are only two BLM Rangers who patrol Grand Gulch's 100,000 acres.

8. We recommend a reduced fee schedule, or waiving the fee, for low-income users and special-use groups such as public-school field trips.

9. Due to increased visitation and inadequate staff, BLM plans to introduce a reservation system for the Grand Gulch area (BLM 1997c). A fee will accompany the reservation. BLM fee schedules are comparable to those of other public recreation facilities in the area. For example, Dead Horse Point State Park charges $4 per car. Canyonlands National Park has a permit fee system that charges $5 for day use, $10 for backpacking, and $25 for whitewater rafting (U.S. General Accounting Office 1997).

10. Representative James Hansen (R-Utah) tried to create a National Park System Review Commission to study national parks and monuments for closures, transfers, or mergers (U.S. Congress, House 1995, H.R. 9083-86). A commission focusing on public land preservation designations would be much different from Representative Hansen's proposal. The main focus would be not on closing wilderness areas but rather on resolving conflicts, establishing clear guidelines for designation, and improving management.

11. In addition to the examples cited above, there are other successful collaborative efforts in public land management; for example, there is the Malpai Borderlands Group in Arizona (Dagget 1995a and 1995b; Klinkenborg 1995) and the Cosummes River Preserve in California (Emory 1995), to name a few.

## ℭ  REFERENCES TO CHAPTER 14

Aplet, Gregory. 1998. Amazing space. *Wilderness*, 27–30.

Armey, Richard. 1988. Base maneuvers: the games Congress plays with the military pork barrel. *Policy Review* 43: 70–75.

Barber, Brad. 1994. Southwest Utah Planning Authorities Council (SUPAC): A case study in interagency planning. In *Challenges to Natural Resource Sustainability in the Colorado River Basin*, edited by Kathleen Truman, Christine Chairsell, and James Deacon. UNLV Environmental Studies Program. Mimeograph.

BLM (Bureau of Land Management of the U.S. Department of the Interior). 1997a. Public land statistics 1996.

———. 1997b. "Grand Staircase–Escalante National Monument: How You Can Participate in Planning for the Monument." http://www.blm.gov/nhp/news/alerts/EscIPubPart.html.

———. 1997c. "San Juan Resource Area: Recreation." http://www.blm.gov/utah/monticello/rec_fr.htm.

BLM Utah (Utah State Office, Bureau of Land Management of the U.S. Department of the Interior). 1990. *Utah BLM Statewide Wilderness Final Environmental Impact Statement.* Salt Lake City, UT.

Clarke, Jeanne, and Daniel McCool. 1996. *Staking Out the Terrain: Power and Performance Among Natural Resource Management Agencies,* 2d ed. New York: SUNY Press.

Dagget, D. 1995a. *Beyond the Rangeland Conflict: Toward a West that Works.* Flagstaff, AZ: Grand Canyon Trust.

———. 1995b. From adversaries to allies. *Range Magazine* (Summer): 14–19, 27.

*Emery County Progress.* 1998. April 7: 1.

Emory, J. 1995. Cattle, rice . . . and biodiversity. *The Nature Conservancy of California Newsletter* (Winter): 1–2.

Freemuth, John. 1991. *Islands Under Siege: National Parks and the Politics of External Threats.* Lawrence: University Press of Kansas.

GAO (General Accounting Office). 1998a. "Revenue sharing payments to states and counties." GAO/RCED-98-261, September 17.

———. 1998b. "Demonstration fee program successful in raising revenues but could be improved." GAO/RCED-99-7, November 20.

Goodman, Doug. 1997. "Overcoming Military Job Losses: How Tooele, Utah Accepted the Challenge." Western Political Science Association, Tucson, AZ, March 13–15.

Grace, Peter J. 1984. *Burning Money: The Waste of your Tax Dollars.* New York: Macmillan Publishing Company.

Johnson, Kenneth M., and Calvin L. Beale. 1995. Nonmetropolitan recreational counties: identification and fiscal concerns. Working paper for Demographic Change and Fiscal Stress Project, Loyola University, Chicago.

Johnson, Kenneth, John P. Pelissero, David B. Holian, and Michael T. Maly. 1995. Local government fiscal burden in nonmetropolitan America. *Rural Sociology* 60 (Fall): 381–98.

Klinkenborg, V. 1995. Crossing borders: a group of innovative ranchers have banded together to preserve a million acres of New Mexico and Arizona. *Audubon* (September/October): 34–47.

Madsen, Reed L. 1997. "Garfield to Get $100,000 in Staircase Aid," *Deseret News*, September 7.

McCool, Stephen F. 1985. Does wilderness designation lead to increased recreational use? *Journal of Forestry* (January): 39-41.

Northwest Power Planning Council. N.d. Brochure. 851 S.W. Sixth Ave., Portland, OR 97204.

Power, Thomas Michael. 1996. *Lost Landscapes and Failed Economies*. Washington, DC: Island Press.

Radin, Beryl, Robert Agranoff, Ann Bowman, Gregory Buntz, J. Steven Ott, Barbara Romzek, and Robert Wilson. 1996. *New Governance for Rural America*. Lawrence: University Press of Kansas.

Reid, Norman, and Robert Lovan. 1993. "Reinventing Rural America: 'The New Governance.'" Paper presented at the annual conference of the American Planning Association, Chicago, IL, May 4.

Sierra Nevada Ecosystem Project. 1996. "Executive Summary: Management Strategies for Ecosystem Sustainability." Copyright, University of California.

Smart, Christopher. 1998. "New Battle Plan: SUWA Ups the Ante—Calling for Even More Wilderness in the War over Utah's Public Lands," *City Weekly*, June 4, 12.

State of Utah. Governor's Office of Planning and Budget. 1992. Estimated land ownership in Utah: 1992. Computer file.

———. 1995. State of Utah wilderness acres by county—draft. Computer file.

———. 1998. *Economic report to the Governor*. Salt Lake City, UT.

Stone, Deborah. 1997. *Policy Paradox: The Art of Political Decision Making*. New York: W. W. Norton.

SUWA. 1998. *SUWA Newsletter* 15 (2): 28.

Twight, Charlotte. 1989. Institutional underpinnings of parochialism: the case of military base closures. *Cato Journal* 9: 73–106.

———. 1990. Department of Defense attempts to close military bases: the political economy of congressional resistance. In *Arms, Politics, and the Economy: Historical and Contemporary Perspectives*, edited by Robert Higgs, 236–80. New York: Holmes and Meier.

U.S. Congress, House. 1995. 104th Cong., 1st. sess. *Congressional Record*, September 18, vol. 141, no. 145.

U.S. Department of Defense. Office of Economic Adjustment. 1995. Community guide to base reuse. Washington, DC: Office of Economic Adjustment.

U.S. General Accounting Office. 1997. "Similarities and Differences in the Management of Selected State and Federal Land Units." GAO/RCED-97-158 (June).

*Wilderness Society News*. 1998. "Utah Wilderness," April 9.

# Index

FRONT ROW (L to R): Joshua Footer, Amber Ayers, Sara McCormick, Dan McCool, Robin Clegg, Doug Goodman

MIDDLE ROW: Andrew Fitzgerald, Lucas Smart, Deborah Schwabach, Tina Compton, Kirsten Jansen, Jerold Willmore, Richard Warnick

BACK ROW: Christian Senf, David Harward, Cyrus McKell, Chris Perri, Buck Swaney

SIDE ROW, from top to bottom: Brent Osiek, Christa Powell, Chris Wehrli

NOT SHOWN: J. T. VonLunen, Janelle Eurick, Christopher Krueger, Meredith Graff, and R. Kelly Beck